FEMINISMS:
WITHIN AND WITHOUT

First published May, 2006
Women's Studies Centre
National University of Ireland
Galway
Republic of Ireland

ISBN 0-9549924-3-1

Cover Design: A & D, Envision House, Flood Street, Galway
Cover Image: Rita Duffy. By permission of the artist.

Typesetting and Design: Women's Studies Centre, NUI, Galway
Printed by Cahill Printers, East Wall Road, Dublin 3

FEMINISMS:
WITHIN AND WITHOUT

Papers Delivered at the Women's Studies Conference,
National University of Ireland, Galway.
July 2005.

Rebecca Pelan, Editor

CONTENTS

CULTURE

Introduction

This collection includes a selection of papers presented at the *Feminisms: Within and Without* conference, hosted by the Women's Studies Centre, National University of Ireland, Galway, in July 2005. The conference was non-themed, and the title (and subsequent papers) represent our efforts not to limit contributions, but to permit as broad a range of topics and perspectives as possible on any aspect of women's political, social, cultural and creative lives. The result was a lively and stimulating conference that generally reflected many of the approaches to Women's Studies and feminist politics that exist today: some are quite clearly discipline-based, while others provide a fascinating view of the field of Women's Studies as a developing (inter)discipline; some are by established scholars in the field, while others are from new researchers.

A source of great enjoyment at the conference was the number of countries represented – some near, some far, and some very far indeed: Ireland, England, Wales, Canary Islands, Italy, Spain, Turkey, Canada, the United States, Australia, Aotearoa/New Zealand, and Mongolia. The wonderful experience of sharing in the company of representatives of such a variety of cultures was matched by the enthusiasm with which the delegates participated in conference events – including a sean nós (traditional Irish singing) workshop facilitated by Pádraigín Ní Uallachán, Aíne Ní Dhroighneáin and Sorcha Ní Chéilleachair, and a Feminist Writing for Performance Workshop facilitated by Georgia Rhodes (USA). We were also treated to selected readings by award-winning poet, Colleen Z. Burke (Australia), and by the participants of Domestic Violence Response's 'Out of the Darkness, Into the Light' project. In conjunction with the Galway Film Fleadh, the conference also sponsored the screening of Mystelle Barbée's *Highway Courtesans* (USA), which ultimately won the Fleadh's award for best documentary film, and Martina Hynan's 'Stitch-up,' an exhibition of contemporary paintings of women thinkers. The next Women's Studies conference is planned for 2007.

Rebecca Pelan
Director/Convener

POLITICS

Gendering on Down: Reflections on Gender, Equality, and Politics in Ireland

Ailbhe Smyth

EQUALITY! (the must-have accessory for a politician in 2005!)

I'd like to start by emphasising that, in this paper, I'm drawing on my personal, political and intellectual experiences as a 'self-confessed' feminist lesbian activist and academic. I'm aware of how my 'multiple subjectivities' – as white, European, middle class, professional and radical – inform one another, and I try as honestly as I can to recognise how the biases, deficits and contradictions they give rise to shape my thinking and my politics. This means that any propositions I make must be tentative, tested through dialogue, and always conditional on their usefulness to others.

What I want to do here is take a short, sharp look at gender and equality in Ireland, focusing in particular on their discursive construction, and reflect on the implications for feminist politics. This is a 'mood' piece, certainly political, possibly polemical. My observations and questions arise from growing feelings of disquiet, frustration, and an acute sense of being blocked, limited and contained by a political consensus that is becoming more and more difficult to contest and counteract.

I have never liked being managed and, increasingly, I have a sense of being managed, semi-benignly tolerated, not-so subtly sidelined, or altogether ignored as a critical and dissenting voice in this society. Although dispositionally skeptical of establishment politics, I'm not particularly given to paranoia, so I don't (actually) think this is personal. What worries me more is that while I don't expect to find a radical analysis of power relations in the mouths of establishment politicians and decision-makers, I do expect and look for it when feminists speak – and especially when we speak up in public. Over the past several years, and at an accelerating pace, I've noticed how feminist political discourse has become markedly more accommodating and euphemistic. I'm aware of being equipped with altogether the wrong discursive accessories when I use terms like 'patriarchy', or – the ultimate *faux pas* – 'feminism', to account for the persistence of women's complex oppression, to ground claims for women's freedom and autonomy, to formulate strategies for social transformation, and even to locate myself on the political spectrum.

I'm worried because I think debate about the political directions, strategies and tactics of feminism by feminists is in danger of disappearing from the public arena, or of being shifted and osmosed in ways that make it unrecognisable as feminist. I'm worried because the space for feminist politics seems to be decreasingly political (if that's not oxymoronic), and because the language of feminism is being replaced by anodyne 'gender speak'. I'm very worried indeed about the displacement of feminist politics by 'gender politics', which is not the same thing at all, despite certain surface similarities. As Kamla Bhasin (2004) points out in her forthright way in a review of gender and women's rights in a major development organisation, "if we wish to work on causes of poverty and women's subordination, then it is necessary to call a spade a spade" (14). So, in an important sense, this paper is a plea to start calling spades spades again, wherever we are and whoever our interlocutors may be. And to keep on digging.

At least in this part of the world, feminist politics is increasingly being directed towards integrating the mainstream, joining in the consensus and not rocking the boat. In an extensive discussion of the implications of gender mainstreaming in the EU, Sylvia Walby (2004) observes that it is "a contested concept and practice [involving] the re-invention, restructuring and re-branding of a key part of feminism in the contemporary era" (1). There are, in my view, important issues to be discussed and debated as a consequence of the shift from the 'strong' social movement politics of contestation and opposition of the 1970s to a 'weak' integrationist politics of consensus and partnership, including: the appropriation and dilution of many of the central concepts of feminism; the discrediting of feminists and of radical feminist activism; the marginalisation of critique and dissent; and, above all, a worsening of the life-situations and potential of women in many different locations and contexts.

My argument is neither original nor particular to Ireland, although these trends do get worked out in site-specific ways in different places. Feminists elsewhere within the EU and the minority world have, of course, been tracking and analysing the evolution of feminism in diverse arenas. While it is by no means the case that such analyses all draw the same conclusions or delineate identical directions for the future, there is a widespread view that over the past decade the scope for instrumental activism has narrowed sharply, and that 'mainstreaming' strategies have led to a significant deradicalisation of feminist politics. As Roberta Guerrina observes:

> Despite the increase in political rhetoric associated with gender] mainstreaming, it is questionable whether it has engendered a greater degree of equality. [...] It is questionable whether it can achieve the aims of substantive equality [because] mainstreaming as endorsed by EU law focuses on integrating women into existing policies rather than allowing gender discourses to inform these policy areas. In this context, mainstreaming can be used to silence women and remove gender from the political agenda. (Guerrina, 2003, 104)

Join the Evolution!
In Ireland, the shift from an oppositional mode of feminist politics to a more integrationist *modus operandi* has been significant and visible. The most consequential moves have been the insertion of activist groups and individuals within more institutionalised frameworks; the increasing professionalisation of organisations accompanied by a quasi-inevitable weakening of their grassroots bases; their increasing reliance on state legitimation and funding; and their discursive incorporation in a neo-liberal politics of social inclusion and partnership.

Whether such moves are seen as progressive or regressive for the achievement of feminist objectives (always plural and complex in any case) is a matter of political (self)-location. I would argue that the tangible gains which have been made in the policy and legislative arenas have been typically either undermined by a failure to deliver adequate infrastructural supports for their appropriate implementation and further development, or tightly controlled and restricted to limited areas. In their study of gender mainstreaming policies and their implementation in the EU, Pollack and Hafner-Burton (2000) note that while "EU equal opportunities policy has indeed pushed forward with an ambitious agenda of legally enforceable rights for European women, [...] it has done so along the comparatively narrow, neoliberal front of workplace legislation" (1).

In Ireland, a major report on men's violence against women by Amnesty International (2005) sharply criticises the State's 'extensive failure' to implement the key recommendations of the 1997 report of a taskforce the State itself had set up to address the issue (Healy). This example is particularly telling since men's violence against women is widely considered to be the issue that feminists have most successfully moved onto the policy-making agenda. On foot of the Amnesty findings, the State has publicly acknowledged that funding for service development has in fact been static for several years.

The debate as to whether feminists should or should not enter into a relationship with the state is, of course, not new. It is a dilemma that has been constitutive of the formation and development of feminist identities, theories and politics since the 1970s (Maddison, 2002). I believe that what has changed, however, over the past ten years or so is the possibility for feminist organisations (and for individual activists) to remain autonomous, substantially non-aligned and outside the web of state partnership and the politics of social inclusion.

'Social Inclusion', to be achieved largely through the mechanism of 'Social Partnership', is a key mantra within Irish policy-making elites, and much of the third sector (Mullan and Cox, nd). I have my reservations. Inclusion has an oddly hollow sound when defined by the included. What concerns me about 'inclusion' is its political weakness, conceptually and practically: 'inclusion' effectively disallows the fundamental critiques of the existing order that are crucial to transformative action, and leave binary systems of 'insiders' and 'outsiders' intact.

'Social Partnership' is similarly problematic, since the discourse and conditions of partnership are substantially State-defined and controlled, and are typically and purposefully manipulative of the language and strategies of feminist and other radical politics. Partnershipping enables the State 'to put its shape' on social movements by deploying a range of tactics which include, *inter alia*:

- creating sectoral divisions through competition for always-scarce funding;

- draining activists of creative energy and resources through relentless bureaucracy;

- detaching movement leadership from the grassroots through the need for a professionalised elite capable of playing the partnership game;

- tying organisations ineluctably into national and EU policy processes by offering carrots to the compliant and punishing those reluctant to partner (Mullan and Cox, nd).

The recent experience of the National Women's Council of Ireland (NWCI) is a useful case in point. The Council refused to sign up to the current Social Partnership agreement, 'Sustaining Progress', on the grounds that "it contained minimal progress for women's equality" (NWCI), highlighting the important point that what current policy agendas do not say is as, if not even more important than, what they do say. As a result, the Council was excluded from the Social Partnership decision-making and consultative fora. The Council has now learned that because of its present stance it will not be invited to participate in the negotiation of a new agreement when the current one ends in December 2005. This places the NWCI in a difficult position since the National Women's Strategy (NWS) is scheduled for inclusion in the agenda of the new agreement, and will very likely be the key – perhaps even the only – element relating to women's equality within it. If the Council refuses to cooperate they will have no direct input into the monitoring of the NWS, while if they sign up to the new agreement, they will effectively be capitulating to State bullying.

Willy-nilly therefore, in order to achieve changes in policy and practice, it would seem that activist organisations must enter into what Mullan and Cox (nd) have described as "an increasingly dysfunctional and coercive relationship" (9) with the State if they are to remain in existence. What can be achieved, however, under such conditions is another question entirely. Ironically, 'capacity-building' is a stated aim of partnershipping in Ireland. But for what purpose, exactly, is capacity being built?

Revolution has indeed evolved. But who removed the R, and where have they put it? Patriarchy is not old hat!

While it is not my purpose here to examine the complex reasons for this 'evolved' state of affairs, I want very briefly to suggest two major grounds.

Firstly, the very success of the women's movement in the 1970s and the 1980s, its immediate and far-reaching socio-cultural and political impacts, generated new forms of control and containment by the State, including recuperation, institutionalisation and the 're-branding' of feminist concepts, issues and agendas. While I don't want to over-generalise or simplify complex and localised processes of social change, feminists in many different environments have analysed the extent and ways in which reformist strands of feminism came to dominate women's movement politics. Sarah Maddison (2000) argues that, over time, reformism succeeded in "virtually silencing the more revolutionary liberationists" (5), with the expression of radical theory and ideas typically being discouraged by reformists as potentially disruptive of the emergent new relationship with the State.

Don't rock the boat – we might fall out!

Secondly, newly prosperous Ireland has embraced neo-liberalism with astonishing speed and comprehensiveness, and is now one of the most globalised countries in the world. In the market-driven, consumerist and individualist 2000s, the key word is growth, with profit as the main objective and motor of the (social) economy. In this politically conservative climate, equality has become a commodity to be mainstreamed, and diversity a reality to be managed. Inclusion (for some), not systemic transformation, is the overriding political strategy. Consensus is the preferred political mode, and protest and confrontation have become impolite, imprudent and increasingly heavily policed.

Does he who pays the piper not always and inevitably call the tune – and the shots?

In this environment, it is hardly surprising that feminist politics in Ireland has become (has arguably been forced to become) increasingly polite and decreasingly radical. For more than a decade now, it has been predominantly reform-oriented, narrowly focused on following a broadly mainstreaming or integrationist approach, in which a gender perspective is advanced "without challenging the existing policy paradigm", but rather (re)packaged and sold as a way of "more effectively achieving existing policy goals" (Walby, 2004: 4). It is during this period that the discourses of gender, equality, rights and citizenship have become ubiquitous in the social policy arena. From a revolutionary, or at least contestatory politics of the 1970s, feminism has downsized to making claims for inclusion.

But these claims seem previous to many for, as Cynthia Enloe reminds us (if we need reminding), "patriarchy is not old hat!" (Enloe, 2003, 6). The inequalities (ie, oppression, othering, marginalisation, exploitation) diversely experienced by women (and regardless, by the way, of their 'rights') are generated by a social, cultural, economic and political system premised on a world where patriarchy remains foundational and normative, although all too rarely named and challenged as such. In her research on the sexual trafficking of women in Ireland, Julia Long (2005) expresses her increasing frustration with the limitations of the current gender mainstreaming agenda which, she argues, focuses almost exclusively on women's participation in the labour market, whilst failing to incorporate in its analysis critical issues relating to women in other areas.

A politics of access and inclusion is not liberation, transformation or even disruption. Who exactly are we disrupting or transforming by asking (politely) to be let in?

Women don't want equality with men. We're far more ambitious
'Managing equality' and 'managing diversity' are terms we have become increasingly familiar with in Ireland over the past decade in both the public and private sectors. It seems that an egalitarian society is merely a matter of organisational style. Whether in relation to socio-economic policy, workplace practices, or in media and cultural representations, the overriding drive is to 'manage' differences (whether in relation to voters, workers, social welfare beneficiaries, TV pundits, lovers, single parents, lesbians and gay men, people with disabilities, women or what have you), so that they're no longer noticeable, visible or audible as difference; so that they cannot disrupt hegemonic norms; so that no action needs to be taken. All that is resistant to assimilation is deemed to be 'unmanageable' (and punished), or irrelevant (and ignored or discarded).

'Celebrating diversity' is another much-used phrase, which functions, up to a point, to encourage people to become more accepting of difference. However, it is not clear to me how celebration can transform the social and economic structures of inequality, or power relations premised on dominance and subordination. So, people with disabilities who cannot participate in the structurally and physically unchanged workforce, will be deemed 'unproductive', and ignored or condescended to; immigrants who insist on giving birth to children in Ireland (horror of horrors) will be denied citizenship rights, and deported; people of colour who persist in naming and resisting racism will be seen as 'difficult', and also possibly deported; lesbians and gay men who choose not to marry or form 'civil unions' will be deemed 'sexual outlaws'; feminists who refuse to 'gender mainstream' will (definitely) not have their projects funded. And old people – what will happen to old people? And to those who remain poor, despite the 'fact' that we have a prosperous, egalitarian, fair and just society? What is to be done with all these people who just won't fit in? A society which claims to be 'managing' equality means that individuals can be blamed for failing to achieve it: since the law says you can, if you do not, it's your fault. In everyday discourse in Ireland, including that of the large majority of politicians and decision-makers, 'equality' remains a curiously uncontested idea whose meaning is rarely, if ever, a matter of public debate. 'Equality' is a powerful concept, but it is not *per se* a politics, programme or agenda. Furthermore, in its current, uniquely discursive formulation by the State, it cannot shift the social and material relations of power between people. It does not make women more independent or protect them from men's violence; it does not increase their participation in political, social and cultural life; it does not ensure recognition and social esteem; and it does not effect an equitable redistribution of roles and resources.

Momin Rahman (2000) suggests that words "like equality, citizenship and rights carry such moral weight or authority that we are conditioned not to question them, but rather to see them automatically as 'good' without examining their content and meaning" (56) and, therefore, not to think about them in relation to what we want and need, and about how our aspirations are to be realised. In fact, despite the institution of formal equality in our laws, many socio-economic disparities have become more pronounced, with the rhetoric of equality serving to mask the continuing reality of multiple and intersecting inequalities (O'Toole, 2003; Kirby, 2004). In other words, substantive equality has not been achieved. As some are included, new 'others' are left – or emerge – to function as the new edges that define the (same) centre. There has been no shifting of the relation of periphery to centre, merely substitution. 'Inclusion' does not eradicate inequality any more than it creates true consensus. It functions, rather, to generate new minorities and out-groups. There are always other others. And the closer one moves to the centre, the less one is likely to know, or care about, who has been left languishing on the edge.

Plus ça change....

I have noticed that alarm appears on reformist faces when you ask pointed questions about 'equality politics'. What exactly will be achieved by this report? These recommendations? This negotiation? This measure? What will be gained for whom, for how long, and at what cost? How will inequalities be erased? What norms will be changed (eg racist, imperialist, hetero, patriarchal, ableist, (post)capitalist, and so on)? Precisely which resources will be redistributed and exactly how much?

A rights-based politics is inept at bringing about systemic socio-economic change and cannot be relied upon to do so. The dangers of an over-reliance on liberal, rights-based approaches need to be publicly debated rather than brushed under the carpet. I should make it very clear that I believe that Equal Rights legislation is a basic and necessary framework for a society in which equality can be achieved. However, it is precisely that, a framework, and no more. Laws, even good ones, are not laurels to be rested upon. Equality laws function primarily to protect and safeguard individuals against discrimination, they do not guarantee equality of outcome. Indeed, such legislation is not intended to do this, and should not be expected to do so.

Formal equality does not redistribute resources. It does not break the overriding binary templates of hierarchical relations of power. It does not propose (perish the thought) a transformative strategy for social organisation and human relations. Formal equality is an abstraction which generally avoids taking account of contexts and experiences and, therefore, rather importantly, of the material inequalities between people. The provision of formal equality in law tends to extend systems and structures rather than to radically alter or remove them. It typically functions as a containment or management strategy, suggesting that application of the law will lead to equality of social conditions and outcomes. But why would it achieve that since that is not its function or its capacity? A revolution by case law seems to me to be an unlikely event.

It has become very difficult of late to raise these sorts of questions in the mainstream of Irish political and social life, including feminist life. Challenging the deployment of equality discourse is likely to run you into problems for several reasons:

- The assumption that 'we all' know what equality is, and agree that it is always and for everyone the 'same' good thing. So what's to be debated?

- The heavy moral weight with which the concept is non-innocently freighted effectively forestalls critique: You're surely not questioning people's right to equality?

- Its embeddedness at the centre of liberalism: of course 'we're all' good practicing neo-liberals in Ireland, in favour of equality, social justice, citizenship, individuality, and nice social aspirations that don't cost the taxpayer ('us') more than a cent or two.

The looseness of this discourse works to pre-empt or foreclose public debate and, therefore, to maintain the very structures of inequality that serve hegemonic interests. In my view, we urgently need to take a much more challenging approach. We need to examine the assumptions built in to policy and practice and to consistently contest normative, formalistic, and hyper-individualising constructions of equality that fail to deliver substantive social and economic change. We need to widen the scope of equality (Walzer, 1983), to sharpen and strengthen our strategic understandings, and to 'fine tune' our analyses of the complexities that underlie its apparent simplicity. At the present time, we need above all to contest the vacuity of national and transnational formulations of equality because this evacuation of effective meaning is politically willed and motivated.

There is a vital political job of discursive de/re-construction to be done: to expose the gap between the rhetoric of formal equality on the one hand, and the continuing reality of substantive inequalities and oppressive social systems on the other. We need to ask whose interests are served by the disparity (or simply, who is in the gap and why), and to examine how the rhetoric is itself constitutive of that gap (ie supporting existing power hierarchies). For, as Nancy Fraser (1995) argues, a politics of recognition (recognition of the equal rights of all citizens) is meaningless unless it is accompanied by a simultaneous politics of redistribution of power and resources. Recognition cannot be given lived expression unless it is underscored and supported by redistributive politics and practices that require far more than rhetoric and the reiteration of high-sounding mantras. Such practices require profound systemic and structural transformations.

This is a particularly urgent challenge for feminism, at least in its quasi-institutionalised forms in Ireland and the EU at present. It is vital to ensure that feminism not be hijacked and neutralised, and drowned in the neo-liberal mainstream. It is vital to resist the discursive appropriation and manipulation of feminist concepts and political practices. That gender is a key descriptor and analytical tool in feminist thinking is obvious (Jackson and Scott 2002). However, its ubiquitous substitution for 'women' in legislation, social policy, services, and in educational and cultural contexts is a politically strategic sleight of hand designed to disappear real-life women, and to discredit those anachronistic creatures who insist on calling themselves 'feminist'.

"The problem with gender", Nighat Khan observes, "is that it can mean both men and women or either man or woman. The specificity of women's oppression disappears" (cit. in Adelye-Fayemi, 1999, 10). Naming that specificity and the complex inscription of patriarchal systems in women's lives is crucial to feminist politics.

I'll be a post-feminist in post-patriarchy!
Feminist politics is in acute danger of being genderised out of existence, at least where I live. Increasingly, feminism is being appropriated by an assimilationist politics and reconfigured so as to serve the interests of the neo-liberal 'gender agenda'.

> This new model (ie mainstreaming) is not threatening, [...] it does not speak about women's struggle, power relationships between the sexes. The rhetoric changes from a women-and power-centered rhetoric to a less politicized discourse of partnership and consensus, where equality is genuinely 'good' for men too'. (Les Penelopes, 2005)

It involves forming new kinds of relationships (working with the State in partnership) and new modalities of action (advocacy), both of which mean learning to speak the language of consensus and acquiescence. While it is argued that there are real gains to be made from and through this shift in attention, focus and discursive style, something vitally important is lost.

What is lost, in my view, is an agonistic practice of politics and, thus, perhaps, politics itself. Because what is politics if it is not agonistic? By this I mean a political arena where opposition, challenge and contest are represented and practiced as the most healthy, invigorating and constructive expression of a contemporary democracy. A space in which multiple counter-publics, to use Nancy Fraser's term, are constantly in dialogue – polylogue – with one another (Fraser 1995). A space in which open debate and multiple, healthily critical and dissenting voices are actively welcomed as enabling the on-going construction of a genuinely egalitarian and fluid polis.

One of the most urgent challenges for feminists – and not only in Ireland – is to resist genderisation, and to continue the profoundly political work of calling spades spades. Seeking to be part of the conversation of the new orthodoxies is not our role. Critique and dissent are feminist business, and we must resist their suppression. We must speak out, and on our own political terms.

Rules of 'Dissent Management' to be Observed and Resisted by Feminists:

- Firstly, 'out of sight, out of mind': refuse to name women at all, and simply call them something else. For example, substitute 'gender' for 'women' at all times, even when it is wildly inaccurate. This enables you to behave as if women don't really exist at all.

- Appropriate and dilute feminist language and aims. "Gender is safe. Feminism is threatening" (Adelye-Fayemi, 2000, 10), and women – above all – are unmentionable. So women's movement and feminist politics become 'gender politics'; equality for women becomes 'gender equality'; men's violence becomes 'gender violence'; 'women's studies' becomes 'gender studies'; 'liberation' becomes 'equality-rights-and-citizenship'; struggle becomes 'advocacy' and 'lobbying'. This will distract attention from the awkward, disruptive and transformative goals of the unmentionables.

- Force feminists to adopt and adapt to your tactics, language, rituals, conventions, lifestyles (and suits). Ignore, prohibit or hive off all forms of challenge and resistance.

- Systematically dilute and delay all claims, legislative and otherwise. Set up committees, expert groups, fora, conferences *et tutti frutti* to explore the same issues in the same ways, *ad infinitum*.

- Use any and all methods of recuperation and co-option: 'buy them off' with occasional meetings, promotions, appointments, promises and – if absolutely necessary – a handful of euro, plus the threat of no more funding for bad behaviour.

- Divide and rule is an excellent dissent management tactic. Keep them busy fighting one another (on- and off-air). Deride and disempower all coalitions as a matter of course.

- Never turn your back for a moment. Be there, infiltrate. Open their conferences, attend their meetings, launch their books and research reports so they can't oppose you behind your back.

- Wear them down with talk, bureaucracy, meetings, endless fund raising. Keep them busy and off the streets at all costs.

- If that doesn't work, cut them off. Refuse to meet them, give them air-time, or funding. They will probably disappear.

- If they still won't desist from resistance, discredit and demonise them (in a rising crescendo) as *passé*, *outré*, incompetent, unqualified, disruptive, destructive, dishonest, negligent, criminal, difficult, mad.

- If they take to the streets, nonetheless, in frustration and anger, use forceful means to silence or disappear them: strong-arm them at protests; close off the streets; refuse permission for protests; refuse them permission to even poster information for protests; just refuse.

- If all these tactics fail (and they rarely do), ignore them altogether and carry on regardless, telling 'the people', that the reason why there's no dissent is that all's well in fairy land, although it won't be if people insist on causing trouble because we all need to pull together, stay in the mainstream and not rock the boat: after all, you are the one who may fall out and drown.

'We don't want all this revolutionary stuff. We just want equality'

A while ago, during a debate on gay legal partnerships (civil union is the model being lobbied for in Ireland at present), I remarked – rather mildly and briefly for once – that it could be useful for lesbians and gay men to think about feminist critiques of marriage, when up stood a fine young fellow who announced: 'We don't want all this revolutionary stuff. We just want equality'. As if it grows on trees, there for the picking. Which troubles me greatly, because it doesn't, and even if it did, how would this new version of 'equality without tears' go down on the streets – and at home, at work, at play, at war?

Polite claims for inclusion are a far cry from the revolution that my generation of activists dreamed of and fought for, with our (never singular or simple) goals of human relations structured in radically different ways, of shifting the centre, of breaking the hierarchical, asymmetrical binaries, of blasting open the straight-jacket of hetero-patriarchal-normativity, of exposing and combating the systemic control, othering and oppression of the many by the few, of the need, in short, for a revolutionary re-thinking and re-making of this world we inhabit.

Utopian? Perhaps. But it does seem (at the very least) to be something of a come-down to be fighting to be 'let in', for inclusion in a system so mined and riven by material inequalities, ie, founded in the very principle of unequal power relations, in the unequal distribution of sexual, material, social and cultural benefits and privileges, however 'dispersed'

Certainly, we were ambitious and idealistic, but not stupid or lazy. Because it is both (they may be the same thing in this case) to behave as if equality is a ready-made, always-waiting commodity ripe for the picking; to behave as if unequal and altogether materially deployed relations of power can be transformed by desire, the flick of a government whip, legislative fiat, or a cultural (half)turn. Claiming the right to inclusion in a system which can only continue to function if benefits, privileges, commodities and conveniences are not equally available to and enjoyed by all is self-deluding, to put it politely. It is, on the whole, rare for people who have power and resources (and the one because they have the other) to hand them over without an unholy row. If and when they appear to do so, one is well advised, as a general rule of thumb, to read the small print.

If me and me and me and mine are now the included, who's taking my place out on the periphery?

But it isn't just about me and mine, is it? Way beyond my immediate self-interest, there's a world full of people who matter, living lives that should matter, but don't. People whose lives should be at least as full of the potential for well-being and well-living as mine, but are not. People I will never encounter, might well not love, like, agree with or understand if I did, but with whom I am connected nonetheless, and whether I choose to acknowledge it or not. What I think and what I do, in the position of immense privilege I occupy as a white intellectual in the rich world, have a massive impact on the flourishing and perishing of people who are strangers to me.

Trying to think through the (complex) reasons which may explain the shocking disparities between people, the injustices, exploitation and oppression (micro and macro) that we can only avoid seeing if we decide not to look, is one of the things I can do as a feminist radical academic. Working out how to transform the systems and structures that generate widespread, morally obscene and technically unnecessary human distress is another. Famine and drought are not necessary; bombing is not necessary; the sexual trafficking of women and children is not necessary; rape is not necessary; deporting refugees and asylum -seekers from rich countries is not necessary. Yet another thing I can do is ask where the knowledge-making I'm involved in gets those other than me and mine (strangers), whether it can be useful to them and if not, what would better serve their flourishing? And working to translate ideas, theories, insights, understandings, observations, findings *et al.* into radical political actions, ie acts designed to interrupt hegemonic discourses and to transform oppressive, brutalising structures so as to lead to a greater chance of some (more) freedom and human dignity for more people.

But we can only do that if we have a sturdy belief, all uncertainties notwithstanding, that acting to make a difference does make a difference. And that doing nothing will accomplish precisely that. A transformed world will never grow on trees.

I know it's not hip to go on about political activism in academic milieux (feminist or whatever), because that's so 1970s, and it's different for the new generation. Yes it is different, and in both exhilarating and troubling ways. But the shape of things as they are didn't fall off a tree. Stuff doesn't just 'happen'. It gets made, produced, generated. How convenient to have a generation of young minority worlders that prefers watching to doing; that's getting fatter and greedier and lazier and unhappier because consuming is the most satisfying thing in their lives; that doesn't care what happens to people down the street, much less a thousand kilometres away, because they've got the message that me, me, me and me matters most, comes first and everyone else has to look out for themselves and their own.

But it's not only a generational thing. It was never cool for more than five minutes to be an activist academic (or academic activist), the oxymoron being altogether too complicated probably, or destabilising (more likely). I speak (as ever) from personal experience. Sometimes, to cheer myself up – lunacy is never far away – I sing tunes in my head, usually very bad ones with ridiculous lyrics. The other day, up surged an absurd 'Guys and Dolls' number, with a great chorus line:

'Sit down, sit down, sit down, sit down, sit down, you're rockin' the boat'.
Mind you, for a boat to be rocked so hard it overturns, you need a lot more people than are rockin' right now.

So let's rock!

It's vital for the sake of humanity.

A Note on the Section Headings
Gendering on down: A play on the US idiom 'motoring on down'. Although idioms are notoriously resistant to (cultural) translation, I think the overall drift of my reformulation of the phrase is clear: increasingly ubiquitous 'gender politics' is not getting women anywhere.

Equality! The must-have accessory for a politician in 2005! This was the (possibly ironic?) text of an advertisement created by the Australian Gay and Lesbian Rights Lobby earlier this year. See www.glrl.org.au.

Join the Evolution! A billboard advertisement put out by the mobile phone company Meteor in Dublin in 2005.

Patriarchy is not old hat! In *The Curious Feminist* by Cynthia Enloe.

Women don't want equality with men. We're far more ambitious. 1970s Women's Liberation Movement widely printed on Cath Tate postcards. I'm not sure if it originated in the USA or the UK.

I'll be a post-feminist in post-patriarchy! Also a postcard, although dating from the late 1990s.

References
Adelye-Fayemi, Bisi. "Creating and Sustaining Feminist Space in Africa: Local-global Challenges in the 21st Century." 4th Dame Nita Barrow Annual Lecture, Toronto, 2000.

Amnesty International. *AI Report 2005: The State of the World's Human Rights.* Amnesty International, 2005.

Amnesty Ireland. *Justice and Accountability: Stop Violence Against Women in Ireland.* Dublin. Amnesty International, Irish Section, 2005.

Armstrong, Chris. "Complex Equality: Beyond Equality and Difference." *Feminist Theory*, 3(1), 2003: 67-82.

Bacik, Ivana."The Criminal Justice Bill 2004." Dublin, *GCN* (*Gay Community News*, July, 2005.

Baker, John *et al. Equality: From Theory to Action*. London: Palgrave, 2003.

Bhasin, Kamla. *Taking Stock II: A Review of Gender and Women's Rights in ActionAid International*. ActionAid International, 2004.

Bulbeck, Chilla. "How Women's Studies Students Express Their Relationships with Feminism." *Women's Studies International Forum*. 24 (2), 2001: 141-156.

Burke, Michael. "Radicalising Liberal Feminism by Playing the Games that Men Play." *Australian Feminist Studies*. 19 (44), 2004: 169-183.

Charlesworth, Hilary and Christine Chinkin. *The Boundaries of International Law: A Feminist Analysis*. Manchester: Juris Publishing/ Manchester UP, 2000.

Colebrook, Claire. *Gender*. London: Palgrave Macmillan, 2004. Cox, Laurence. "Globalisation From Below? 'Ordinary People', Movements and Intellectuals." www.iol.ie/~mazzoldi/toolsforchange/rev/firkin (2001).

Devins, Neal and Davison M Douglas, eds. *Redefining Equality*. Oxford: Oxford UP, 1998.

Enloe, Cynthia. *The Curious Feminist: Searching for Women in a New Age of Empire*. California: U of California Press, 2004.

Equality News. Dublin: The Equality Authority, (Summer) 2005.

European Women's Lobby (EWL). "European Women's Lobby Proposals for the New Social Policy Agenda 2006-2010." www.womenlobby-org/Document.asp (2004).

Fraser, Nancy. "Recognition or Redistribution? A Critical Reading of Iris Young's *Justice and the Politics of Difference*." *Journal of Political Philosophy*, 3 (2) 1995: 166-180.

Guerrina, Roberta. 'Gender, Mainstreaming and Fundamental Rights: Challenging the Foundations of Democratic Governance in the EU Debate.' *Policy, Organisation and Society*, 22(1) 2003.

Healy, Alison. *Irish Times*. 28 June 2005.

Hughes, Kate. "I've Been Pondering Whether You Can Be a Part-Feminist'. Young Australian Women's Studies Students Discuss Gender'. *Women's Studies International Forum*, (28) 2005:1, 37-49.

Jackson, Stevi and Sue Scott, eds. *Gender: A Sociological Reader*. London: Routledge, 2002.

Kirby, Peader. "Globalization, the Celtic Tiger and Social Outcomes: Is Ireland a Model or a Mirage?" *Globalizations.* Vol. 1, No 2, 2004: 205-222.

Les Penelopes. "Men and Feminism." www.penelopes.org.anglais/xarticle (2005).

Long, Julia. "'Al is for to selle': An Investigation into the Trafficking of Women into Ireland for Commercial Sexual Exploitation". MA Dissertation, WERRC, University College Dublin, 2005.

Maddison, Sarah. "Bombing the Patriarchy or Just Trying to Get a Cab: Challenges Facing the Next Generation of Feminist Activists." *Outskirts.* 10 www.chloe.uwa.edu.auoutskirts/archive/VOL.10/article3.html (2002).

Mullan, Caitriona and Laurence Cox (nd). "Social Movements Never Die: Community Politics and the Social Economy in the Irish Republic'. www.iol.ie/~mazzoldi/toolsforchange/afpp/isa.html

National Women's Council of Ireland. Letter from Director to affiliated organisations, 19 July 2005.

O'Toole, Fintan. *After the Ball.* Dublin: New Island, 2003.

Phelan, Shane. *Sexual Strangers: Gays, Lesbians and Dilemmas of Citizenship.* Philadelphia: Temple UP, 2001.

Pollack, Mark A. and Emilie Hafner-Burton. "Mainstreaming Gender in the European Union." Massachusetts: Harvard Law School. Harvard Jean Monnet Working Paper, 2000.

Rahman, Momin. *Sexuality and Democracy: Identities and Strategies in Lesbian and Gay Politics.* Edinburgh: Edinburgh UP, 2000.

Randriamaro, Zo. "Gender and Economic Reforms in Africa: The Hidden Political and Ideological Agenda" www.twnside.org.sg/title (nd).

Sen, Amartya. *The Argumentative Indian: Writings on Indian History, Culture and Identity.* London: Allen Lane, 2005.

Signs. Special issue on Eastern Europe. 29(3) 2004.

Smith, Nicola Jo-Anne. "Deconstructing 'Globalization' in Ireland." *Policy & Politics.* 32 4 (2004): 503-19.

Walby, Sylvia. "Gender Mainstreaming: Productive Tensions in Theory and Practice." ESRC Gender Mainstreaming Seminars, 2004.

Walzer, Michael. *Spheres of Justice: A Defence of Pluralism and Equality.* New York: Basic Books, 1983.

Young, Iris Marion. "Unruly Categories: A Critique of Nancy Fraser's Duals Systems Theory.' *New Left Review.* 222 (1997).

Progressive Politics and the Ethics of Care

Ornaith O'Dowd

The ethics of care has been a central theme of feminist thought for roughly the last quarter century. In this paper I will sketch the main trajectories of the care debate, and suggest my own interpretation of care, from a Kantian perspective. In doing this, I will focus on two questions: first, how care and justice are related in moral and political theory, and, secondly, what a political reading of care should look like. In this connection, I will argue that the conception of care that I offer can help to provide progressive thinkers and activists with some valuable theoretical tools with which to argue coherently against the intertwined and mutually-supporting systems of global capitalism, neo-imperialism, and patriarchy.

The care approach was inspired by a radical feminist critique of the neglect of women's experience in patriarchal cultures – in politics, art, the academy, and so on. In particular, moral and political philosophy was seen to have based its conception of moral personhood on a false universalisation of male experience. Yet, how could moral and political philosophy guide human action if it ignored the historical experience of women, specifically, their role as primary caregivers? Early care theorists, in the 1970s and 80s, argued that ethics should take account of this kind of distinct historical experience, and further, that ethics would be changed quite fundamentally as a result. The developmental psychologist Carol Gilligan suggested that there were significant differences in the way men and women tended to approach moral problems, and that these differences might reflect a gendered "different voice" (2) as she put it, in ethics, or, indeed, two different and possibly incommensurable moral frameworks. The approach that Gilligan's female subjects tended to take reflected what became known as a 'care perspective' or an ethics of care: a perspective concerned more with maintaining relationships than protecting individual rights or autonomy, and based more on feeling and context-dependent assessments of need than on abstract moral principles. The approach that male subjects tended to take, on the other hand, reflected what became known as a 'justice perspective' or justice ethics, and was grounded, more or less, on abstract principles and respect for individuals' rights and autonomy, prioritising reason rather than feeling as a basis for moral judgment. This 'justice perspective,' of course, also reflected the dominant approach in philosophical ethics, and the care approach, rooted as it seemingly was in women's historical experiences as caregivers, was relatively ignored in philosophy. Gilligan suggests that justice and care were two distinct moral frameworks that one could not think from simultaneously (1, 62-63, 164-165 *passim*): one might adopt one perspective at one time and the other perspective at another time, but one could not adopt both at the same time, and each might recommend conflicting courses of action. These, of course, were basically empirical claims — and her findings and interpretations have been criticised, but they were highly influential for moral philosophers.

One of the most prominent of these was Nel Noddings, who offered a complete moral theory based on care, eschewing the justice perspective entirely. This care ethic existed without the standard language of rights, duties, and justice, and claimed instead that morality's central concern was the maintenance of caring relations and the responsiveness of the carer for the cared-for in such relations. In Noddings's view, 'ethical caring' emerges from our remembrance of our "best moments of caring and being cared for" (10): this remembrance, by causing in us a feeling of obligation, prompts us to meet the needs of the other as they present themselves to us, even though we might not feel the 'natural' impulse to care, and this is what gives caring its moral value. These kinds of judgements do not appeal to abstract principles, but are highly context-dependent, and rely more on feeling than on reason.

This is a radical view, and there are, I think, several serious problems with it, which reflect difficulties with the general project of constructing a 'care-only' ethical theory. Firstly, it is unclear how such a theory can avoid at least tacitly appealing to some kind of principle or rule which can enable us to identify our best moments of caring and being cared for. This seems to imply some kind of objective standard for assessing acts of caring: if so, we need to specify what it is, and if not, we risk making the dangerous claim that any kind of relation in which caring takes place is beyond moral criticism. Surely the moral philosopher must be able to criticise relations in which care is given, but which are unequal, exploitative, or abusive and, for this, we need a standard beyond care itself: we need justice. I think this is a point that should be particularly resonant for feminists.

A second problem— and, again, one that should be of particular concern to feminists — is that the carer's care for herself seems to be justified only on the grounds that it enables her to continue caring for others. It is only with the language of justice that we can make moral claims on the carer's behalf on the grounds that she deserves consideration in her own right.

A third problem concerns our moral obligations to distant others. Noddings's version of care, based on maintaining face-to-face caring relations, and meeting the needs for care of 'particular others,' rather than on respecting persons in the abstract, cannot apply to distant others, and since hers is a 'care-only' ethic, it cannot guide our dispositions or actions towards them at all. The moral costs of such a position should be clear. Clearly, we cannot have a personal caring relationship with everyone in the world: this is why we need universal moral principles or rules. Our obligations to care about distant others cannot be articulated without the language of justice. It is quite wrong to deny that I am morally connected to distant others. In the context of globalisation, in particular, it borders on the absurd to claim that we do not have obligations, let's say, to the exploited worker in China who made our shoes.

With these kinds of criticisms in mind, many later care theorists have attempted to accommodate both care and justice in an overall moral theory. Grace Clement, for example, thinks that justice and care, while distinct, can and should be integrated in our moral lives, each correcting limitations in the other. The justice perspective gives us the framework for setting out the rights and obligations of individuals (including our obligations to distant others), while the care perspective sets those rights in the context of human interrelatedness and motivates us to respect them. While this is an advance from a 'care-only' approach, serious problems remain for a theory like Clement's, which attempts to balance or integrate justice and care, seen as radically different kinds of moral framework. Any conception of morality that drives a wedge between justice and care, and allows for situations in which morality offers conflicting directions through these two perspectives that form part of it, is problematic.

In spite of these problems, I think that the care theorists have diagnosed a serious deficiency in traditional, male-dominated western moral theory or, at least, traditional interpretations of the canon of moral theory and, therefore, I think that any adequate moral theory must take care very seriously. Before advancing my own interpretation of care and its relation to justice, let me sketch some of the elements that appear to be common to most of the very varied interpretations of care already in the literature, of which I have only been able to give a very brief sketch here.

First, an ethic of care suggests that caring relations have moral value (of some kind), and that, therefore, their maintenance is a central imperative of morality. Secondly, an ethic of care emphasises active engagement with the other, rather than disinterested calculation of rights and obligations. Thirdly, the cared-for is seen not as an abstract representative of humanity, but as a particular, unique individual with needs that should be responded to with flexibility and sensitivity to context.

My own conception of care takes account of each of these concerns, but in a modified way, and in the context of a wider view that takes justice and care to be equally essential components of morality. Care, as I see it, is an attitude of active moral concern for persons, viewed always as particular others, although they may not be personally known to us, and to whom we stand in some kind of relation as fellow members of the moral community. This attitude of active moral concern for others is always manifested in practice to whatever degree is possible, subject to reasonable practicability and considerations of justice.

This interpretation of care views human beings as both social and autonomous, with both rational and sensuous natures; therefore, morally recommendable care respects and nurtures all of these capacities. Care, as I understand it, directs our moral attention primarily to all particular others who are members of the moral community, whether or not we are in face-to-face relations with them, and this membership is constituted by a broadly Kantian criterion of autonomy, or having a self-governing will. Of course, when applying the moral law to human persons, who are, as far as we know, the only kinds of creatures who satisfy this criterion, the Kantian rightly acknowledges that we must take into account our sensuous, vulnerable, embodied nature too. This is an important and insufficiently appreciated point.

In my view, justice and care are not two distinct ethics, but two fundamental elements of morality, deeply intertwined at its heart. Morality cannot do without either: I think attempts to treat them as 'stand-alone' ethical frameworks are deeply problematic. Any coherent conception of morality must take both care and justice seriously.

Active moral concern, to return to the first part of my definition, is central to Kantian ethics properly understood. One of the most important features of Kant's ethics is the emphasis on the intentions of the moral agent or, more precisely, the maxim or policy for action that arises or can be inferred from these intentions: not only must one do the right thing, but one must do the right thing for the right reason or, more precisely, one's maxim or policy for action must agree with the moral law. Responding with respect to the moral law—which is what the moral agent should do— means that we care about doing the right thing for its own sake. Now, the care theorist may well object here that care demands not that we care about doing the right thing for its own sake, but that we care about the particular other with whom we are confronted in a given situation. However, if we examine closely what is implied in the notion of 'caring about doing the right thing', we see that it does not make much sense unless one cares about the persons involved. I do not think that Kant is suggesting that our devotion should be to the rules as mere rules: that reduces morality to the level of a game, and one of Kant's central claims is that morality is something of quite a different order to anything else, something unique and exalted that demands a special kind of respect. This special respect is due precisely because the moral law arises from the unconditional moral worth of persons. So, albeit in a somewhat abstract sense, Kant would agree that caring about doing the right thing is caring about the other. Very importantly, it must be an active moral concern, manifested in practice as far as possible. After all, if one is truly concerned about others, one will act to help them where possible and to whatever extent is possible.

However, I do not go as far as care theorists who claim that care is both practice and value (Noddings) or practice and disposition (Tronto). Care, understood as a fundamental category of morality cannot at the same time be identified with one specific practice, namely, the care work associated with women in patriarchal societies. To be sure, care as a basis for moral theory has been inspired by many characteristics of care work, but it does not follow that they are the same thing. Moral theory must apply to all action; care can, therefore, only serve as a basis for moral theory if it can provide a means by which we can make moral judgments about all action, and this kind of generalisation is very difficult if one kind of practice is identified with the theory.

My position about the relationship of practice and value is more modest: care is a value and an element of morality that emphasises the need for action and practice, and acts as a necessary corrective to traditional interpretations of the canon of ethical theory that seemed to suggest that morality amounts to mere rational calculation about duty. Now, I think this sort of account is a serious misrepresentation of Kant, who is usually the principal target in these critiques of 'justice ethics,' but, in my view, care suggests not an abandonment of Kantian ethics, but a re-interpretation; one that is, indeed, more faithful to the spirit of the Kantian project.

So what does all of this mean for political theory? I think that something like my version of care, as I have suggested already, not only allows for but demands a political interpretation. It avoids the difficulty that particularistic versions of care run into in expanding beyond the personal. In my interpretation, distant others are particular others, and they demand our moral attention, our care, in virtue of their moral personhood. Paying attention to the particularity and unique moral worth of all persons leads precisely away from the parochialism towards which a Noddings-style theory tends, and instead recommends political engagement as a moral imperative, since it is only through political engagement, broadly construed, that we can carry out our duties of care to distant others. If one really cares about particular others, one will surely care about the economic, social and political structures that affect their lives. To extend our moral scope, as we must, beyond those with whom we have 'face-to-face' relations, we must think politically. This gives rise to a related moral duty, which is a duty to be informed about politics, and informed about the effects of our actions as citizens, consumers, members of society. Do we buy goods produced by exploited workers? Do we let our political representatives off the hook about debt relief and aid? Even as acquiescent parts of 'the system,' we have effects: we tacitly support the *status quo*, whatever that may be, and for that we must take responsibility. Citizens in democracies with relative freedom of expression and association have a moral obligation to watch the news, and watch it critically, to read the newspaper and read it critically, and even to discuss important political matters with those around us. Politics is not a pastime, a blood sport, a preference: it is a moral duty. Care helps to make this duty vivid to us. Political morality, much as is the case in individual morality, is quite fundamentally a matter of caring about justice.

Caring about justice requires us, then, to be informed, to recognise our own political and social responsibilities, and to act on them where we can; in short, to be active citizens. We can see some good examples of this kind of engagement at the moment with 'Live8' and the 'Make Poverty History' campaign: I think they reflect quite nicely the claim that care and justice are inseparable and form basic elements of political as well as individual morality. After all, one of their clearest messages has been that poverty in Africa is a moral concern for us, not only insofar as we must respond to suffering with charity and care that meets basic needs, but, more fundamentally, as a matter of justice: hence, the current campaign's emphasis on debt and trade as well as aid. The manner in which people are participating in these campaigns also reflects the same point: care is what drives and motivates them to act on their principles of justice by protesting in Edinburgh, for example. Taking care seriously as a political value means not that we replace our notions of justice, but that we commit ourselves to act on them, that we bring them out from their abstract groundings and into our lives.

A political theory that takes care seriously will have another central feature: an emphasis on political community and solidarity, based on care's view of people as both autonomous and interrelated, and based also on care's emphasis on action, which is best interpreted as an emphasis on positive duties or obligations to others. This complex view of people yields a political theory that helps us to avoid the extremes of libertarianism and communitarianism; a theory that demands the creation and maintenance of a sense of community among autonomous and interrelated persons. What I have in mind here is a community of persons who care about justice, which is another way of saying that they respect the moral personhood of others in that community. My interpretation of political care is strongly influenced by the work of John Rawls. Unlike many commentators, I think Rawlsian justice satisfies many of the demands of political care.

Consider, for example, the difference principle as expressing the value of social solidarity, and equally intriguingly for the care theorist, as also demanding very specific action. The difference principle says that the primary social goods (especially economic ones) must be equally distributed unless an inequality would benefit the worst-off in society. It is important to note that it is a conditional argument: Rawls does not claim that there are, in fact, any circumstances under which an unequal distribution of primary goods would benefit the worst-off, but he does argue that if there were, then the inequality would be justified. The just 'baseline' is equality, but there is a sense that the political community as a whole has a special obligation of care to the least privileged, and that obligation trumps a formal commitment to equality. People in a Rawlsian just society do not simply 'make their own way.' Although Rawls is anxious to avoid the term 'community,' and at one point uses the unfortunate gendered term 'fraternity', I think he is indeed talking about a kind of political community, albeit one not based on shared comprehensive doctrines (religious, political, and so on), but on a shared commitment to basic principles of justice and a shared conception of public reason as a basis for politics. All of this is very congruent with a political reading of care.

In conclusion, I want to suggest that the kind of political theory I advocate, incorporating care and justice as equally foundational, inseparable elements, can help progressives to give more coherent responses to the mutually supporting systems of US-led global capitalism, neo-imperialism, and patriarchy, by exposing their deep anti-humanism, and constructing an alternative, true, inclusive humanism based on respecting not a false model of humanity modelled on its most privileged members, but on respecting the autonomous and interrelated nature of all persons.

How can all of this be of any use in political debate and activism? First, activism requires theory. In particular, I think the alter-globalisation movement requires a theoretical basis, an answer to the neoliberal's question: 'what's your alternative?' If it can offer a robust, coherent theory, it can defeat that well-worn refrain, that the ideological debate about capitalism is over, that there is no way but the third way, so to speak. A political theory along the lines I have suggested here—a theory that values political community, but is based on respect for individual persons, a theory that demands engagement and action, and has something to say not only about our economic and political rights, but about our duties and obligations—might be the source of an alternative vision. A theory that values both autonomy and interrelatedness, individual rights and solidarity, carries in it a powerful moral critique of capitalism, of patriarchy, and all the systems of oppression intertwined with them and nourished by them. Such a theory can make a difference, because activism is not just about being on the streets, but about ideas, and ideas can, in a real sense, create the 'other world' which progressives must believe is possible.

References

Gilligan, Carol. *In A Different Voice: Psychological Theory and Women's Development.* Cambridge, Mass.: Harvard UP, 1982.

Herman, Barbara. *The Practice of Moral Judgment.* Cambridge, Mass.: Harvard UP, 1993.

Kant, Immanuel. *Critique of Practical Reason.* Trans. Werner S. Pluhar. Indianapolis and Cambridge: Hackett, 2002.

-----. *Groundwork for the Metaphysics of Morals.* Trans. Arnulf Zweig. Oxford: Oxford UP, 2002.

-----. *The Metaphysics of Morals.* Trans. Mary Gregor. Cambridge: Cambridge UP, 1996.

Clement, Grace. *Care, Autonomy and Justice: Feminism and the Ethics of Care.* Boulder, CO: Westview Press, 1996.

Noddings, Nel. *'Caring' Justice and Care: Essential Readings in Feminist Ethics.* Virginia Held, ed. Boulder, CO: Westview Press, 1995.

O'Neill, Onora. *Constructions of Reason.* Cambridge: Cambridge UP, 1989.

Rawls, John. *A Theory of Justice* (Rev. Ed.) Cambridge, Mass.: Belknap Press of the Harvard UP, 1999.

-----. *Political Liberalism.* New York: Columbia UP, 1996.

Tronto, Joan. *Moral Boundaries: A Political Argument for Care.* New York and London: Routledge, 1993.

Is There Such a Thing as a Mediterranean Feminism?
A Contribution from the Margin

Elisabetta Bertolino

The dominant positions within western feminism can be summarised as the 'equality' and 'difference' approaches and, more recently, as the deconstructive perspective. Although it is not possible to make generalisations about streams of feminism and define them within geographical areas, it is true that the privileged positions of Anglo-American and French feminism are by far the most disseminated within western thought.

This paper is an attempt to investigate the direction taken by feminism in the margin of the mainstream. It looks at the Mediterranean area around the western centre and focuses, in particular, on the sexual difference stream of thought developed in Italy and, specifically, on the theory of a contemporary Italian feminist philosopher, Adriana Cavarero. The idea behind this is that by moving the focus away from the centre, a broader conversation can be opened within feminism and different ways of opposing the phallogocentric order can be explored. To be argued is that, while the equality, difference and even the deconstructive perspectives remain within a phallogocentric position, Adriana Cavarero's theory seeks to avoid the phallogocentric logic of sameness, and its reduction of plurality to unity and binary thinking.

The question of the metaphysical construction of the subject in philosophy needs to be brought to the surface to understand why, within feminism, there has been a production or reaction confined to the equality/difference thinking and to a deconstructive position. The term 'subject' in philosophy is directly related to the *cogito* of Cartesio, in which the subject is constructed, metaphysically, as rational. The Cartesian subject reflects an abstract rationality that is thought as 'man' and within a binary logic based on the mind/body opposition. Consequently, 'man' as a rational subject is constituted precisely in opposition to a woman, who is instead considered a corporeal object.

This thinking of the subject as male, and the consequent reduction of woman to object or corporeal element, has given origin to what is called a phal-logo-centric system, a system founded on both the logos or reason and the perspective of the phallus. The perspective of the phallus is a perspective constructed and described from the phallic or male point of view and constitutes a kind of male thinking, which insists on telling, as absolute truth, one and only one story.

The phallogocentric subjectivity/logic is constituted of language and thought and is used as a framework for all discourses. Although the phallogocentric subjectivity is deeply masculine, it presents itself as neutral. Any attempt to formulate a discourse outside it needs necessarily to speak in masculine terms. Consequently, feminists have found themselves either trying to reflect this symbolic system with an 'equality' discourse or trying to oppose it with a 'difference' approach that emphasises the positivity of the feminine subjectivity or, recently, they have sought to deconstruct this phallogocentric system by reinterpreting it.

In particular, equality and difference have been reductively understood to be alternative concepts in the phallogocentric political tradition. But, while an equality perspective implies an acceptance for women of the conditions in which men live and work and the reduction of plurality to unity, the difference alternative, although empowering for women, still defines women in relation to a male identity, within a very limited sphere of actions and reduces otherness or difference to sameness. In other words, the terms of the question have been asked either in relation to how women can be included within the phallogocentric subjectivity or how a specific subjectivity for women might be affirmed. In the absence of alternative models, women have been, thus, constrained to think and argue about equality or difference within the same logic of phallogocentrism. Women are asked either to share men's standards of efficiency, competitiveness and individualistic lifestyle or to be marginalised within their mothering and familial roles.

I shall, therefore, analyse the main points of an equality feminist approach, such as the current liberal feminist perspective, which is anchored in rights and gender equality, and a difference feminist perspective as it has been theorised by the French feminist of sexual difference, Luce Irigaray. I shall also consider the deconstructive perspective of the American feminist Judith Butler. Finally, I shall conclude with the Italian sexual difference theory of Adriana Cavarero, which explains how sexual difference can avoid the logic of sameness and the binarism of the phallologocentric system.

Liberalism and Equality Feminism

To understand what an equality approach implies, it is necessary to go back to the subject that shapes it. The modern notion of the free and autonomous individual of liberalism reflects directly the logic of the phallogocentric subject of philosophy. The abstract universal, presumably neutral, individual is based on a standard notion of 'man,' which excludes any singularity and "replicates (...) itself in everybody" (Cavarero 1999: 136). Liberal feminists have tried to challenge the gender unbalance produced by the phallogocentric system by focusing on the abstract individualism of liberalism and by seeking to include women within the same system through the principle of equality.

Liberalism based on this subjectivity focuses on an understanding of reason as universal and on a dualistic mode of thinking. The mind is conceived as distinct and superior to the body. This mind and body separation emphasises a subjectivity based on male reason. Men have traditionally been associated with the disembodied or transcendent human existence, and women with the bodily and immanent components of human existence. Women are 'others' as defined by a masculine perspective. Within this dialectical system, the masculine disembodiment is possible only if women occupy their bodies, only if women constitute the excluded, other or absent.

Liberalism is the model adopted by western democracies and by mainstream feminism. Thanks to feminist requests for equality, the core ideas of liberalism have recently been extended to include women. For liberal feminism, the main achievement has been to secure equality of opportunity and equal rights for women (Weedon 13). Whilst, on the one hand, equality feminism reflects women's desire to share men's individualistic lifestyle; on the other, women face the difficulty of combining marriage and paid work (Bacchi 1990: 28). Within liberalism, feminism has also adopted and elaborated the concept of gender to emphasise the constructed cultural differences between men and women in opposition to the previous biological reductionism and with the aim of freeing women from previous forms of constraints and eliminating differences.

Especially during the early phase of 'second wave' feminism in the 1960s, there was a striving for equal rights and opportunities for women and a focus on gender and gender equality. Egalitarian feminists claim that women are as able-bodied as men, and that women's roles are the result of culture and social organisation rather than nature. They look to gender, in other words, rather than sex, and focus on the gender construction of women within society.

This focus on gender is not without problems. Gender remains within the same logic of sameness of the phallologocentric system. Within gender categories, it is women that are compared to men and not men to women. Therefore, the comparison is hierarchical with men remaining the standard. Gender focuses on more general and neutral concerns of the structures and practices of social inequalities and social life; it also functions as an undifferentiated attribute of the subject that, at the same time, affirms and ignores women's difference.

Whilst the notion of equality does have a liberatory and emancipatory force and, through equality, women have gained the same political rights as men and have enabled equal rights legislation to be passed, which prevents the arbitrary treatment of women, an equality approach is also limited, restrictive and not without a few problems. There is, in particular, the impossibility of relying upon the concept of equality as a driving force for women's liberation. Equal rights, gender equality and the subjectivity constructed on the rational, autonomous and self-fulfilling agent of the individual do not fit women's needs. The neutral individual necessarily presupposes categorisations of sex or even gender as secondary. This is because the principle of equality functions within notions of similarity and sameness. People that differ are compared within the same parameters assumed to be valid for everybody.

Moving from formal equality to the latest policy of substantive equality, within which welfare liberalism takes account of disadvantages, is also problematic. Substantive equality co-exists, in fact, within the classical liberal concept of equality, thereby reducing its potential. For example, affirmative actions that are a direct outcome of substantive equality and welfare liberalism are a contradiction within the equality approach. The equality approach of liberalism tries to recuperate the excluded through affirmative actions such as quotas in order to ensure that men and women are forwarded in equal numbers. However, quotas as strong affirmative actions, are often opposed in the very name of equality, justice and fairness.

In relation to the principle of equality, Cavarero provides an interesting critique of the concept as revolutionary for men and conservative for women (Cavarero 1999: 122). This is because equality has the capacity to subvert the public sphere, but it does not challenge the distinction made between the public and private spheres. Equality, in fact, dismantles only the hierarchical order within the public sphere as it has been directed explicitly, solely to men. In the recent past, talk of universal suffrage, as related only to men, is a clear example of the way in which the equality principle has been constructed on the phallogocentric universal subjectivity. Therefore, the formal principle of equality has been played, at least for a while, on an exclusive phallogocentric position. Recently, women have been included but, and here is the paradox, only as if they were men. Cavarero writes of a paradoxical position of the principle of equality (1999: 125). The late inclusion of women contradicts, in a sense, its origins in exclusive logic. But this is possible because at the base of the principle of equality there is a paradoxical logic that reconciles exclusion with homologation (Cavarero 1999: 127).

Speaking more specifically of politics, we can say that the liberal democratic system based on the principle of equality requires as its condition that people transcend their localised and partial concerns. Clearly this, if imposed on an unequal society, can allow some people to count more than others. Equality, in fact, is not guaranteed by the neutrality and the abstraction of the liberal individual (Phillips 90). The abstract individual imposes a unitary conception of human needs and, to the contrary, this can have the effect of marginalising people from the dominant norm.

Liberalism and equality feminism, thus, have not provided an adequate understanding of human differences and of women's differences. In treating men as the universal, those theories impose a false universal standard, requiring women to become like men and they fail to include women's concerns.

By reflecting the same phallogocentric subjectivity, both liberalism and equality feminism construct women once more as others; women are offered either assimilation to the current situation or segregation from it and asked to abandon or minimise their mothering role and its characteristics in order to gain equality with men. Biological differences and reproductive roles are seen as obstacles to women's emancipation and bodily concerns are excluded within this perspective. Equality means aspiring to masculine qualities, having men as the standard and, therefore, an acceptance of the conditions in which men live and work (Bacchi xvi).

To summarise, in today's liberalist policies, there is a phallogocentric and masculine subject that functions within either the old mechanism of exclusion or the new one of assimilation. Therefore, considering the patriarchal order as a fact in the past for women, even in western countries, it is very naïve, and even dangerous, to push feminism towards the continuous adjustment of the principle of equality. Awareness of those limits has brought the need, within feminism, to resist the phallogocentric subjectivity discourse offered through a difference approach.

Luce Irigaray and Difference Feminism

Starting from the phallogocentric critique of subjectivity, where men have become the only subjects and women are assimilated, French sexual difference philosopher, Luce Irigaray attacks the system based on equality. She writes: "Becoming a man seems to correspond to distancing oneself from one's concrete, living environment, entering into a coded universe that more or less accurately duplicates reality" (Irigaray 1994: 48).

Irigaray opposes the sexual indifference of the neutral subject of equality, which is a male subject. "Gender neutralization", says Irigaray, "puts us, individually and collectively, in danger of death" (Irigaray 1993: 80). Within the current symbolic system, the feminine has been considered as the other of the masculine subject. Irigaray suggests, instead, that the concept of equality may presuppose inequality. For Irigaray, the focus upon rights (and gender) means that women have subjected themselves to a phallocratic order and are simply trying to mirror the male equivalent. Women, instead, need to speak as women because the demand to be equal always presupposes a point of comparison. "To whom or to what do women want to be equalized? To men? To a salary? To a public office? To what standard? Why not to themselves?" (Irigaray 1993: 12).

To move herself outside the phallogocentric discursive system, without being contaminated, Irigaray attempts to reveal the specular logic of such a system through what she calls 'specular deconstruction'. In other words, she explains how phallogocentric subjectivity projects its representation in the mirror producing a feminine that is actually just a masculine reflection. Irigaray deconstructs precisely this game of internal reflection of the phallogocentric logic.

Irigaray's strategy consists, thus, of the mimesis of the male symbolic, which allows re-appropriation of the attributes of the other-feminine. She believes that there is something that exceeds the margins and the normative power of the logos, something that is outside the discursive phallogocentric system. The inside of the system is the phallogocentric intelligible that shapes, represents and produces meanings and, in so doing, is able to control the outside that cannot be captured. Consequently, Irigaray seeks to posit the feminine, through the morphology of the female body, as outside the phallogocentric system of thought and language, outside words and language which are structured upon the phallogocentric system of masculine subjectivity.

All this is done by Irigaray with the intent of disrupting the phallogocentric system and the internal representation of the feminine (Deutscher 69-77; see also Cornell 16, 142); despite this, Irigaray appears to reappropriate traditional ideas about femininty and create a new positive identity and specific subjectivity for women (Burke, Schor and Whitford 17). Irigaray questions the structure of the logic in which the female as concept has been suppressed, and then displaces the construction of a feminine symbolic system by promoting a mode of being that is opposed to the phallic mode of discourse.

Irigaray is theorising in dangerous zones here, risking the reproduction of patriarchal stereotypes regarding women. Women are categorised on the basis of elements of commonality, essences that become new metaphysical and abstract representations in which singularities between women are erased. "Women", argues Irigaray, for example:

> Do not have the same relationship to entropy, to homoeostasis, to release. Their internal regulation is much stronger, and it maintains them in a constant, irreversible process of growth...A woman reaches puberty, loses her virginity, is pregnant one or more times, reaches menopause...All these events mark a much more continuous temporality than do the ruptures of male sexuality or its continuum without irreversible momentum" (Irigaray 1994: 25).

She also writes: "Women care more about the qualities of people, things, actions. Their speech contains more adjectives and adverbs than men do" (Irigaray 1994: 49).

Thus, while Irigaray attempts to exit the binary logic of the phallogocentric system by positioning herself outside the system, at the same time, she naively reproduces the binary logic (Cavarero 1999: 144). To the masculine subjectivity, Irigaray adds, in fact, that of the feminine, or, in other words, together with the universal and abstract subject of man, we have now the universal and abstract subject of woman. Created once more is a subject that excludes and produces indifference. Irigaray also reinforces in this way the existence of separate spheres for men and women. Comparing women with nature, body, emotions or appealing to a superiority of women leads to the opportunity to equate women again with family and domestic life or, in any case, with essentialised, fixed categories of sameness that are assumed to be valid for all women.

One should not underestimate the benefits of difference feminism to women. To be categorised and essentialised as woman, rather than as a duplicate of the essence of man, has surely been more significant for women and has probably helped bring confidence and empowerment to them. To view women as active rather than passive has helped activate the shift from women as victims to women as subjects who can change their condition. Also, to oppose the female subject to the male subject has been, in any case, a strategic move not predicted by the phallogocentric order (Cavarero 1999: 136).

However, one has also to be critical of this new type of essentialism. The common space for women, which difference feminism has found, can easily become an essence or a metaphysical perspective of the category 'woman' as it produces necessarily an internal non-differentiation between women and, therefore, reproduces once again relations of sameness based on phallogocentric thought. But Cavarero invites us to think this type of difference feminism as a temporary and necessary strategy in order to deconstruct the persistent androcentric and phallogocentric logic (Cavarero 1999: 136). Ultimately, a feminism of difference, such as the one proposed by Irigaray, stresses women's differences from men's by reflecting upon existing definitions and categories and reduces differences between women to essentialised concepts of sameness.

Judith Butler and Deconstructive Feminism

The deconstructive or poststructuralist position focuses on identity formation and on the ways meanings are negotiated within the phallogocentric logic, seeking to deconstruct differences and identities. The essentialised concept of woman is rejected in favour of fractured identities and multiple subjectivities; meanings and subjectivity are seen as culturally produced and changeable. Here, the individual is never fully coherent as in liberalism, but is, instead, contradictory. The aim of a deconstructive perspective is to move through the phallogocentric symbolic in order to obtain a position of alterity/difference from which to subvert the symbolic itself (Critchley 1999a: 28).

Within this context, the theory of Judith Butler shows affinities with a deconstructive perspective. Butler (1987, 1990, 1993) focuses, in particular, on gender, but her thought can be applied to other identity categories as well. Gender is commonly rigidified and internalised within discourses. The power of language has, in fact, a normalising effect and, through iteration, performativity and repetition, the meaning of language is made stable, normal and natural. Language constructs identities and differences through processes of subordination and exclusion. This process of normalising is part of the binary logic of the phallogocentric system.

Butler interrogates precisely those regulatory mechanisms of language through which the subject is produced, starting from the Hegelian dialectic, seen not from a totality perspective, but, rather, in its mode of becoming. Power, for Butler, is never merely a condition external or prior to the subject. The subject enjoys its subjectivity because there is necessarily another which is the excluded. It is the very mechanism of exclusion that allows the subject to be formed through rupture and re-signification.

Re-signification entails seeking instabilities within a discourse upon which it is possible to generate crisis in order to limit and define the subject. That means that within the logic of discourses there are opportunities for the subject to reinvent itself and other discourses. That is, Butler theorises re-signification in order to oppose the violence of discourse against differently constituted subjects. Thus, within this logic, Butler is able to push the feminist understanding of gender identity beyond the polarities of the essentialist debate.

Important for Butler is the concept of performativity. Performativity and repetition contain the possibility for a reconfiguration of the discursive embodiment. Therefore, there are no men or women, only performativity and repetition in accordance with social rules. By repetition, one inevitably finds a position of alterity or difference, which, although always remaining within the phallogocentric system, allows one to rearticulate the symbolic system in new ways (Critchley 1999a: 28). The deconstructive approach of Butler is surely a new perspective that avoids the equality/difference binarism, and might prove very useful to feminism. Feminism can, in fact, exploit these mechanisms of subversion and instability of identity and difference through iteration in language. However, the application of Butler's deconstructive perspective does not avoid phallogocentric thinking.

Butler argues that the hegemony of the phallogocentric system, which operates through exclusions, contains the potential for expanding democratic possibilities and, therefore, for rendering liberalism as more inclusive and dynamic. As a result, both gender and rights relate dialectically, through mechanisms of inclusion-exclusion, to the abstract neutrality of democratic theories that are thought of in terms of man as a constitutive subject.

Within gender and rights discourses, women are maintained in a continuing interaction with the phallogocentric system of power and within relations of sameness. Therefore, the gender element and the rights approach, even though theorised as never-fixed constructions, may work to produce the very universal subjectivity and achieve only limited change. One should, in fact, not forget the limits of a discourse that tries to rearticulate the same phallogocentric construction. The normative dominant power may be able to reconsolidate itself through cycles of crisis and resolution and might be capable of incorporating feminist requests for change (Modeski 1991). Identity categories may be reproduced without achieving real transformation. And the rearticulation of discourses often produces new legal, social or cultural subjects that are very similar to those of which others have been critical (see, for example, Loizidou 1999). Also, rearticulation requires highly abstract skills and may be unsuitable to provide agency to all women.

A further problem involves the focus of Butler solely on the textual or symbolic and, therefore, again on the logos of the phallogocentric system. The system can be resignified and rearticulated while the material and corporeal is not addressed. Matter and body, as is sex, are, in fact, only prediscursive effects of discourses and cannot be accessed outside the symbolic for Butler (Costera 1998). This is problematic for human beings, and for women in particular. Many women's issues are actually directly related to women's bodies and cannot be reduced solely to textual discourses.

Ultimately, then, although Butler's thought appears to be radical, it shares the fundamental premise of the phallogocentric system. The focus is on the phallogocentric infrastructure and, although difference and identity can become disruptive and subversive, the assumption remains that discourses and subjectivity constructions must go through a never-ending repression of differences and identites in order to function. The normativity of language still constructs itself from the processes of exclusion within the logic of sameness. The phallogocentrism of the fixed metaphysical identity of the subject is not negated, only reinterpreted. The phallogocentric system is simply deconstructed and its positions made unstable.

Adriana Cavarero and Her Different Difference Feminism of One's Uniqueness

The Mediterranean perspective of the Italian sexual difference stream and, in particular, the thought of Adriana Cavarero is based on a radical separatist practice outside the male-female dialectic. The key idea of the *pensiero della differenza sessuale* (the thought of sexual difference), is that women should not aim for equality with men; nor should they attempt to achieve emancipation within a relation of sameness with the neutral male universal. Rather, women should focus on their difference, starting from themselves.

The Italian *pensiero della differenza sessuale* and, in particular, Cavarero's thought, has developed an anomalous way of theorising difference and separatism from the phallogocentric perspective. Italian feminism starts from the single woman in relation to other women. There is the self of each woman in a situation of practical communication with other female selves. It is not a theory of essentialised feminine subjectivity, but a confrontation with a structure of relations. There is no subject or identity, only a self that is human.

Although sexual difference in Italy has been inspired by the work of Luce Irigaray (her books were translated immediately into Italian), the *pensiero della differenza sessuale* seems to depart both from the feminine subjectivity construction of Irigaray and the dialectic that sustains Butler's thought. The dialectic of the self that includes the other or necessitates the exclusion of the other as a condition for its own freedom, which is maintained in the deconstructive perspective, is avoided. Recognition happens within herself and in relation to other female selves. This is an unavoidable journey for *il pensiero della differenza sessuale* in order to recuperate female self-confidence and evade the trap of the relation of sameness within which the male is assumed to be neutral universality.

At the same time, as in a deconstructive perspective, the fixed phallogocentric subjectivity is dismantled. The *pensiero della differenza sessuale* refutes the separation between the symbolic and corporality and opens itself up to the multiplicity of differences beyond sexual difference itself. The concept of materiality is important for *il pensiero della differenza sessuale* as it is mainly in regard to the material differences between women and men that the inequality between the two sexes has been constructed and legitimated through the appropriation and the control of the female body (Vaccaro 20). Also, this perspective is not binary, but focused instead on the uniqueness of the self; it commences from inside her-self rather than assuming the self as a given symbolic or natural entity. Cavarero similarly focuses on the uniqueness of each existent human being, which is revealed during communication through the voice and, therefore, moves from inside/outside by breaking the mind/body binarism of the phallogocentric logic.

Cavarero's philosophy offers a fundamental non-metaphysical challenge to phallogocentric discourses. People are not viewed as the abstract autonomous individuals of liberal theory; instead, they are constituted in their relational uniqueness, whose differences need to be taken into account. As Critchley writes, in regard to the subjectivity construction, one can either remain in a state of permanent deconstruction or seek a way to think people in a non-metaphysical subjectivity as fallible and mortal (Critchley 1999b: 73). And this is precisely what Cavarero attempts to achieve.

Cavarero reduces the conscious self to a living subject who exists. This is an operation that she shares with philosophers such as

Emmanuel Levinas or Jean-Luc Nancy. In Levinas (1993, 1998), the ethical subject takes place at the level of sensitivity, and the subject is a sensible subject rather than a conscious subject. There exists a desire towards the Other. Levinas speaks of the face-to-face as a means of opposing the metaphysical subject. In Nancy (2000) also, there exists a sharing of humanity and an attempt to avoid the symbolism of meaning. Meaning, for Nancy, is no longer meaningful as it refers to its closure. Meaning can instead be found in the being-together, rather than in discourses and the symbolic.

There is in Cavarero, then, as in Levinas and Nancy, the attempt to theorise existence rather than essence. In Cavarero, the uniqueness of each one of us has a relational character that allows the multiplicity of experience. People are seen as concrete human beings rather than as subjects who suppress their own needs, giving space to universalities.

Cavarero also utilises the thought of Hannah Arendt in order to displace the binarism of gender via Arendt's concept of action (Dietz 17; Arendt 1958, 1971). In *The Human Condition*, Arendt rejects gender in favour of 'unique distinctiveness' and action. In Arendt there is the beginning of this unique difference that has been elaborated by Cavarero. By focusing on unique difference, particularity and contingency rather than sameness, universality and fixity, Arendt prepares feminism for the dissolution of identities; by focusing on action instead of being, and unique difference instead of equality and sameness, she emphasises plurality over identity politics and subjectivity. Arendt detaches freedom from the static language of gender identity and considers it as the 'whoness of acting' rather than the 'whatness of being'. By acting and speaking, women can achieve liberation.

Similarly, for Cavarero, to speak of woman is, above all, not to speak about the universal phallogocentric subject and its logic of sameness where the subject is indifferent, generalisable, neutral, founded upon common equality and universality. Focusing on one's uniqueness and its relationality can be, instead, a breakthrough term in contesting patriarchal conceptions of woman and femininity. In particular, while Irigaray's sexual difference fails to acknowledge the differences between women and claims that women enjoy specific attributes, Cavarero focuses on the singularity and particularity of each woman and human being. The idea of uniqueness in Cavarero allows the focus on the embodied singular particularities of people and women in a relational context, rather than on the sameness of the phallogocentric system.

By contrast, both the equality and difference frameworks offer perspectives that remain within the phallogocentric grid. If the equality approach is applied, women are offered an identity as men's equals. If a difference framework is used, women's identity is conceived in completely different ways from the male identity, but using the same logic. Those two frameworks of equality and difference are not adequate for characterising the singularity of sexed human beings, or for what women share with men and what particularises them.

Cavarero rejects the terms by which equality and difference are measured and proposes one's uniqueness as embodied singularity in plurality. For Cavarero, then, difference consists in this uniqueness of the self as existent human being in relation with the uniqueness of other selves. Within the impossibility of representing a fully feminist vision, Cavarero focuses on the non-representable or, more specifically, on what has been excluded from the symbolic and semiotic, what exceeds, but also participates in, the symbolic. Language, as universal, has been devocalised for Cavarero and the voice is the element that can lead back to the uniqueness of the human being.

One's uniqueness can precisely transform the metaphysical strategy that subordinates speech to thought (Cavarero 2005:173-174). For Cavarero, this means opposing speaking to thinking. Thinking is precisely a timeless solitary activity that reflects the consciousness of the self. By contrast, speaking happens in communication between live human beings and in a specific time. Speaking involves mouth and ears and, therefore, involves also listening; it consists of an interlocution between existent speakers. The ear, in particular, perceives the vocal vibration of each human being.

Cavarero is talking precisely of a singularity in flesh and bone that philosophy considers unimportant as it does not belong to the universal abstract subject. When one speaks to another human being, one cannot be abstract, but has to necessarily be there, existent. For Cavarero, the voice has the potential to oppose the metaphysical silence of existent singularities. And it is also important that this is done through the vocal rather than the visual way of philosophy.

According to Cavarero, it is possible to reorient speech towards its vocalic side by suspending the semantic that is used by metaphysics. The logos has focused on a relationality that consists only in linking ideas. Connecting this critique to politics, Cavarero shows how the vocalic can help to think in corporeal terms the possibility of emphasising our uniqueness and modify the political system by thinking politics as a contextual relation (Cavarero 2005: 209).

While politics is a space of confrontation and discussion, paradoxically modern liberal democratic politics thinks individuals as free and autonomous without intersubjective relations, and views them through the principle of equality in a relation of sameness. Equality means the denial of plurality and, therefore, of politics (Cavarero 2005: 191), and it becomes a logic in which "each is worth one" (Cavarero 2005: 186). But this is a model of depoliticisation that excludes the plural and the relational in favour of the abstract 'one'. Therefore, what should be a bond within democracy becomes the unbinding individual. From a logocentric or phallogocentric perspective, people are considered political because they speak of political things. Speaking and its relationality become a secondary function of signifying. What has to be emphasised instead, for Cavarero, is the political being of people because they speak to one another.

Logos, in itself, cannot bind; only logos as speech can constitute a natural bond of association, as what is lacking is a community in which each human being can count and be recognised. Logos, for Cavarero, signifies political community, but it cannot make that community. The devocalisation within language means that language is thought of only as a rational sphere. In comparison, a focus on the voice could redress the lost uniqueness and singularity that is part of the universality of language and could, therefore, emphasise the Saying to the Said within logos and politics.

Here, the legacy of Arendt in Cavarero's thought is again evident. For Arendt (1958, 1971), what makes speech political is not its signification but, rather, the fact that the uniqueness of the speaker is revealed. One's uniqueness becomes political through words and deeds. This sharing of words and deeds is what produces the political realm. Consequently, what is important is the plurality of unique beings. Here is this shift, in Arendt as well as in Cavarero, from speech to the speaker: "The speakers are not political because of what they say, but because they say it to others who share an interactive space of reciprocal exposure. To speak to one another is to communicate to one another the unrepeatable uniqueness of each speaker" (Cavarero 2005: 190). Arendt links plurality to politics. Plurality, for Arendt, means that we are all distinctive and more than one. This is precisely in opposition to the phallogocentric order within which there is only an abstract universal male viewpoint. Cavarero derives from Arendt this attention to the 'who', to the distinctiveness and the relational character of one's uniqueness.

And there is a difference between this concept of plurality of Cavarero and the pluralism that is practiced in modern democracies. The pluralism of modern democracies remains, in fact, based on the abstract universal subjectivity of the individual. The abstract individual is still the standard upon which various groups of people with different identities are recognised. Rather, Cavarero talks of one's uniqueness in plurality, which means that there is a relational space between human beings, unique and plural. The Saying becomes the privileging aspect; those who communicate are not individuals, but unique human beings in flesh and bone, unrepeatable and singular. This is clearly opposed to the phal-logo-centric discourse of the individual, which is incommunicable. And this privileging does not remain embedded in the phallogocentric binary thinking either, as it happens as a moment of suspension of the phallogocentric construction of the Said.

This is a position that is framed within the relationality of the Saying. The political is precisely this being-in-common. What determines politics is precisely uniqueness, relation and plurality. In Cavarero, human beings can expose and reveal their uniqueness only when they communicate to one another; otherwise their uniqueness remains a mere ontological given: "Nothing communicates uniqueness more than the voice" (Cavarero 2005: 197). And "the drive of the bodies, of which the voice is an expression, makes the voice ideal for subverting the order of language and thus of politics" (Cavarero 2005: 199). The aim is, thus, "to think a politics that does not continue to expunge the vocal from the realm of speech" (Cavarero 2005: 200).

A politics of Saying is, for Cavarero, the revaluation of the vocalic, which is a different way of thinking the relation between politics and speech. It means focusing on speech from its vocal site as, "what counts the most is not the words, which are usually ridiculous or rhetorical, but rather the fusion of individuals" (Cavarero 2005: 202). Cavarero calls this relational space of the event of communication the 'absolute local', which does not depend on communal substance or territory, but, rather, it can take place anywhere as it is a condition of human plurality; it is where human beings actively communicate their uniqueness, an ontology of plural uniqueness and relation.

One's uniqueness in Cavarero's thought is not a common essence but, rather, the relational context in which singular differences can be expressed. Focusing on speech as communication between human beings is not a new essence, subjectivity or identity of the feminine:

> it is not woman, which is just as fictitious as man, which is here expressed and represented. Rather, this politics consists in the relational context or better, the absolute local where reciprocal speech signifies the sexed uniqueness of each speaker in spite of patriarchal prohibition. (Cavarero 2005: 206)

"It is not woman who makes herself heard; rather it is the embodied uniqueness of the speaker and his or her convocation of another voice" (Cavarero 2005: 207). In Cavarero, difference is not thought of as opposition or symmetry; rather it is uniqueness, which is to say asymmetry and excess in relationality. The attention here is on the acoustic sphere, on the vocal, the Saying and on uniqueness and singularity.

Conclusion

Cavarero appears to avoid the repetition of the phallogocentric order, in which other approaches within western feminism seem to remain trapped. Her focus on one's uniqueness signifies the emphasis on the embodied singularity of each human being in relation with other singular human beings and avoids sameness, binarism and the reduction of plurality to unity. She escapes the economy of the same, which carries with it this essential ingratitude and violence towards materiality, via the voice that reveals one's uniqueness, and she proposes a way towards the singularity and difference of each human being without returning to the logic of sameness. She suggests a way to interrupt logocentrism from within and outside logocentrism itself. The Saying, within which one's uniqueness carries, can interrupt and suspend the Said of logocentrism. And, although this logic may sound close to a deconstructive position, it avoids the textual logocentric indifference for sexual difference of the deconstructive perspective. Cavarero's fresh way of thinking is perhaps better suited to the various needs of women, as it avoids reproducing constructed commonalities between women themselves that may function as a forced grid of thought.

References

Arendt, H. *The Human Condition*. Chicago: U of Chicago Press, 1958.

-----. *The Life of the Mind*. London: A Harvest Book, 1971.

Bacchi, L.C. *Same Difference*. London: Allen & Unwin, 1990.

Bacchi, C.L. *Affirmative Action*. London: Sage Publication, 1996.

Bock, G. and James, S. *Beyond Equality and Difference, Citizenship,Feminist Politics and Female Subjectivity*. London: Routledge, 1992.

Bono, P. and Kemp, S. *Italian Feminist Thought: A Reader*. Oxford: Basil Blackwell, 1991.

Braidotti, R. *Nomadic Subjects*. New York: Columbia UP, 1994.

Burke, C. Schor, N. and Whitford, M. *Engaging with Irigaray*. New York: Columbia UP, 1994.

Butler, J. *Subjects of Desire*. New York: Columbia UP, 1987.

Butler, J. *Gender Trouble: Feminism and the Subversion of Identity*. New York: Routledge, 1990.

Butler, J. *Bodies that Matter*. London: Routledge, 1993.

Cavarero, A. and Restaino, F. *Le Filosofie Femministe*. Torino: Paravia, 1999.

-----. *Tu Che Mi Guardi, Tu Che Mi Racconti*. Milano: Feltrinelli, 1997. Trans. as *Relating Narratives, Storytelling and Selfhoood*. California: Stanford UP, 2000.

-----. *A Piu' Voci, Filosofia dell' Espressione Vocale*. Milano: Feltrinelli, 2003. Trans. as *For more than one Voice, Toward a Philosophy of Vocal Expression*. California: Stanford UP, 2005.

Cornell, D. *Beyond Accommodation*. Oxford: Rowman & Littlefield, 1999.

Costera, I. and Prins, B. "How Bodies Come to Matter: An Interview with Judith Butler." *Signs* 23, N.2 (Winter 1998): 275.

Critchley, S. and Dews, P. *Deconstructive Subjectivities*. New York: State U of New York, 1996.

Critchley, S. *The Ethics of Deconstruction*. Edinburgh: Edinburgh UP, 1999a.

Critchley, S. *Ethics, Politics, Subjectivity*. London: Verso, 1999b.

Derrida, J. *Of Grammatology*, Baltimore: The Johns Hopkins UP, 1976.

Deutscher, P. *A Politics of Impossible Difference*. London: Cornell UP, 2002.

Dietz, M. G. (1995) "Feminist Receptions of Hannah Arendt." In *Feminist Interpretations of Hannah Arendt*. Honig, ed., Pennsylvania: The Pennsylvania State UP, 1995.

Diotima, *Il Pensiero della Differenza Sessuale*. Milano: La Tartaruga, 1987.

Fuss, D. *Essentially Speaking*. London: Routledge, 1989.

Guzzoni, U. "Do We Still Want to Be Subjects?" In *Deconstructive Subjectivities*. Critchley and Dews, eds. New York: State U of New York, 1996.

Honig, B. *Feminist Interpretations of Hannah Arendt*. Pennsylvania: The Pennsylvania State UP.

Irigaray, L. *This Sex Which is Not One*, New York: Cornell UP, 1985.

Irigaray, L. *Je, Tu, Nous, Towards a Culture of Sexual Difference*. London: Routledge, 1993.

Irigaray, L. *Thinking the Difference for a Peaceful Revolution*. London: The Athlone Press, 1994.

Levinas, E. *Outside the Subject*. London: The Athlone Press, 1993.

Levinas, E. *Otherwise than Being or Beyond Essence*. Pennsylvania: Duquesne UP, 1998.

Levinas, E. *On Thinking the Other*. London: The Athlone Press, 1998.

Loizidou, E. "The Trouble with Rape: Gender Matters and Legal Transformations." *Feminist Legal Studies*, 7. 3. 1999: 275.

Modeski, T. *Feminism Without Women*. New York: Routledge, 1991.

Nancy, J.L. *Being Singular Plural*, California: Stanford UP, 2000.

Phillips, A. *Democracy and Difference*. Cambridge: Polity Press, 1993.

Sandel, M. J. *Liberalism and the Limits of Justice*. Cambridge UP, 1982.

Schor, N and Weed, E. *The Essential Difference*, Indianopolis: Indiana UP, 1994.

Schor, N. "This Essentialism Which is Not One: Coming to Grips With Irigaray." In *The Essential Difference*, Schor and Weeds, eds., Indianopolis: Indiana UP, 1994.

The Milan Women's Bookstore Collective. *Sexual Difference*. Indianopolis: Indiana UP. Trans. Libreria delle Donne di Milano *Non Credere di Averedei Diritti*, Torino: Rosenberg & Sellier.

Vaccaro, S and Coglitore, M. *Michel Foucault e il Divenire Donna,*   Milano: Associazione Culturale Mimesis, 1997.

Weedon, C. *Feminism, Theory and the Politics*, Malden: Blackwell, 1999.

Zerilli, L. M. G. "The Arendtian Body", in *Feminist Interpretation of Hannah Arendt,* Honig, ed., Pennsylvania: The Pennsylvania State UP, 1995.

A Case Apart: The Evolution of Spanish Feminism

Lorraine Ryan

The Spanish feminist movement stands as a marked exception to the European paradigm of feminist movements, its vicissitudes having only been equalled by the turbulent history of Spain itself in the twentieth century. From half-hearted attempts at suffragism in the 1920s to the plethora of feminist organisations in the 1930s; from excessively reticent organisations under Franco to the fragmented women's movement of the Transition, the prevailing ethos of feminism has been heavily influenced by the socio-cultural shifts of twentieth century Spain. In this paper, I shall examine each of these shifts in feminism and also analyse the socio-cultural contexts in which they occurred.

A feminist movement first originated in Spain as early as 1915, with the establishment of the *Asociación Nacional de Mujeres Españolas* (the National Association of Women). Claiming women's increased participation in the workforce and equal wages, it was also an unashamedly political movement, manifesting an unapologetic jingoism in its literature. Although it proclaimed its membership open to all political creeds, in reality, its members were predominantly right-wing (González Calbet 54). This imbrication of political concerns with feminism, which I will classify as dual activism, was to become a permanent feature of Spanish feminism, and one that was ultimately to hinder the progress of the movement by relegating feminist issues to a secondary position.

This pioneering feminism, although largely ineffectual, did succeed in raising the novel idea of rights for women and, as such, contributed towards a form of gender awareness. However, it was with the establishment of the Spanish Second Republic in 1931 that Spanish feminism reached its zenith. The Second Republic, in keeping with its liberal and progressive ethos, created optimum conditions for women's advancement in society (Abella 33). The Constitution of 1931 not only granted women the right to maternity insurance and legalised civil marriage, but it also sought to eradicate discrimination in the workplace by legislating pro-feminist labour laws (Martín Carretero 14). A woman's reproductive freedom was safeguarded by the legalisation of contraception, and women also began to participate in political life (Graham 184). Not surprisingly, such innovative measures created a situation in which an enormous amount of women's organisations flourished. It is necessary, however, to qualify this image of a feminist utopia since, although the Second Republic conceded much freedom to women, theorists concur that this did not eradicate traditional thinking and, moreover, did not expedite equality in the workplace. Divorce was only availed of in traditional, left-wing cities; in Madrid, a relatively liberal city, only eight out of every 1000 troubled marriages ended in divorce (Bussy Genévoise 182). The tendency to irreconcilable political views, which, in turn, created trenchant divisions within the feminist movement – thus, substantially reducing the movement's capacity for consensus on key issues – once again plagued the movement during this period. The aims of the two main groups, the Female Republican Union, led by Clara Campoamor, and the Foundation for Women, led by the radical socialists Victoria Kent and Margarita Nelken, were so different as to be mutually exclusive. While Campoamor was solely concerned with women's suffrage, Kent and Nelken were enmeshed in party politics, an affiliation to which their feminist leanings were decidedly subservient. Indeed, both women were vehemently opposed to the enfranchisement of women, astutely recognising that giving the combination of the Catholic Church's avowed hatred of the secular Second Republic and the blind obedience of the majority of women to the dictates of the prelates, the granting of the vote to women could very well precipitate the collapse of the Second Republic. Their intuition was to prove remarkably prescient with the Conservatives winning the elections in 1933, due to the clerically-influenced vote of the female electorate (Mangini 25).

Challenging as it did the hegemony of the Catholic Church in Spain and the omnipotence of the land-owning classes, the Second Republic was faced with a serious threat from both these groups (Schatz 146). Possessing only a rudimentary grasp of socialism, they equated it with atheism and dissoluteness that was antithetical to their vision of an ultra-Catholic Spain (Grugel and Rees 25). The outbreak of the Spanish Civil War in 1936 was to act as the prelude to a new chapter in the history of the feminist movement in Spain. Groups such as the republican *Mujeres Libres* (Free Women) propounded an ambitious agenda, stating their objective "to combat the triple enslavement to which (women) have been subject: enslavement to ignorance, enslavement as women and enslavement as workers" (Smith 476). How innovative this feminist group was can be deduced from the fact that it was the only group during the Civil War to really prioritise the 'woman question', going even as far as critiquing gender inequities within the anarchist movement itself, an inconceivable act of daring in the Spain of that time. Not restricting themselves to disseminating highly inflammable rhetoric in its journal, *Mujeres Libres* also sought to ameliorate the living conditions of working class women by initiating literacy and medical schemes (Kaplan 415). Albeit groundbreaking in its demands, the association never focused on contraception and abortion, a deviation from their radical policy on all other feminist issues which, again, demonstrates the irreversible influence of the Catholic Church on the evolution of feminism in Spain. Offen contends that due to the spectre of punitive counteraction by the Church, these questions did not even arise in that period (Offen 326).

In a country convulsed with violence and seething with political passions, as was Spain during the Civil War, it is of small surprise that most feminist groups followed the by now familiar pattern of letting political dreams supersede their feminist aspirations. Bridenthal and Koonz observe that, although women on the Republican side were involved in war production and even construction work, this reversal of gender roles was effected at the price of their feminist ideals (472). Of further significance is the fact that women's participation in the republican cause took place, for the most part, at the beginning of the Civil War, when the Republican side were desperately searching for volunteers (Bussy Genévois 189). After this initial threat had subsided, the battalions of female fighters were disbanded.

Certainly, the republican movement had no qualms in using stereotypical images of women in order to gain support. The *Agrupación de Mujeres Antifascistas* (Antifascist Women's Organisation of the Spanish Communist Party) and the Feminine Secretariat of the Dissident Marxist Party targeted women with emotive poster campaigns, designed to spark a decidedly maternal outrage against the atrocities being committed against their sons and husbands by the fascists (Nash 235). Therefore, even radical political affiliations did not help Spanish women to escape the pervasiveness of traditional thinking, as the co-option of women into these movements translated into a worryingly high proportion of women occupying ancillary roles. While the republican attitude towards women's involvement in the war effort was not as progressive as one would expect considering their liberal ethos, the nationalists' stance was the very opposite, prescribing motherhood and domesticity as not only the unique functions of women, but also as their only possible patriotic contribution (Gallégo Méndez 1983). The accession to power of General Francisco Franco in 1939 effectively signalled the death-knell for the egalitarian expectations fostered by the Second Republic. Furthermore, the ideological clash between Francoism and the Second Republic meant that the policies of the Regime, especially those relating to the social domain, were engendered from their fear of liberalism, a political conviction which they equated with moral dissoluteness (Bahamonde and Martinez 19). Further, instigated by their alliance with the Catholic Church, they implemented legislation that can only be described as inimical to women's progress on a social, economic and personal level; thus, an essentialist, polarised concept of gender relations came to govern Spanish life. Logically, in such an atmosphere, feminist groups suffered a severe setback. Highly distrustful of any splinter groups, the Regime instilled in the Spanish national psyche the notion of 'anti-España' (against-Spain), which vilified all forms of otherness, such as socialism, feminism, communism and liberalism (Corkill 50). Posing a formidable threat to the Regime's social policies, which, at the time, were primarily concerned with demographic growth, feminist organisations were in fact considered a potentially subversive group by the State. Harsh conditions were laid down for their legalisation and, not surprisingly, only four feminist organisations succeeded in gaining official approval. Unfortunately, having diluted their aims to a very languid version of feminism in order to obtain the necessary approval, these organisations soon showed themselves to be unwilling to challenge the *status quo*, and did not even dare to question the prevailing gender structure (Threlfall 139).

At this juncture, a significant problem arises. Up to this point, I have been using Rodríguez *et al's* definition of feminism, which involves women "challenging the relations between men and women and rebelling against all power structures, laws and conventions that keep women servile and subordinate" (3). The women's movement that I am about to analysis, and which undoubtedly had the most influence on Spanish women during the Francoist era, stood in proud and defiant opposition to any such ideals: *La Sección Femenina*, (Falange Women's Section), which incessantly propounded the silent and docile stereotype of the supposedly innately maternal Catholic woman, hardly qualifies as a feminist movement within most definitions (Pérez Moreno 182). However, various theorists, applying a revisionist framework to the study of the movement, have unearthed feminist elements within it. Kaplan argues that, although traditionalist in outlook, the *Falange's* women's section did precipitate a quasi-entry of women into the public sphere by obliging them to do six months Social Service (Kaplan 96). Furthermore, if we reflect on the following speech made by José Antonio Primo de Rivera, whose sister Pilar was leader of the *Sección Femenina* and remained doggedly faithful to her brother's ideals throughout her life, we can also perceive an attempt to improve the public perception of traditional womanly duties: "True feminism should consist in surrounding feminine functions with increased human and social dignity" (Enders 676).

Thus, *Sección Femenina* embarked on its educational mission, founding agricultural and adult schools, cultural groups, sports centres and libraries, publishing magazines, organising discussion groups, awarding scholarships and preserving oral traditions such as folk songs. Therefore, conservative ethos aside, *Sección Femenina* elevated womanly functions to an unprecedented, honorific level: indeed, from interviews I have conducted with former members of the *Sección Femenina*, I can actually conclude that the organisation gave them a sense of pride in their domestic abilities and their patriotic contribution, findings which validate Guiliana Di Febo's formulation of a "Christian feminism", which is "the regenerating" and "reChristianising" mission confided to feminine masses in the reconstruction of the arm of values dislodged by the Republic and the Civil War and recuperated by the "New State" (cited in Enders 678). My own research was conducted in the summer of 2004 in the village of Zalamea la Real in the province of Huelva. The women I interviewed fondly remembered the camaraderie of the *Sección Femenina* and, indeed, credited it with their lifelong passion for domestic pursuits, an interest which they felt had enriched their lives immeasurably.

Granted, this is a paltry version of feminism by some definitions, but, when judging it, one has to take into account that this was a country with one of the highest illiteracy rates in the world and under the repressive domination of the Catholic Church, so equality feminism was never destined to flourish.

However, as Spain experienced industrialisation in the 1960s, so too did *Sección Feminina* adopt a different, altogether more modern, ethos. The *Ley de Derechos Políticos, profesionales y laborales* (Political, Labour and Professional law) exemplifies this: the law, proposed by *Sección Femenina*, granted more privileges to women. Its subsequent approval was much vaunted by *Sección Femenina* as a measure of its commitment to ensuring an improved quality of life for women (Sánchez López 44). Furthermore, in its magazine, *Teresa*, it featured debates and interviews with modern, successful young women who were university-educated. Indeed, *Teresa* took to supporting the idea of women working outside the home, boldly featuring a weekly column entitled *"Las Mujeres quieren trabajar"* (women want to work). But its finest hour came in 1969 with the recommendation of Betty Friedan's *The Feminist Mystique*, which was praised precisely because of its subversive feminist qualities; women, the writer held, could overcome what she referred to as "this con-trick", which held that a woman's self-realisation was only obtainable in the home, by "leaving behind [their] small, enclosed world, becoming more outward-looking" (Coca Hernando 9). Therefore, as the socio-cultural parameters widened to allow *Sección Femenina* greater agency, it became a more liberal, modern movement.

Although the barriers to female emancipation were lifted somewhat by the rapid economic growth of the 1960s, ardent feminists recognised that in order to achieve their aims they would have to infiltrate other government-approved organisations, such as the Association of Homemakers, thus surmounting the constraints imposed by its illegality.[1] However, attempts to influence government policy proved to be their undoing, and the government refused to legalise any other branches of the Homemakers movement. Undaunted, the most powerful women's organisation, the MDM (Movement of Women) turned its attentions to the Castilian Association of Homemakers and Consumers, a collaboration which resulted in the building of nineteen new centres and the launching of

---

[1] The Association of Homemakers was, as the name suggests, a group which prioritised homemaking skills such as sewing and cooking, and had no feminist ethos.

many previously unthinkable initiatives. These Housewives' Associations were, in their own right, and despite their purportedly domestic function, highly political: working class members voiced their unhappiness with the paucity of services provided by the State, and, in this way, dissatisfaction with the Regime became the predominant mood within the movement (Threlfall 1996, 121). Thus, a woman's organisation approved by the Regime became a conduit for political awareness, and was thereby transformed into a locus of political dissent.

The death of Francisco Franco in 1975 ushered in a new era in Spanish politics and society. The feminist movement, now unfettered by any legal restrictions, experienced a dramatic upsurge in the 1975-1978 period as it campaigned vigorously for anti-discriminatory measures to be stipulated in the new Constitution, a demand partially met by the 1978 Constitution, which legalised contraception and penalised sexual discrimination (Montero 382). The immediate aftermath of the new Consitution was something of an anti-climax for the feminist movement, mainly due to two factors, which I shall analyse respectively: the failure of the different feminist bodies to coalesce, and disagreement as to the pertinence of politics to the movement. Due to the polarisation between older feminists (who viewed the feminist struggle and the political struggle as inextricably linked), and young feminists (untroubled by memories of repression) no single, co-ordinating Spanish feminist body was created. As the years went by, competing visions of equality and, paradoxically, the lack of a single goal, such as the fight for democracy, made that possibility chimerical: at present, the movement consists of small, autonomous regional units.

As I have continually emphasised throughout this paper, the cause of the seemingly irreparably fragmented state of the Spanish feminist movement is intrinsically political, and never was the movement more political than in the early years of the Transition to democracy in Spain when the so-called femocrats (feminists who were involved in party politics) emerged as a formidable political force. Naturally, divisions between dual and single activists resurrected themselves in this period, as dual activists found themselves torn between party loyalties and their feminist goals, as well as earning the wrath of single activists who viewed them as irredeemably compromised by their party affiliations. In fact, the very idea of politics, with its patriarchal orientation, was anathema to these single activists who, having been heavily influenced by French feminist thought, advocated difference and personal experience as paramount to the feminist struggle. The politicisation of the feminist movement in Spain, they further argued, had only one function: namely, to assert control over the movement's activities (Brooksbank-Jones 11). Certainly, there was a certain amount of credibility in the accusations they levelled against party feminists. These feminists were invariably attracted to politics, representing as it did a possibility for promoting the feminist cause in a powerful forum. However, once enmeshed in political machinations, they were forced to perform a delicate balancing act between maintaining their position within the party and remaining loyal to their feminist ideals. The victories achieved by the femocrats were, for the most part, only minor concessions designed to placate feminist demands, which inevitably fell short of the long-term investment required to solve deep-rooted social problems. More often than not, the goals of the feminists and their political colleagues were incompatible, so, in order to achieve these minor victories, the femocrats began to subdue their demands, thereby neglecting key issues of the feminist agenda and decreasing the autonomy of the feminist movement.

Despite the internal difficulties of the feminist movement, the situation of Spanish women has undoubtedly improved, with the PSOE (Socialist government), which came to power in 1982, giving funding to women's groups. A governmental organisation specifically addressing the question of women's status in society, the *Instituto de la Mujer* (Women's Institute), was established in 1982 under the tutelage of the Ministry of Culture, and was to seek to promote women's increased involvement in all spheres of life. However, problems remain. Notwithstanding the fact that Spain has morphed into a liberal, advanced society, tinctures of misogyny simmer under the surface, and female underemployment continues to be a problem (Threlfall 124). Neither has the *Instituto de la Mujer* delivered on the reforms it pledged to implement in the sanguine atmosphere of the early years of the Transition; inadequate financial resources, a failure to coalesce with the feminist movement, and bureaucracy have all impeded its progress. Its accomplishments tend to be vicarious as it functions primarily as a lobby group of other state bodies and, even in that regard, fails to make a significant impact, as it usually placidly accepts party policy on the issue in question (Valiente 225).

Clearly, the evolution of Spanish feminism has been fraught with difficulties. Hindered as it was by a dictatorial regime and an overarching *machismo*, its progress is nonetheless commendable: academic feminism is flourishing and women's issues now receive extensive media coverage. However, its history continues to exert an influence on its development. After all, throughout the Francoist era, the fundamental implications of gender equality were completely ignored as the necessity for basic survival eclipsed such abstract concepts. Angela Glasner asserts that "extreme levels of poverty and low levels of industrial development" (Glasner 79) are almost insurmountable obstacles to the progress of a feminist movement, a contention verified by the evolution of Spanish feminism.

Certainly an entitlement to equal treatment was inconceivable for Spanish women until 1975 as, until then, domestic violence was a taboo topic, exempt from the retribution of the public sphere (Falcón 20). Therefore, the struggle to enshrine a perception of gender equality in the public consciousness was always destined to be arduous. In many ways, feminism has been a victim of the greater political struggles of twentieth century Spain, as its objectives were subsumed into higher-profile rubrics, such as the fight for democracy, which had the effect of confusing the essence of the movement. The politicisation of the movement eclipsed the feminist cause itself, and also caused it to lose a certain amount of credibility with supporters. Furthermore, the fact that the Francoist Regime discredited the majority of feminist organisations as 'anti-Spain' instilled in the Spanish subconscious a view of feminists as troublemakers, one which unfortunately prevails today (Hooper 83). Although its principal purpose was clarified somewhat by the return to democracy, the feminist movement at present is characterised by disunity and, consequently, has failed to attain the stature and public recognition accorded to other national feminist movements. Only, it would seem, with greater unity is the Spanish feminist movement ever really going to prosper. Let's hope that the events of this century prove more beneficial for its progress than the previous one.

References

Abella, Rafael. *La vida amorosa en la Segunda República*. Madrid: Ediciones Tema de Hoy, 1996.

Bahamonde, Ángel and Jesús A. Martínez. "La configuración de la dictadura de Franco" in Jesús A. Martínez, ed. *Historia de España siglo XX: 1939-1996*. Madrid: Ediciones Cátedra, 1999: 19-23.

Bridenthal, Renate and Claudia Koonz. *Becoming Visible: Women in European History*. Boston: Houghton Mifflin, 1998: Third Edition. For some very interesting personal accounts of how the Civil War affected women's lives, see: Ronald Fraser, *Blood of Spain: The Experience of Civil War*. London: Penguin Books, 1988: 286-291.

Brooksbank-Jones, Anny. Women in Contemporary Spain. Manchester: Manchester UP, 1995.

Bussy Genevois, Daniéle. "The Women of Spain from the Republic to Franco" in George Duby, Michelle Perrot, Françoise Thébaud, eds. *A History of Women in the West V: Towards a Cultural Identity in the Twentieth Century*. Cambridge, Massachusetts: The Belknap Press of Harvard UP, 1994: 177-193.

Coca Hernando, Rosario. "Towards a New Image of Women under Franco: the Role of Sección Femenina." *International Journal of Iberian Studies* 11:1: 5-13.

Corkill, Dave. "Race, Immigration and Multiculturalism in Spain" in Barry Jordan and Rikki Morgan-Tamosunas, eds. *Contemporary Spanish Cultural Studies*. London: Arnold, 2000: 48-57.

Enders, Victoria L. "Nationalism and Feminism: the Sección Femenina of the Falange." *History of European Ideas*, 15: 4-6, 673-680.

Falcón, Lidia. "Violent Democracy." *Journal of Spanish Cultural Studies* 3:1: 15-28.

Gallégo Méndez, María Teresa. *Mujer, falange y franquismo*. Madrid: Taurus Ediciones, 1983.

Glasner, Angela. "Gender and Europe: Cultural and Structural Impediments to Change" in Joe Bailey, ed. *Social Europe*. London: Longman Sociology Series, 1992: 70-99.

González Calbet, María Teresa "El surgimiento del movimiento feminista" in Pilar Folguera, ed. *El feminismo en España: Dos siglos de historia*. Madrid: Alianza Editorial, 1988: 51-56.

Graham, Helen. "Gender and the State: Women in the 1940s" in Helen Graham and Jo Labanyi, eds. *Spanish Cultural Studies: An Introduction: The Struggle for Modernity*. Oxford: Oxford UP, 1995: 182-195.

Grugel, Jean and Tim Rees. *Franco's Spain*. London: Arnold, 1997.

Hooper, John. *The New Spaniards*. London: Penguin Books, 1995.

Kaplan, Temma. "Luchar por la democracia: formas de organización de las mujeres entre los años cincuenta y setenta" in A. Aguado, ed. *Mujeres, regulación de conflictos sociales y cultura de la paz*. Valencia: Universidad de Valencia, 1999: 89-108.

-----. "Women and Spanish Anarchism" in Renate Bridenthal and Claudia Koonz, eds. *Becoming Visible: Women in European History*. Boston: Houghton Mifflin, 1978 (First Edition): 402-420.

Mangini, Shirley. *Memories of Resistance: Women's Voices from the Spanish Civil War*. New Haven: Yale UP, 1995.

Martín Carretero, Carolina. *Las mujeres jóvenes: empleo, educación y familia*. Avances y retrocesos en la igualdad de oportunidades. Madrid: Instituto de la Juventud, 1999.

Montero, Rosa. "The Silent Revolution: The Social and Cultural Advances of Women in Democratic Spain" in Helen Graham and Jo Labanyi, eds. *Spanish Cultural Studies: an Introduction*. Oxford: Oxford UP: 381-385.

Nash, Mary. "Milicianas and Homefront Heroines: Images of Women in Revolutionary Spain (1936-1939)." *History of European Ideas*. 11: 235-244.

Offen, Karen. *European Feminisms, 1700-1950: A Political History*. California: Stanford UP, 2000.

Pérez Moreno, Heliodoro Manuel. "La misión formativa de la Sección Femenina (1939-1977): Evolución, referente teleológico y medios formativos." *Revista de Ciéncies de Éducacio*, XXV11: 175-199.

Rodríguez, Marta, Marisa Rueda, and Susan Alice Watkins. *Introducing Feminism*. Duxford, England: Icon Books, 1999.

Sánchez López, Rosario. *Mujer española, una sombra de destino en lo universal: Trayectoria histórica de Sección Femenina de Falange (1934-1977)*. Murcia: Secretariado de Publicaciones de la Universidad de Murcia, 1990.

Schatz, Sara. "Democracy's Breakdown and the Rise of Fascism: The Case of the Spanish Second Republic, 1931-1936." *Social History* 26: 2 145-166. For further discussion on the ideological conflict underlying the Spanish Civil War, see: Stephen J. Lee, *The European Dictatorships, 1918-1945*. New York: Routledge: 1987: 231-245.

Smith, Bonnie G. *Changing Lives: Women in European History since 1700*. Lexington, Massachusetts: Heath and Company, 1989.

Threlfall, Monica. "Gendering the Transition to Democracy: Reassessing the Impact of Women's Activism" in Christine Cousins, Monica Threlfall and Celia Valiente, eds. *Gendering Spanish Democracy*. London and New York: Routledge, 2004: 11-55.

-----. "Feminist Politics and Social Change in Spain" in Monica Threlfall, ed. *Mapping the Women's Movement: Feminist Politics and Social Transformation in the North*. London: Verso, 1996: 115-152.

Valiente, Celia. "The Power of Persuasion: The Instituto de la Mujer in Spain" in Amy G. Mazur and Dorothy Stetson McBride, eds. *Comparative State Feminism*. London: SAGE Publications, 1995: 221-237.

Surfing Feminism's Third Wave?

Katherine Side

There is a prevailing tendency to categorise periods of feminist activism and theorising using a wave metaphor. While this tendency has been challenged for its simplicity and ethnocentrism, it continues to stand as a marker of some convenience. To date, undergraduate courses in Gender and/or Women's Studies in Canada and the United States have tended to focus on analyses of First and Second Wave feminism; however, increasingly, universities now offer separate courses on the topic of Third Wave feminism. In this paper, I set out to do three things: 1) to briefly consider how Third Wave feminism is being conceptualised and constituted; 2) to examine some possible reasons that account for its emergence at this particular point in time; and 3) to build a case for the inclusion of Third Wave feminism, where possible, into Women's Studies curricula.

Conceptualising Third Wave Feminism
Marsha Lear's introduction of the wave metaphor, and specifically her phrase 'the Second Wave', was intended to characterise the activities of groups of women under specific sets of historical, social and economic circumstances, and to demonstrate continuity with women's historical struggles (Kimser 2004). This wave metaphor is fraught with limitations. Its retroactive application to suffrage struggles obliterates entire periods of feminist thinking and resistance to gendered oppression. Kimberly Springer (2002) argues that it excludes women of colour from feminist movement history and theorising. It oversimplifies the complexities of feminist thought, depicts feminist knowledge production as a linear project, and evokes a generational model that is based in simplistic distinctions that mask political differences and perpetuate a reproductive, familial narrative (Purvis 106, 109). Furthermore, it lends credibility to rhetoric about feminism's inactivity and ineffectiveness by perpetuating the belief that abated periods of inactivity between waves of action are natural and to be expected (Gillis and Munford 2001).

In light of these criticisms, building a case for the inclusion of feminism's Third Wave is challenging, and Judith Lorber (2005) candidly questions whether, in fact, a 'new' feminism is needed. While I acknowledge the limitations of this wave metaphor, I have nevertheless chosen to retain it here because it is an already recognisable shorthand in feminist scholarly literature in Anglo-American feminisms (Alarcón 1997), specifically in Canada, the United States and Australia (Else-Mitchell and Flutter 1998, Maddison 2004, 2004a), and because its currency as a term with which feminist scholars are familiar, but about which they do not necessarily agree, opens up some important, future possibilities for Women's Studies. Third Wave feminism appears contradictory – as an ever-shifting terrain, inherently and intentionally unstable and, at the same time, a secure site of new considerations and emphases, an innovator of new methods and a forum for novel forms of expression.

There is no uniform basis in which Third Wave feminism is being defined. A cursory survey of contributions to feminist scholarly journals on the topic of Third Wave feminism reveals a range of definitions that hinge on theoretical considerations, on whom its practitioners are and on the locations in which their feminism is practiced. Colleen Mack-Canty (2004) defines Third Wave feminism based on its affiliation with theoretical perspectives, specifically postmodernism, post-colonialism and ecofeminism; while not explicitly stated, its disassociation from other feminist, theoretical perspectives is suggested (158). Amber Kimser (2004) maps out the terrain of Third Wave feminism based on a set of circumstances, assumed to be shared by its practitioners. Third Wave feminists, she claims: came to adulthood as feminists; inhabit a cultural milieu that practices feminism and, at the same time, resists it; demonstrate pluralistic thinking about the diversity of women's lives, undermining the uniform definition of feminism; and live with the tensions of post-feminism (133). Candis Steenbergen (2001) distinguishes Third Wave feminism by its locations of practice; she argues that "the complexities of everyday experiences and the personal and structural relationships affecting them" (9) are addressed in locations that include:

> independently produced zines, in book reviews hidden at the backs of journals, on walls, across public advertisements, in non-mainstream publications and in other less conspicuous places. (9)

Feminist scholars who remain suspicious, or at least uncertain, about the existence of this subsequent wave and/or its distinctiveness, have criticised both its definition and its practice. Third Wave feminists have been criticised for the locations in which they practice feminism (Gillis and Munford 2001, 165), for their lack of a collective mass movement (Ellis 2001), and for their inadequate development of a distinguishable body of political and theoretical analyses, at least when held up against an often unspecified body of Second Wave texts (Jensen 2000, Purvis 2004). Conceptualisations of feminism's Third Wave remain slippery and elusive, in part because the task of devising a fixed definition is an untenable one for some Third Wave feminists. But its conceptualisation also remains slippery and elusive, I suggest, because it remains firmly entrenched in ongoing, and yet unresolved, debates about authenticity and what constitutes legitimate forms of feminist activism, theorising and knowledge production, and how feminists should understand and respond to ever-shifting social contexts.

Accounting for the Emergence of a Third Wave

The emergence of Third Wave feminism at this particular moment in time can be read in response to the successes and the limitations of feminism. In a North American context, the emergence of Third Wave feminism demonstrates the extent to which feminism, or at least some forms of it, has become part of the mainstream. Third Wave feminism has been embraced by individuals for whom feminist ideas have both always existed and have always been critiqued (Friedman 1992, Fillion 1995, LaFramboise 1996), in popular literature (Baumgardner and Richards 2000 in Purvis 120), and in the Women's Studies courses that have always formed a part of the university curriculum. Its limitations are also challenged and Third Wave feminists often come to Women's Studies courses already critical of the ways that contemporary feminism thought has been shaped by the experiences of select groups of women, conversant in critiques of essentialism and universalism and willing to construct their own everyday realities as separate from the body of feminist thought and ideas presented to them.

Constructions of these everyday realities as separate and distinct from existing bodies of feminist thought run two risks: first, the development of "historical amnesia" in feminist thought (Springer 1063) and, second, the construction of 'presentism' in Women's

Studies curriculum, understood as a preoccupation with the present so as to render histories less significant and portray key ideas in feminism as emerging during the 1970s (and in an almost exclusively American context), and only moving forward since then (Newman 144).

Neither, however, is inevitable. In a recent article about teaching feminist theories, Canadian feminist scholar, Lesley Biggs suggests:

> as learners, in order to comprehend contemporary debates, we need to appreciate their intellectual, social, political and economic origins. Critical analysis entails understanding epistemological assumptions of theories and concepts, the conditions [and] social locations under which the ideas were generated and the strategies for change undertaken. (32)

Ideas in Third Wave feminism can explore feminisms' imbricating natures and in ways that are attentive to feminisms' multiple sites of development and locations and to the multiple ways of being a feminist (Budgeon 26). Theorising can be presented as a non-linear project, replete with contradictions, backsliding and tensions. It is important that debates about the existence and/or legitimacy of Third Wave feminism be located in a broader context that includes: the construction of generational conflict among feminists (Henry 2004; Mack-Canty 2004), the uneven spaces between Second and Third Wave feminisms (Kimser 2004), and our flawed institutional structures as a site of feminist theorising. Debates about Third Wave feminism cannot be properly entered into without knowledge of and attention to the origin myths of Women's Studies, and debates about which knowledge projects, theory formations and activist agendas are worthy of 'passing on' (Braithwaite *et al.* 2004, Newman 2002), as well as sites of resistance.

Acknowledging the Contributions of Third Wave Feminism to Gender and/Women's Studies

Reservations about Third Wave feminism in Women's Studies curricula should be balanced by considerations of its contributions. Third Wave feminism, through written, visual and performed texts, provides opportunities to analyse scholarly and popular feminist questions. It opens up intellectual spaces that provide further "site[s] of convergence and contestation" (Purvis 119), and offers tools through which to understand and address the social and political dynamics of everyday experiences (Altman 2001, Steenbergen 8). Third Wave feminism offers sites of expression through which to explore changing social contexts, and to analyse relevant concepts and theoretical subjects. Importantly, it offers space for the construction of individual identities and feminist political spaces without conceding to persistent backlash forces (Braithwaite 2002, Gillis and Munford 2001, Maddison 2004), fostering vital networks for feminist thought and action in which the students in Women's Studies classrooms are positioned as possible agents of change, not simply as repositories for information about other agents of change.

Third Wave feminist accounts have kept pace with the vibrancy of feminist publishing for popular, academic and alternative audiences, although these accounts have frequently been criticised for their individualistic focus and for political engagement that is unrecognisable to critics (Greer 1999, Jensen 2000, Steinem 1995). The majority of Third Wave feminist collections have been published, not individually, but jointly and collectively, and with multiple contributors, by those whose background has been shaped by Women's Studies. Recouping the self in the interests of historical continuity constitutes an important political project that draws on the significance of personal experiences from a multiplicity of social locations through which to understand gendered society (Springer 1061, Mack-Canty 156). These collections address how one "does feminism[s]" (Kimser 37). Kimser contends that, as personal narratives, they explore "how it feels to live a feminist life, how feminism informs and complicates one's sense of identity and how one stabilizes that identity while being knocked about by post-feminist and backlash forces" (137).

However, Third Wave feminism must also acknowledge and address its present limitations, inside and outside of the classroom, the most obvious being its inability to transcend a limited Anglo-American context. Winnie Woodhull suggests that "if anything can be said with certainty about Third Wave feminism, it is that it is mainly a first world phenomenon, generated by women who, like their second wave counterparts, have limited interests in women's struggles elsewhere on the planet" (76). In the well-intentioned effort to corral

Third Wave feminism into Women's Studies classrooms and curricula, its complicity in knowledge reproduction as an intellectual project that solidifies mostly North American biases, remains under examined (May 146).

The contributions and limitations of the inclusion of courses about Third Wave feminism in Women's Studies curricula pose some pressing questions: whose interests are being served by (the always limited) project of defining and distinguishing periods of feminist thought and activism? Whose interests are not served? How do Women's Studies curricula reflect students' experiences of feminism as everyday social reality? How are feminist intellectual debates and practices reflected in what we teach, and how we teach, Women's Studies? And, how are the contributions of Women's Studies students recognised in the production of feminist knowledge?

Conclusion

Third Wave feminist thought might be served well to remember that 'new' feminisms can very quickly seem 'old' (Lorber 2005). The knowledge project of Women's Studies will not be well served if time and energy are invested in expressing doubt and concerns about the possibility of an "[inevitable] failure of the future" of feminism, instead of taking up its many possibilities (Weigman 807). If Women's Studies students are to be sufficiently equipped with the intellectual tools to respond to feminism's dynamic constructions and its ever-changing expressions, then we must also be flexible enough to chart 'new waters' in Women's Studies curriculum and to recognise that doing so, however difficult and contested, is a valuable intellectual endeavour.

References

Alarcón, Norma. "The Theoretical Subject(s) of *This Bridge Called My Back* and Anglo-American Feminism" in Linda Nicholson, ed. *The Second Wave: A Reader in Feminist Thought.* New York: Routledge, 1997: 288-299.

Altman, Meryl. "Beyond Trashiness: The Sexual Language of 1970s Feminist Fiction." *Journal of International Women's Studies* 4 (2) 2001: 7-19.

Baumgardner, Jennifer and Amy Richards. *Manifesta: Young Women, Feminism and the Future.* New York: Farrar, Straus and Giroux, 2000.

Baumgardner, Jennifer and Amy Richards. *Grassroots: A Field Guide to Feminist Activism.* New York: Farrar, Straus and Giroux, 2005.

Biggs, C. Lesley. "If I Can't Sing, I Don't Want to Belong to Your Revolution: Teaching Feminist Theory Through Music" in C. Lesley Biggs and Pamela Downe, eds. *Gendered Intersections: An Introduction to Gender and Women's Studies.* Halifax: Fernwood, 2005: 32-36.

Braithwaite, Ann. "The Personal, the Political, Third Wave and Post-Feminism." *Feminist Theory: An International Interdisciplinary Journal* 3(3) 2002: 335- 344.

Braithwaite, Ann, Susan Heald, Susanne Luhmann and Sharon Rosenberg. *Troubling Women's Studies: Pasts, Presents and Possibilities.* Toronto: Sumach Press, 2004.

Brooks, Ann. *Postfeminisms: Feminism, Cultural Theory and Cultural Form.* London: Routledge, 1997.

Budgeon, Shelley. "Emerging Feminist (?) Identities: Young Women and the Practice of Micropolitics." *European Journal of Women's Studies* 8 (1) 2001: 7-28.

Dicker, Rory and Alison Peipmeier, eds. *Catching a Wave: Reclaiming Feminism for the 21st Century.* Boston: Northeastern UP, 2002.

Ellis, Rebecca. "Second Thoughts about a Third Wave." *Canadian Woman Studies* 20/21 (1/4) 2001: 24-26.

Else-Mitchell, Rosalind and Naomi Flutter, eds. *Talking Up: Young Women's Take on Feminism.* Melbourne: Spinifex, 1998.

Faludi, Susan. *Backlash: The Undeclared War Against American Women.* New York: Andrew Books, 1991.

Fillion, Kate. *Lip Service: The Truth about Women's Darker Side in Love, Sex and Friendship.* Toronto: Harper Collins, 1995.

Friedman, Amy. *Nothing Sacred: A Conversation with Feminism.* Ottawa: Oberon Press, 1992.

Gillis, Stacey, Gillian Howe and Rebecca Munford, eds. *Third Wave Feminism: A Critical Exploration.* London: Palgrave Macmillan, 2004.

Gillis, Stacey and Rebecca Munford. "Genealogies and Generations: The Politics and Praxis of the Third Wave." *Women's History Review* 13 (2) 2001: 165-183.

Greer, Germaine. *The Whole Woman.* London: Doubleday, 1999.

Hernández, Daisy and Bushra Rehman, eds. *Colonize This! Young Women of Color on Today's Feminism.* New York: Seal Press, 2002.

Heywood, Leslie and Jennifer Drake, eds. *Third Wave Agenda: Being Feminism, Doing Feminism.* Minneapolis: U of Minnesota Press, 1997.

Henry, Astrid. *Not My Mother's Keeper: Generational Conflict and Third Wave Feminism.* Bloomington: Indiana UP, 2004.

Humm, Maggie. *Feminism: A Reader.* New York: Harvester Wheatsheaf, 1992.

Jensen, Michele. "Riding the Third Wave." *The Nation.* 11 Dec. 2000. Web site available at: http://www.thenation.com Retrieved 28 June, 2005.

Kimser, Amber. "Negotiating Spaces For/Through Third-Wave Feminism." *NWSA Journal* 16(3) 2004: 124-155.

LaFramboise, Donna. *The Princess in the Window: A New Gender Morality.* Toronto: Penguin, 1996.

Lorber, Judith. "Third-Wave Feminism." *Gender Inequality: Feminist Theories and Politics.* Los Angeles: Roxbury, 2005: 279-301.

Maddison, Sarah. "Young Women in the Australian Women's Movement." *International Feminist Journal of Politics* 6 (20) 2004: 234-256.

Maddison, Sarah. 2004a. "A Part of Living Feminism-Intergenerational Feminism in A Working Class Area." *Journal of Interdisciplinary Gender Studies* 8 2004a (1 & 2).

Mack-Canty, Colleen. "Third-Wave Feminism and the Need to Reweave the Nature/Culture Duality." *NWSA Journal* 16 (3) 2004: 154-179.

May, Vivian. "Disciplining Desires and Undisciplined Daughters: Negotiating the Politics of a Women's Studies Doctoral Education." *NWSA Journal* 14 (1) 2002: 134-159.

Mitchell, Allyson, Lisa Bryn Rundle and Lara Karaian, eds. *Turbo Chicks: Talking Young Feminism.* Toronto: Sumach Press, 2001.

Newman, Jane. "The Present and Our Past: Simone de Beauviour, Descartes and Presentism in the Historiography of Women's Studies" in Robyn Weigman, ed. *Women's Studies on Its Own.* Durham: Duke UP, 2002: 141-173.

Purvis, Jennifer. "Grrrls and Women Together in the Third Wave: Embracing the Challenges of Intergenerational Feminism(s)." *NWSA Journal* 16 (3) 2004: 93- 123.

Springer, Kimberly. "Third Wave Black Feminism." *Signs: Journal of Women and Culture in Society* 27 (4) 2002: 1059-98.

Steinem, Gloria. "Forward" in *To Be Real: Telling the Truth and Changing the Face of Feminism*, ed. Rebecca Walker, New York: Anchor Books, 1995: xxix-x.

Steenbergen, Candis. "Feminism and Young Women: Alive and Well and Still Kicking." *Canadian Woman Studies* 20/21 (1/4) 2001: 6-14.

Weigman, Robyn. "Feminism's Apocalyptic Future." *New Literary History.* 31. 4 (2000): 805-825.

Woodhull, Winnie. "Global Feminisms, Transnational Political Economies and Third World Cultural Production." *Journal of International Women's Studies* 4 (2) 2001: 76-90.

Biased Balloting:
An Investigation of the Role of Gender in Voter Choice

Fiona Buckley, Neil Collins, and Theresa Reidy

Elections are special occasions because of their centrality to the democratic process, importance for the legitimacy of government and symbolism of the sovereignty of the people. The academic literature on elections stresses the impact of social and political cleavages, ideologies and early socialisation on voter choice (Lipset and Rokkan 1967). Various models lay more or less emphasis on the rationality of the voter's decision and, in the Republic of Ireland, clientelism, brokerage, localism and other cultural peculiarities are also rehearsed.

The popular experience of elections is strikingly different. A quasi-military rhetoric of 'battle grounds', electoral strategy and local tactics are used to describe a reality of 'family' seats, long term loyalties and significant voter disinterest. This is particularly true for local elections. Tellingly, candidates at all levels generally place great reliance on pictures, posters and pressing the flesh. The picture of the candidate, accompanied by the briefest of slogans and, often, the least obtrusive style of party logo is given pride of place in all forms of publicity.

Gender equality is not an issue that is given any great consideration. In fact, the problems of low female representation can often be traced to unwillingness amongst party activists to pick female candidates at selection conventions, a point confirmed by this research.

This paper will present the findings of an election survey undertaken at the June 2004 local elections. It used a ballot paper photograph survey to investigate gender and age patterns in Irish politics. Voters were asked to vote for candidates using only ballot paper photographs. The opportunity to do this research systematically and away from the experimental contexts of previous studies presented itself with the recent introduction of photographs on ballot papers in Ireland. Together with the end of dual mandate, which excluded parliamentarians from the local elections, the local government contests of 2004 were elections without well-known political faces on the ballot papers. The importance of the research is affirmed by the experimental social psychology findings, which suggests that, shown only photographs, people are prepared to judge a person's emotional state, personality traits and probable employment (Rosenberg *et al* 1986; Rosenberg *et al* 1991; and Bartle and Griffiths 2002).

Gender and Politics

The representation of women at all levels of politics in Ireland falls far short of the European average. In 2002, only 13.3% of Dail deputies were women. This figure is an embarrassment when compared with European notables such as Sweden at 45.3% and Denmark at 37.9% (Inter-Parliamentary Union). Galligan reports similarly low levels of female representation at local government level (Coakley and Gallagher 279).

There are many reasons cited for the poor representation of women in politics but, currently, there is a strong belief that the major difficulty lies at the candidate selection level. Galligan highlights this factor and explains that many party activists believe that the electorate prefer male candidates (Gallagher and Marsh 289). In earlier research, O'Kelly (2000) points to this same reluctance to promote female candidates. In particular, he identified a residual bias against female candidates amongst Fianna Fail supporters.

The female disadvantage is further underlined by White, who points out that:

> There is a belief out there that women vote for women. It's far from the truth. There is a tendency among older women to support male politicians, in the belief that they are more capable in the rough, tough terrain that is our political culture. Younger women–who have always had "equality" in their lives–do not understand the 'Women's Lib' aspect of it all and tend to vote for men as there is always "something about that particular women candidate that is not right. (26)

Generational differences have also been highlighted by many authors. Campbell (2004) suggests that for women, at least, generational differences are important. She shows, for example, that in Britain, women who were politically socialised after WWII were significantly more feminist than men of the same generation, and this had a significant effect on vote choice.

Henn *et al.* similarly draw attention to the importance of generational differences, but warn against accepting the conventional wisdom that young people are alienated from politics. Drawing on British data, they assert that:

> Young people are interested in political matters, and do support the democratic process. However, they feel a sense of anti-climax having voted for the first time, and are critical of those who have been elected to positions of political power. If they are a generation apart, this is less to do with apathy, and more to do with their engaged scepticism about 'formal' politics. (167)

To date, generational research has not received a great deal of attention in Ireland. Sinnott (2002) suggests a life cycle hypothesis which posits that voters become politicised when politics starts to impact upon their lives, however, how this politicisation manifests in voting patterns remains largely unstudied. This research will attempt to provide some insights into age and gender effects on voting.

Ballot Paper Experiment

The research design employed in this study is outlined below, but the context of the study needs to be noted. Local elections in the Republic of Ireland are clearly second order elections in the sense employed by Reif and Schmitt (1980). There are interesting questions about different voter choice criteria, the significance of personality rather than issues, potential impacts of postering strategies, and a possibly more pronounced candidate-centred campaign. The trend in voter turnout also indicates that these are quite distinct from general elections though they are run under the same PR-STV system.

An election survey was conducted for this research at the June 2004 local elections. Two replica ballot papers were developed. The first contained only photographs of local election candidates: names and party logos were removed. The photographs were of candidates from a different electoral area than that surveyed and, as a result, the candidates would have been unknown to the survey respondents. In the second ballot paper, the same candidates appeared but with their party affiliations. This ballot paper acted as a control. In all, there were twelve candidates on the paper, nine men and three women. Respondents were asked to give their own gender and age. Information on the time of voting and the weather conditions were recorded for each response.

The survey was administered at three polling stations on the day of the election. Two urban polling stations and a rural polling station were used. Turnout on the day of the election exceeded 60% in all three polling stations and over 650 respondents completed the survey. A refusal rate of just over 3% was recorded. Turnout was unusually high in June 2004 in comparison to previous local elections. European parliament elections and a constitutional referendum were held on that day, in part explaining the higher turnout.

There are a number of additional remarks that must be made in relation to the data. Firstly and most significantly, the respondents of the survey were voters. Respondents were approached outside the polling station, after they had completed their voting. Secondly, the photographs on the ballot paper were of actual local election candidates. All of the data was collected on the same day. The final point is that, in using actual voters and candidates, the external validity of the research is increased.

Research Findings

The most notable outcome of the survey was the similarity of the results of the actual election and the survey. PR-STV counts were undertaken for each of the polling stations. Table 1 labels candidates alphabetically and includes gender labels. This is the order in which the candidates appeared on the ballot paper.

Table 1: Candidate Information

Candidate Label	Gender
Candidate A	Male
Candidate B	Male
Candidate C	Male
Candidate D	Female
Candidate E	Male
Candidate F	Female
Candidate G	Female
Candidate H	Male

Candidate I	Male
Candidate J	Male
Candidate K	Male
Candidate L	Male

Table 2 outlines the results of the election count from June 2004 in column two. Columns three and four outline the final results of the PR-STV counts that were conducted on the sample ballot papers. Column three outlines the results for the polling stations where only photographs appeared on the paper and column four details the results for the polling station where photographs and party affiliation were included.

Table 2: Election Results

Order of Election	Local Election Result (June 2004)	Survey Result (Photos only)	Survey Result (Photos and Party Affiliation)
1	Candidate I	Candidate I	Candidate G
2	Candidate K	Candidate G	Candidate F
3	Candidate A	Candidate B	Candidate I
4	Candidate G	Candidate D (elected with the same vote as K)	Candidate D
5	Candidate D	Candidate K (elected with the same vote as D)	Candidate A

There is a remarkable similarity between the election results and the results of the ballot paper survey. Four out of the five candidates elected in the real election were selected in the survey. These results (column 3) were obtained from the sample ballot papers, which contained only photographs of the candidates. The second sample ballot paper was deployed in an urban polling station and included party affiliations. Here, also, four out of the five candidates were selected. An additional female candidate was selected.

In addition to comparing election results, there are a number of other patterns which can be discerned from the data. On breaking the voting patterns down by gender and age, striking patterns emerge. Table 3 outlines the breakdown of first preference voting by gender. The figure in italics refers to the outcome in the polling station where party affiliation was known.

Table 3: First Preference Trends by Gender

	Female Voters	Male Voters
Female Candidates	41%(*56%*)	26%(*38%*)
Male Candidates	59%(*44%*)	74%(*62%*)

Male voters are less likely to vote for women when party affiliation is unknown. The number of male voters expressing a preference for female candidates is low in both instances (although it must be admitted that only one quarter of the candidates were female). The number of female voters expressing a first preference for female candidates is higher than the figure for male voters when party is either known or unknown, indicating that there is some level of a female vote. Due to the small number of women appearing on the ballot paper, the female vote is concentrated among only three candidates, increasing their chances of election. The indication from these trends and the counts above is that the small number of women contesting elections is currently advantaged by the fact that the female vote is concentrated and their chances of election are thus increased.

Tables 4 to 7 outline the trends by gender in the second to fifth preferences of voters. There is a high fall-off amongst voters at the fourth preference as is evident in Graph 1. Votes beyond the fifth preference are not analysed in this paper due to the low numbers of voters expressing higher preferences.

Preferences 2 to 5 are examined to determine whether there is a consistent pattern expressed by voters through their preferences. The tables indicate that there is no major deviation from the patterns identified in the first preference of the voters. This is perhaps most evident from Graphs 2 and 3. As with Table 3, the figures in italics refer to outcomes in the polling station where party affiliation was known. Graph 2 presents the analysis of the polling stations where only photographs appeared on the survey ballot paper. Graph 3 presents the evidence from the polling station where photographs and party affiliation were included on the survey ballot paper. Both graphs confirm that there is little significant change in pattern across the preferences.

Graph 1

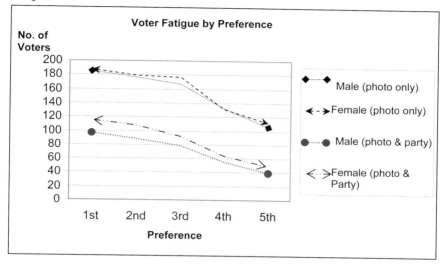

Table 4: Second Preference Trends by Gender

	Female Voters	Male Voters
Female Candidates	49%(41%)	29%(34%)
Male Candidates	51%(59%)	71%(66%)

Table 5: Third Preference Trends by Gender

	Female Voters	Male Voters
Female Candidates	46%(36%)	36%(37%)
Male Candidates	54%(64%)	64%(63%)

Table 6: Fourth Preference Trends by Gender

	Female Voters	Male Voters
Female Candidates	40%(37%)	34%(24%)
Male Candidates	60%(63%)	66%(76%)

Table 7: Fifth Preference Trends by Gender

	Female Voters	Male Voters
Female Candidates	26%(35%)	32%(31%)
Male Candidates	74%(65%)	68%(69%)

The tables indicate that party affiliation does have an impact on voting preferences. In the first and fifth preferences, female voters are more likely to select a female candidate when the party is known. The pattern is reversed in the second to fourth preferences. In the first to third preferences, male voters are more likely to select a female candidate when party affiliation is known. This pattern is then reversed for the fourth and fifth preferences when male voters are less likely to vote for a female candidate when party is known. The results suggest that party affiliation does have an effect on voter decision-making, but it is difficult to interpret this effect as it is not consistent across voters or preferences. The trends in the preferences are more easily represented from Graphs 2 and 3.

Graph 2

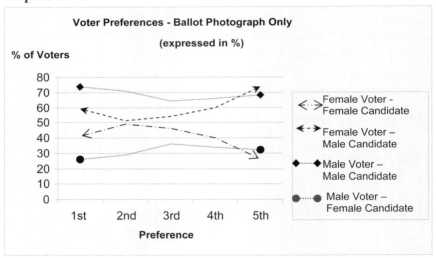

The percentage of female voters voting for female candidates declines after the fourth preference with a corresponding increase in the number of female voters expressing a preference for male candidates. This may be explained by the fact that there were only three women on the ballot paper and those who voted for the three women in their first preferences had to vote for a male candidate by their fourth preference. Again, this suggests that there is some element of a gender vote amongst women. The second preference is the highest in the category of women voting for women. There is little variation evident amongst the male voters. There is a small increase in votes for female candidates at the third and subsequent preferences.

Graph 3

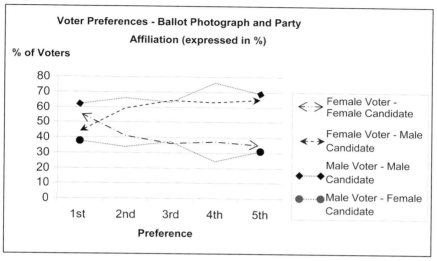

Graph 3 presents the trends when party affiliation is known. There is some variation in the graph and it differs somewhat. The number of male voters expressing a preference for female candidates declines after the third preference, and there is a corresponding increase in votes for male candidates after the third preference. This contrasts with the earlier graph which indicated that female candidates received a greater number of preferences from male voters after the second preference. The difference is slight as the percentage of male voters expressing a preference for female candidates never reaches 40%.

The examination of the first five preferences provides evidence of a number of trends. Voting patterns remain fairly consistent across the first five preferences. Both male and female voters are more likely to vote for male candidates. There is some evidence of a gender vote i.e., female voters voting for female candidates.

Tables 8 and 9 outline voting trends by age and gender. The examination of the age profile of the respondents provides a more nuanced insight into the voting trends. Table 8 outlines the age breakdown for female voters. These figures refer to first preferences only. Women in the 65+ category are more likely to vote for a female candidate with women in the two youngest age categories being most likely to express a first preference for a male candidate. Younger women were least likely to vote for female candidates. This trend is replicated amongst younger men who were also least likely to vote for a female candidate. It must also be pointed out that the 18-24 age category is more populous than the 65+ category, both in our survey and in the electorate as a whole.

Table 8: Female Voters (Age Effect)

	Female Candidates	Male Candidates
18-24	41.4%	58.6%
25-34	30.2%	69.8%
35-49	44.4%	55.6%
50-64	44.4%	55.6%
65+	57.1%	42.9%

Table 9 outlines the patterns for male voters. There is an overwhelming vote for male candidates amongst 18-24 year old men. Men in the middle age categories from 35-64 were most likely to vote for female candidates. This is a somewhat unusual trend as it could be argued that young men have been socialised in a period when female participation in political life has been normal. This has not encouraged young men to vote for female candidates.

Table 9: Male Voters (Age Effect)

	Female Candidates	Male Candidates
18-24	19.4%	80.6%
25-34	21.9%	79.4%
35-49	28.3%	71.7%
50-64	35.6%	64.4%
65+	23.1%	76.9%

Discussion

A number of broad trends have emerged from the analysis of the results. Firstly, gender does have an impact on voting patterns. All voters are more likely to vote for male candidates. This supports Galligans' assertions on party activists' reluctance to select female candidates. Female candidates were more likely to receive votes from female voters, although at a lower level than male candidates.

Examination of the age profile of voters sheds further light on voting behaviour. Younger voters are most likely to vote for male candidates. Voters in the 35+ age categories have a higher propensity to vote for female candidates. There is a clear generational effect in the trend. Voters politically socialised during the feminist movement appear more conscious of the gender issue in their voting behaviour. Younger voters appear ambivalent to the representation of women in politics. Evidence of this is also to be found in the national parliament where the number of women parliamentarians has not improved in the last twenty years. This raises serious questions for the future representation of women in politics in Ireland, as the voting population is one of the youngest in Europe. The young electors were politically socialised during a period in Irish politics when political debate focused exclusively on economic performance. Gender was not an important issue.

Political parties have taken note of the need to encourage more women into politics. Considerable funding has been allocated to parties under the National Development Plan to achieve this goal. However, our survey indicates that consciousness of gender equality has not been transferred to voters.

References

Banducci, S, M. Thrasher, C. Rallings, J.A. Karp. "Candidate Appearance Cues in Low-Information Elections." Paper presented to the American Political Science Association Annual Conference, Philadelphia (21/08/2004).

Bartle, J., and Griffiths, D. "Social-Psychological, Economic and Marketing Models of Voting Behaviour Compared" in I. Nicholas, J. O'Shaughnessy, and S. C. M. Henneberg, *The Idea of Political Marketing*. London: Praeger, 2002.

Campbell, R. "Gender, Ideology and Issue Preference: Is There such a Thing as a Political Women's Interest in Britain?" *British Journal of Politics & International Relations*. Vol. 6 (2004).

Clarke, H., D. Sanders, M. Stewart, and P. Whiteley, P. *Political Choice in Britain*. London: Oxford UP, 2004.

Gallagher, M., M. Marsh and P. Mitchell, eds. *How Ireland Voted 2002*. Basingstoke: Palgrave Macamillan, 2003.

Coakley, J. and M. Gallagher, eds. *Politics in the Republic of Ireland*. London: Routledge, 2005.

Henn, M., Weinstein, M., and Wring, D. "A Generation Apart? Youth and Political Participation in Britain." *British Journal of Politics and International Relations.* Vol. 4 (2002).

Inter-Parliamentary Union. www.ipu.org/parline

Lipset S.M., and Rokkan, S. *Party Systems and Voter Alignments.* New York: Free Press, 1967.

O'Kelly, M. "Gender and Voter Appeal in Irish Elections 1948-1997." *Economic and Social Review,* Vol. 31 (2000).

Reif, K., and Schmitt, H. "Nine Second-order National Elections. A Conceptual Framework for the Analysis of European Election Results." *European Journal of Political Research,* Vol. 8 (1980).

Rosenberg, S.W., Bohan, L., McCafferty, P., and Harris, K. "The Image and the Vote: The Effect of Candidate Presentation on Voter Preference." *American Journal of Political Science,* Vol. 30 (1986).

Rosenberg, S.W., Khan, S., Tran, T., and Minh-Thu, L. "Creating a Political Image: Shaping Appearance and Manipulating the Vote", *Political Behavior.* Vol. 13 (1991).

Gallagher, M., M. Marsh and P. Mitchell, eds. *How Ireland Voted 2002.* Basingstoke: Palgrave Macamillan, 2003.

Kerrigan, M., ed. *That's Politics; A Guide to Politics in Ireland.* Dublin: Quinn Direct, 2004.

LANGUAGE/LITERATURE

Marie E.J. Pitt: Poet and Socialist

Colleen Z. Burke

The life and work of poet and socialist Marie E.J. Pitt (1869-1948), highlights issues of women poets, as well as working class and socialist politics. The landscape of her Gippsland childhood, as well as Tasmania, where she lived for twelve years in isolated mining areas with her miner husband, inspired her creativity, poetry and politics. Strongly anti-war, an outspoken Labor and socialist journalist, she also advocated education and family planning for women.

Marie Elizabeth Josephine McKeown, the eldest of seven children, was born on 6 August, 1869 at Bulumwaal, Boggy Creek, North-East Gippsland, Victoria. Her Irish, Catholic father was from Co. Armagh and her Scots, Presbyterian mother from Ayrshire. When Marie was three, the family took up a small selection at Doherty's Corner, Wy Yung, East Gippsland. From seven to eleven, when farm work permitted, she was educated at the local public school as her father, like many other farmers, regarded the Compulsory Education Act as an interference with his liberty. At twenty, she took what was then seen as a radical step, and moved to Bairnsdale where she was employed as a re-toucher in a photographer's studio. Her first verse was published in the *Bairnsdale Advertiser*.

Marie married William Pitt in March 1893, and they moved to Tasmania's rugged West coast where he obtained work as a miner with the Mt. Read Silver Mining Company. The family lived in a miner's cottage on Mount Hamilton. Bill Pitt also worked at The Magnet, Waratah, and later at Mathinna, a gold mine, in Tasmania's North East. Marie's four children, one stillborn, were born in Tasmania, where she was often the only woman in isolated mining settlements.

Appalled by the working conditions of miners, Marie captured the horror of living outside a mining town:

> To those who have always lived outside the 'vicious circle' of a mining town or centre it would be … (difficult) to convey any conception of the sleepless terror of impending evil – the grisly obsession of 'who   next'– that tugs at the

heart of every woman whose husband, son brother or lover goes 'below'. Particularly is this so when the body or bodies of someone's breadwinner or winners lies at the changing-house waiting for the packed inquest that formality demands – while the grinding gear moans its incessant dirge, and the siren shrieks at the change of shifts 'more blood' – 'more blood'... (Pitt, 1912)

The restrictive political climate forced her to disguise her gender under initials and pseudonyms. It wasn't easy then for women to be published. These years were seminal for Marie's political and literary development – the extreme environmental conditions were a catalyst for her writing:

. . . for more than nine months one has wrestled with rain and spiteful hail, days of fog, that never saw the sun, when men groped through the long twilight night ... and pine-huts rocked in the grip of the sou'wester till they plucked at the 10 inch spikes that held their footplates to the myrtle logs. Suddenly, almost as though a wizard had waved his wand ... Summer has come to the mountains .... Six weeks or so of halcyon calm and as suddenly as it came it will go – a greying of the southern sky; ... stealthy fog wrapping everything in its melancholy mantle through which the brown thrush calls, and the eternal lantern glimmers like a wavering star up and down the twisted tracks where men go to and fro and the tunnels pierce the rocky ribs of the world, above the clouds ... (Pitt 1913)

In 1905, after Bill Pitt contracted the miner's lung disease, phthisis, the family moved to Melbourne, where he got some casual labouring jobs before becoming too ill to work. So, as well as looking after her husband, children, and trying to earn an income by writing, Marie turned her hand to a variety of jobs, including casual clerical work, roll checking, census collecting and part-time reader for a publishing company. Finally, in desperation, she put capitalistic justice to the test by writing an eloquent letter to the Chairman and Board of Directors of the New Golden Gate Mine, Mathinna, whose dividends her husband's labour had helped to raise, explaining her destitute position and asking them, in justice, to make some compensation to help her support her dying husband and three children. The courteous, cold reply came: "We have no fund out of which such help could be given" (Pitt 1913b).

Then Pitt wrote 'The Keening', a strong political poem, critical of a system that placed little value on human life, and the poem that set me on my quest to find out more about Marie Pitt:

> They moiled like gnomes in the 'faces',
> They choked in the 'fracteur' fumes,
> And your dividends paved the pathways
> That led to their early tombs.
> With Death in the sleepless night-shifts
> They diced for the prize ye drew;
> And the Devil loaded the pieces –
> But the stakes were held by you!
>
> Ye have sown the wind, to your sorrow;
> Ye have sown by the coward's code.
> Where the glimmering candles gutters
> And the rock-drill bites on the lode!
> Ye have sown to the jangle of stampers,
> To the brawl of the Stock Exchange,
> And your children shall reap the whirlwind
> On the terms that the gods arrange.
>
> We are the women and children
> Of the men that ye mowed like wheat;
> Some of us slave for a pittance -
> Some of us walk the street;
> Bodies and souls, ye have scourged us;
> Ye have winnowed us flesh from bone:
> But, by the God ye have flouted,
> We will come again for our own. (Burke 1985, 130-32)

In 1999 I was invited to the Rosebery Miners, Axemen, Bush and Blarney Festival in Tasmania to introduce a community play called *The Keening*, inspired by Marie's poem. It was about a strike, instigated and supported by women. This was a creative idea, as it had never happened in real life, nor had Marie written about it. The participants in the play, who came from mining areas, included adults, children and a high percentage of unemployed people. Because of family circumstances, juggling full-time work, babies, writing, I didn't get to Tasmania when I was doing the research for the biography, although I'd been there before on several occasions. So now, fourteen years later, I found myself in Marie's territory.

During my stay in Rosebery I learnt about the history and working conditions of Tasmania's mining areas, and how improvements in working conditions for miners during the twentieth century were being drastically eroded. Recently introduced twelve hour shifts were moving to seven days on, seven days off, impacting negatively on health, personal and family life. Unemployment was high. After the festival, I moved into a miner's house on Mt. Black. Every evening there were underground blasts beneath the house. From the veranda I could see Mt. Read draped with mist, obscuring the TV tower, bare slopes, trees. The mine settlement was on the other side, out of sight.

It was inspirational talking to local people interested in Marie Pitt's poetry, walking and seeing areas where the Pitts lived – mountains, mining environment, stimulus for much of her Tasmanian writing and poetry. It enhanced my understanding of her strong political beliefs, life-long commitment to justice for miners, workers, women, for the underdog.

During Bill Pitt's long illness and after his death in 1912, Marie herself suffered ill-health, although she was still active in the Victorian Socialist Party (VSP), which comprised an eclectic group of people – vegetarians, feminists, writers, poets, socialists, laborites, unionists and anarchists. In 1911, Marie co-edited *The Socialist*, the VSP's weekly newspaper, with the Reverend Sinclaire, a Unitarian Minister. At the VSP she came in contact with a variety of people, including writers and poets, such as Mary E. Fullerton, Nettie Palmer (nee Higgins) and Bernard O'Dowd.

Women's Issues
For many years an outspoken, passionate writer for *The Socialist*, Marie was indignant at injustices suffered by the working class, but still believed that, compared to his wife, the working-class man was well off:

> What a damnable piece of impudence to deny to a woman that which the poorest navvy takes as-his right, but which his wife, if she has a few children never dares to hope for – an eight hour day, a paper or book and a couch when the eight hours are done. (Pitt 1912a, 2)

When my children were small, I worked full-time, did most of the housework, shopping, wrote poetry – sometimes it's difficult to get the balance right. And most of the research on Marie Pitt was done when I was off on maternity leave, rushing into the Mitchell Library, between breast-feeding my daughter. I was usually leaking and sticky with milk by the time I left, perhaps shocking other researchers in that almost sanctified atmosphere.

Marie also realised that domestic servants were in an ever-lower position than wives – they were isolated with no rights, unions and sexual harassment was common:

> The domestic servant is on the lowest rung of the ladder of industrial degradation. Compared with her, the factory hand is noble in her freedom, and dignified in her sturdy independence. (Pitt 1908, 2)

And she felt that:

> until the economic independence of women, as women and not as industrial machines, is secured, the true evolution of women must be at a standstill. Until she is economically independent as man is, she dare not   be   true to her real self. (Pitt 1911, 2)

She also advocated equal pay for equal work – a radical concept then and still not achieved or fully implemented, despite a 1969 Australian Federal ruling.

Marie also advocated a motherhood that was conscious and dignified, impossible when women have too many children, and not enough money, or time. To achieve this perfect motherhood or 'humanhood', Marie advocated 'family limitation' and 'family planning'. Prevention was preferable to abortion, but she knew the reality of a society where abortion was often the last resort for 'desperate women':

> but then desperate people are mostly foolhardy, and the capitalist system is the breeder of desperate people, desperate for gain, desperate for social standing, desperate for most things that, in the truest sense, are worth little or nothing. (Pitt, 1910)

In 1911 Marie covered an abortion trial for *The Socialist*, where the abortionist was convicted of murder:

> . . . this woman was no murderess; the death of the girl was an accident, for which she may or may not have been partly responsible ... It is the quintessence of cant, this whole twaddle about the sanctity of the unborn ... the girl with a baby is an object of ... reproach, a creature to be shunned by women ... exploited by men. (Pitt, 1910)

It is interesting how, in Australia, the issue is again being brought up by conservative politicians and the churches. Yet Marie knew that only women can free themselves:

> until woman ... has found her own specific value and ceased to be an apologist for her own sex, it is folly to talk of the emancipation of woman from bonds that man, in his own interest as master and exploiter, has by long precedent woven into the very fibre of her being. (Pitt, 1911, 2)

These ideas were explored in poems such as 'The Enslavement':

> Not with red rite of sword on Strife's wan hill,
> Mid clash of arms and pomp of war's estate,
> Was Freedom slain, and her strong sons laid low,
> But in some wild red dawning long ago,
> When Man, the savage, took his savage mate,
> And beat, and bent, and broke her to his will. (Burke 1985, 83/84)

Marie and poet Bernard O'Dowd eventually began a relationship, the attraction was there before, but blossomed after the death of her husband. As O'Dowd was still married, the affair was conducted in secrecy. Eventually the situation became untenable for Marie and she gave Bernard an ultimatum – to commit to her and leave his wife, or end the relationship. When O'Dowd eventually left his wife and the two set up house together, Marie still suffered censure, this time through criticism of her as 'the other woman'. She preferred marriage, but O'Dowd's wife, a strict Catholic, wouldn't agree to a divorce. Their partnership lasted until Marie's death.

In 1929 the pair joined Melbourne's Unitarian Church, which was concerned with the here and now and social issues, rather than the hereafter. In 1945 Marie suffered a stroke from which she never recovered. Drifting in and out of consciousness, she was converted back to Catholicism before her death on 20 May 1948, aged 78 years, although friends and family claim she was a Unitarian to the end (Bottomley 1949: 7 and Price 1978). The Catholic Church only had her body, not her independent spirit:

> Thus would I,
> In twilit forest of that day of doom,
> Reckless and sure in such brave company,
> Hunt with the Hounds of Death to the last leap,
> And, from this vale of lingering decline,
> From charnel vault and slow despoiling worm,
> Have those fierce horses I have loved in life
> Back to the Potter bear my broken clay. ("The Last Ride", Pitt 1925: 107)

Change is a long process – the battle never won – the fight for equality, justice for women, working people, humankind is ongoing – never truer than today when everything seems to be going rapidly backwards and so much that has been gained is diluted or lost. But, despite the repressive political climate, we can still be optimistic, as Marie Pitt wrote:

> We can rebel, we women of Australia ... and by all the gods in the calendar of the old (and new) oppression we will rebel. (Pitt 1912: 2)

References

Bottomley, Rev. "Death of Mrs. M.E.J. Pitt." *Beacon*. June 1949, No 104: 7.

Burke, Colleen, *Doherty's Corner: The Life and Work of Marie E.J. Pitt*. Sydney: Angus and Robertson Publishers, 1985.

Burke, Colleen, "Marie E.J. Pitt, Poet and Socialist." *Overland*, 158, (2000): 51-57.

Personal interviews with Kim McDermott, Rosebery, Tasmania, 27 Feb., 2 March and 21 June 1999.

Pitt, Marie E.J. "A State Bureau for the Registration of Domestic Servants." *Socialist*. 17 April 1908: 2.

-----. "The trial of Mrs. Rook – Killing no Murder." *Socialist*. 28 Dec. 1910.

-----a. *Horses of the Hills*, Melbourne: Thomas C. Lothian, 1911.

-----b. "Women in Art and Literature." *Socialist*. 11 August 1911: 2.

-----a. "A Morbid Expression of Class Consciousness." *Socialist*. 5 Jan. 1912.

-----b. "Woman her Duty to her Race." *Socialist*. 15 March 1912: 2.

-----c. "The Greatest Strike in World History." *Socialist*. 8 March 1912: 2.

-----a. "Bauera and Buttongrass." *Lone Hand*, Tasmania, 2 June 1913.

-----b. Letter on Horses of the Hills, *Sydney Morning Herald*, 23 May 1913 from 'One who waited.' Gavutu, 30 March 1913, Solomon Islands, H.H. Pearce Private Papers.

-----. *Bairnsdale and Other Poems*, W.F. Wannan, ed. *Back to Bairnsdale* Back to Bairnsdale Committee, 1922.

-----. *The Poems of Marie E.J. Pitt*, Melbourne: E.A. Vidler, 1925

-----. *Selected Poems of Marie E.J. Pitt*, Sydney and Melbourne: Lothian Publishing Co., 1944.

The Father and Daughter: 'A Simple, Moral Tale'?

Aída Díaz Bild

Since the 1960s feminist literary historians and critics have paid special attention to the way in which eighteenth century women writers contributed to the development of the novel. Long-neglected authors have been recovered and their narratives re-read and 're-visioned' in order to better understand their aims and anxieties as both women and writers. For most of them, sentimental or domestic fiction was not just about courtship, love or romance, but also about interrogating the structures of society that enslaved women: "Thus, the novelist appears to be telling a fashionable tale of love and romance but is actually presenting a vivid picture of the exploitation and frustration of her sex in the eighteenth-century" (Schofield 24). Under the careful manipulation of literary conventions, the novel became a document of female assertion. And, in this process of challenging or questioning the patriarchal order, women writers transformed the scope of the domestic novel, expanding the horizons of fiction and breaking new ground for it. One of the main contributions of female authors to the development of the narrative genre was precisely this shift from romance towards realism in order to offer the readers a more faithful portrait of women's lives. By showing women's real problems in the eighteenth century these writers were not only defending themselves from the accusations of providing young ladies with a romantic and unrealistic view of the world, but were reaffirming their belief that the novel should fulfil a didactic and moral function. For women writers, fiction was the right vehicle to portray everyday life and offer their readers a moral comment on it: "Female art was resolutely *not* transcendental; ethics not aesthetics was its business" (Todd 229).

One of the late eighteenth century writers who better understood the oppression and frustration of women's lives and used her novels or tales to draw a vivid and faithful painting of them was Amelia

Opie.[1] Most twentieth century critics have focused on the subversive aspects of Opie's novels and on how she presented these elements of criticism in an oblique way because she was writing at a time when feminist and revolutionary ideals were strongly questioned (Kelly 1981, Eberle, Johnson. My own point of view is that Opie was not so much interested in undermining the values of her society, as in giving her female readers a realistic and dark lesson on the true situation of women in the eighteenth century. Behind her novels there is more disappointment than anger, as well as an acknowledgement that all doors to personal fulfilment are closed to women in a patriarchal society whose principles and ideals have been reasserted after the revolutionary period. It is precisely because she is aware of the fact that women's predicament is not going to change that, unlike other contemporary women writers, she does not offer her heroines an ideal, fairer and better world in which they would be able to exercise their powers.

By the time Amelia Opie published *The Father and Daughter*, the enthusiasm for the French Revolution had long faded away. In the early stages, many British liberal thinkers – the so-called Jacobins – believed that the French insurrection could serve as a model for a peaceful reform in England. They were convinced that if the French example were followed, British society would become more liberal and egalitarian. Some women writers, such as Mary Wollstonecraft or Mary Hays, believed that the example of France opened up new possibilities for them. Thus, they united in defending their right to be considered moral and rational beings rather than delicate and submissive creatures. But towards the middle years of the 1790s, the revolutionary excitement declined and, by the end of the century, the emphasis had shifted from rebellion and change to reaction and reassertion of traditional values. The Jacobins became increasingly unpopular and their work the main target of many novels and tracts published at the end of eighteenth century. Conservative writers used all the weapons they had to attack the 'modern ideas' and Wollstonecraft's personal life, as represented in William Godwin's *Memoirs of the Author of "A Vindication of the Rights of Woman"* (1798),

---

[1] The realistic bias in Opie's fiction has been outlined by Kelly (1980), Ty (1998), and Howard (1992). Howard affirms that Opie "did offer an intelligent view of contemporary social issues and effectively showed how they impinged on people's lives" (232).

proved to be one of the most useful. She was described in *The Unsex'd Females* (1798), by the conservative theologian Richard Polwhele, as "ripe for every species of licentiousness" (70), and the *Anti-Jacobin Review* of 1798 does not hesitate to list her in the index under the word prostitution. Thus, feminism became associated with being anti-English and with sexual immorality and any kind of reforms, especially those concerning women's equality, was totally rejected.

Conservative conduct books for women, such as James Fordyce's *Sermons to Young Women*, were published in new editions and the female ideal that the conduct books had helped to construct throughout the century was firmly reasserted.[2] A virtuous woman had to be defined by her meekness, submission, chastity, modesty, reserve, delicacy, sympathy, gentleness, as well as a unique capacity for self-control and self-knowledge.[3] The subjection of women was now justified in terms of "a renewed model of 'domestic woman' as professionalized custodian of the 'national' conscience, culture and destiny" (Kelly 21). Although there were no changes in the laws that oppressed women and denied them any autonomy, females were told that they had a vital task to fulfil, that of regenerating the spirit of society. A good example is Hannah More's *Strictures on the Modern System of Female Education,* in which she emphasises both the need to prepare girls for submission and obedience, and their role as moral refiners of society. Interestingly, Kelly argues that by allotting women such an important and decisive role in national and international survival, More "has subverted the hierarchy of patriarchy by inverting it or by turning its inside (subjectivity, domesticity) out (the social, the public)" (Kelly 118).

The new, virtuous domestic woman had to be above all chaste. In *Fictions of Modesty*, Ruth Bernard Yeazell explains how Mary Douglas has pointed out that cults of virginity tend to appear at times of social upheaval and stress (Yeazell 23), and, indeed, the end of the eighteenth century witnessed a reinforcement of the ideology of

---

[2] For the role of conduct books in contributing to creating the new domestic woman and the rise of the middle class in England, see Armstrong (1989).

[3] Many of the passive qualities attached to the new ideologically constructed woman – modesty, meekness, compassion, affability, humility – were already present in conduct books published at the end of the seventeenth century, and beginning of the eighteenth century, such as Richard Allestree's *The Ladies Calling* (1673), the Marquis of Halifax's *The Lady's New-Year's Gift: or Advice to a Daughter* (1688), or *The Whole Duty of a Woman: or a Guide to the Female Sex from the Age of Sixteen to Sixty* (1701).

female chastity and decorum. Fordyce, whose *Sermons to Young Women* was reprinted after the revolutionary period, asserted that chastity was a woman's treasure and *The Whole Duty of a Woman*, by 'a Lady' begins by instructing women "how to obtain the divine and moral virtues of piety, meekness, modesty, chastity, humility, compassion, temperance, and affability with their advantages, and how to avoid the opposite vices" (Bergen Brophy 11). Wilkes, in *A Letter of Genteel and Moral Advice to a Young Lady* (1740), makes a real apologia for this female virtue and does not hesitate to say that, "an immodest woman is a kind of monster, distorted from its proper form" (Wilkes 30). Years later, in the counter-revolutionary period, conservative writers, such as Hannah More, reinforced the validity of these statements. In *Strictures on the Modern System of Female Education* (1799), More affirms that propriety "is to a woman what the great Roman critic says action is to an orator; it is the first, the second, the third requisite" (More 131-2).

Unchastity was a mortal sin which could not be forgiven and which marked a woman's social death. Mandeville summarises it very clearly in *An Enquiry into the Origin of Honour* (1732): "Whereas Honour once routed never rallies; nay, the least *Breach* in Female Reputation is irreparable; and a *Gap* in Chastity, like a *Chasm* in a young Tree, is every day a *Widening*" (cited in Yeazell 17). As Rogers has explained, the fact that woman's entire moral status and fate depended on the observance of a single law clearly restricted her possibilities for self-determination and independence (Rogers 240). Women had not only to be chaste, but preserve the appearance of being chaste. This explains why eighteenth century women were more concerned with avoiding blame than with achieving excellence or cultivating more positive virtues.

But whereas unchastity was unforgivable in women, in men it was just considered a venial sin. Thus, whereas a woman's moral and sexual behaviour had to be above reproach, a much lower standard of conduct was tolerated in men. Radical writers, such as Mary Hays, Catharine Macaulay or Mary Wollstonecraft, strongly criticised this moral double standard that was more flexible towards men and saw no fault in hardly anything they did. They pointed out the irony and absurdity of considering women weak of intellect and reason, unable to control their passions, but expecting a higher standard of conduct of them. Interestingly enough, these radical writers do not want to destroy or ridicule the virtues of modesty and chastity, which, for them, as for their contemporaries, are of paramount importance, but to claim a change in male sexual behaviour. Thus, at the same time that Hays attacks the licentiousness of men, she encourages women to possess the "amiable" and "indispensable" virtue of modesty (Hays 236). Wollstonecraft and Macaulay also praise chastity and modesty and call for equality in moral behaviour. They argue that unless women's minds are cultivated, they will not be able to have and develop purity of mind and chastity, since virtue is based on knowledge and understanding. As Yeazell explains, whereas many eighteenth century writers tried to reduce female modesty to an instinctive shrinking from harm and, thus, celebrated "the glory of a delicate female to be unconscious" of all "unbecoming knowledge'" (56), some women, such as Wollstonecraft, defended that modesty was a rational, active and conscious virtue.

But although both conservative and radical writers celebrate the qualities of modesty and chastity, they greatly differ in their attitude towards fallen women. As would be expected, radical authors are more sympathetic to those who have erred. Thus, for example, Mary Hays asks virtuous women to show humanity and compassion towards the fallen women and, unlike most conservative thinkers, defends that some women are capable of returning to the path of rectitude, thus proving "that in some minds nothing can totally extinguish the love of virtue" (Hays 237).

Catherine Macaulay agrees with Hays that a first fault must not necessarily lead to a woman's destruction and also asks for "benevolence to the frailties of the fair as circumstances invite" (Macaulay 116). Finally, Mary Wollstonecraft admits that she "cannot avoid feeling the most lively compassion for those unfortunate females who are broken off from society, and by one error torn from all those affections and relationships that improve the heart and mind" (Wollstonecraft 150).

Conservative writers were not so benevolent towards fallen women. In their aim to support the *status quo* they heavily criticised anything that could contribute to its destruction. Elizabeth Hamilton considers forgiveness of the fallen woman an "excess of charity" (cited in Todd 209), and Hannah More "an affectation of charity" (More 329). She defended that a fallen woman could not be rehabilitated, an idea shared by many conservative writers, although some of them argued that pity should be shown towards those who had repented of their sins.

If the virtue of chastity was considered sacred, so was the father/daughter bond. It has been argued that the eighteenth century witnessed what Stone has called a "growth of affective individualism" (Stone 149 *passim*) or, in other words, the rise of more egalitarian and warmer affective relations between husband and wife and parents and children. Locke's influence here was quite obvious. In his *Two Treatises of Government* (1690), he argues that a parent has authority over a child as long as the child is too immature to judge for himself. Although he emphasises the child's perpetual obligation to honour the parents, "this is very far from giving Parents a power of command over their Children or an Authority to make Laws and dispose as they please, of their Lives or Liberties" (cited in Gonda 14). The new family type that emerges during the Enlightenment is, thus, less patriarchal and authoritarian and more liberal. This becomes more obvious in the children's increasing freedom to choose their partners for individual, emotional reasons and not for familiar or economic ones (Stone 149-180). There are, nevertheless, two objections to Stone's theory. The first one is that, although it may be true that there was a clear improvement in family relationships, this improvement always depended on the willingness of the husband and father to cede the power society had given him, since there were no changes in the laws or structures that recognised and sustained the superiority and authority of men and expected women to fulfil a dependent and subservient role all their lives. Obviously, conduct books of the age, such as Richard Allestree's *The Ladies Calling* (1673), William Fleetwood's *The Relative Duties of Parents and Children, Husband and Wives, Masters and Servants* (1705), or Patrick Delany's *Fifteen Sermons upon Social Duties* (1744), greatly contributed to this notion of the obedient and submissive daughter.

Filial duty was seriously tested on the question of the daughter's marriage. The 'general rule' was that a girl must never marry without the consent of the parents and that parents must never force the child into a marriage she did not like. As Brophy has explained, while the first condition was considered 'sacred', the second one was very often rather liberally interpreted. Since young girls' experience of the world was very limited, parents thought that they could better judge what was best for them. Echoing this desire to protect young ladies from making the wrong choice, an anonymous pamphleteer in 1753 asserted: "I suppose the human Heart is scarce susceptible of a keener, and more exquisite Anguish than what many a Parent hath felt from the Indiscretion of their Children in that important Circumstance" (Gonda 20). Thus, whereas, theoretically, women had the right to choose, in practice, it was not always so and many ladies were forced into unwanted marriages. The consequences of not fulfilling one's filial duty on the question of marriage were really appalling: women lost their reputation and right to inheritance, thus risking a life of absolute poverty.

Obviously, this emphasis on the father's authority and the child's submissiveness within the family was reinforced at the end of the eighteenth century as a means of correcting the laxity in morals that the revolutionary period had brought about in England (Stone 149-180). Jane West, who was obsessed with the "depravity of the times" defended that "filial and conjugal ties are no remnants of feudal barbarisms, but happy institutions, calculated to promote domestic peace" (West 7). As Johnson has explained, "Clearly the fictions conservative writers contrive do not invite us to inquire when the authority of fathers over children is ever morally compromising, because the debate in which they are engaged requires them to demonstrate that the family itself is preeminently moral and moralizing" (Johnson 10).

The second objection to Stone's argument is of a different kind. We may accept that in the eighteenth century there emerged a new family model based on love and not tyranny. As a matter of fact, many of the novels published during the period idealise the bond between father and daughter as one of emotional closeness and intensity. Richard Steele reflects this tendency when he affirms that, "certain it is, that there is no kind of Affection so pure and angelick as that of Father to a Daughter" (Gonda 1), and even the liberal Mary Hays defends that, "Men in the characters of fathers too, are generally infinitely more amiable, and do more justice to the sex, than in any other character whatever" (Hays 174). This celebration of the father/daughter bond explains why eighteenth century people were so horrified at Mary Blandy's murdering of her father. Her crime represented the destruction of the ideal father/ daughter relationship, especially if we take into account that her father was presented, during the trial, as a tender, loving parent, who did his best to protect his daughter from prosecution (Gonda; Eger *et al*.). But, as writers such as Caroline Gonda, Margaret Anne Doody or Eleanor Wikborg have explained, the introduction of the element of love and tenderness in the father/daughter relationship was just another means of reinforcing paternal authority: "In a situation where patriarchal rulers in both the public and the private sphere were confronted by revolutionary beliefs in the rights of the individual, a daughter figure's deeply felt devotion served to allay anxieties over the legitimacy of their power" (Wikborg 9). Filial love and devotion, thus, became the new weapons to obtain a daughter's obedience and submission in the new sentimental family. As a matter of fact, many of the conduct books of the age dwell on the 'benefits' of inculcating filial love.

The Father and Daughter is the story of a young lady who has violated two sacred rules of society: she has challenged paternal authority, thus destroying the ideal father/daughter bond, and lost a woman's most precious treasure, her chastity. Agnes acknowledges her mistakes and is aware of the great pain she has caused her father. Therefore, she decides to dedicate the rest of her life to alleviate the misery she has produced: "my only wish now is, to live and to suffer" (Opie 98). She works herself almost to death to support herself and her child and to procure her father's release from the madhouse in which he is confined, so that she can personally look after him. She never loses the hope of his recovering his wits, but her anxiety about her father's mental condition, her hard labour and her sense of guilt gradually deteriorate her health. Thus, when her father finally recovers his sanity and recognises and forgives her, the shock kills both of them. In the eyes of society, Agnes becomes the perfect penitent who seeks expiation for what she has done by means of a life of poverty, sorrow, distress and shame. Many twentieth- and twenty-first-century critics consider that Agnes's suffering is excessive and the moral debt overpaid. Thus, Gary Kelly says:

> For whether or not the heroine has transgressed a moral or social code, her suffering and humiliation seem incommensurate with her real or supposed crime, and she remains to be bathed in the reader's sympathy alone. The centre of Opie's tale is this "passion", in the Christian sense: "the sufferings of a martyr". (85)

Kelly believes that this structure helps Opie to portray the ambiguities and contradictions of the female condition in the apparently loving and egalitarian family model that was emerging at that time. He also points out that Opie's concern with excessive moral debt cannot be only explained by reference to the conventions used by other female writers of the time. Although it is true that throughout the eighteenth and nineteenth centuries – but especially during Opie's own lifetime – that many writers dealt with the incurring and repayment of a moral debt, in the case of Opie we must look closely into her personal life, through her poems, to discover a daughter who felt guilty for not having duly respected and appreciated her mother, who died when Opie was only fifteen. Separately, Jane Spender and Eleanor Ty have also underlined how, behind the mother/daughter relationship described in Opie's novels, is a clear autobiographical element (Spender; Ty).

King and Pierce also consider that Agnes is not punished in proportion to her 'sins', especially if we take into account that the narrator emphasises that Agnes's intentions were good and innocent and that she has been the victim of her own shortcomings – she believes that she is an expert at judging other people's motives – and Clifford's manipulating and seducing powers: "As a result, the calamities that befall her seem punishment in excess of her true moral worth, and in excess of her transgression against her father" (King and Pierce 15). Agnes is not excused for her actions, but her life of poverty, sorrow and humiliation clearly overpays her debt to her father and society. For King and Pierce this ambivalence in presenting Agnes's situation – on the one hand, understanding and supporting her and, on the other, severely punishing her – makes clear that Opie was more concerned with Agnes's struggle for moral identity than with preaching proper behaviour.

Like Kelly, Ty points out how, in the novels by women writers of the 1790s and early 1800s, characters are severely punished for violating the rules of female behaviour "and what becomes fascinating in the novels is the disparity between the act of disobedience and the length and harshness of the woman's period of atonement" (Ty 12). Ty analyses *The Father and Daughter* in detail, examining the way in which Opie deconstructs and rewrites the notion of the fallen woman within a socially acceptable framework and discourse of penitence. Opie elevates the stature of Agnes, on the one hand, by comparing her with

Cordelia, the good daughter in *King Lear*: "Agnes, the seduced woman, becomes the one who has been mistakenly condemned by the ruler and by society, but who returns to show her fidelity and devotion" (Ty 138). She is also ennobled by an association that is established between her and the prodigal son in Luke's parable. As in the case of the biblical text, the attitude towards the sinner, in this case a fallen woman, should not be one of censure, but of forgiveness, compassion and charity. Lastly, Opie shows how a fallen woman is not the monster or corrupted person many of her contemporaries considered her to be, but capable of making herself useful by fulfilling her duties as daughter and mother and looking after the poor.

All these insights into *The Father and Daughter* are really interesting, but I partially disagree with them. If there is imbalance in the novel between crime and punishment, it is not so much because Opie wants to redeem the fallen woman or to denounce the way in which women are constrained and oppressed by social rules, but because she wants to give her female readers a useful and harsh lesson on the consequences of not fulfilling one's duties and violating the notions of right conduct and propriety. The novel is didactic, not because it tries to preach duty, chastity, and obedience, but because it offers the audience a realistic and bleak picture of woman's situation in patriarchal society. The message is clear and direct: in a reactionary and conservative environment, women who break the rules are doomed forever, no matter how hard they try to atone for their faults. Agnes has sinned against society by not fulfilling her filial duty and deviating from the path of virtue, two transgressions for which, as we saw in the first part of this article, there is no forgiveness at the time Opie is writing.

In "British Seduced Maidens", Susan Staves compares the representation of seduced maidens in fiction and in law reports and comes to the conclusion that novels do not offer us a very faithful picture of the real situation, since they ignore the legal remedies or actions against seduction available in the eighteenth century. She further adds that although in fiction the fate of the seduced woman was usually that of death, in real life many were capable of returning to decent places in society, as the chronicles of the Magdalen Asylum prove. Maybe, as Staves explains, seduction did not always inevitably cause physical death, but it undoubtedly led to social doom and ostracism. Even those women who redeemed themselves through penitence and useful work could never sit next to the 'decent ladies'. Not even litigation could compensate for a woman's sexual betrayal, since the public exposure of her crime was a fatal blow for her most fragile possession, her reputation. And it is precisely this harshness and cruelty of society towards those who do not adhere to its customs or the female ideal of the age that Opie depicts realistically and without any kind of 'decoration' in *The Father and Daughter*. Society only sees the facts and never takes into consideration how virtuous the sinner may inwardly be.

Staves has pointed out that the great paradox of the seduced maiden is that she resists any categorisation into good or bad, whore or maiden. On the one hand, they are not lascivious whores, but embody the virtues considered essential in a woman: beauty, simplicity, trustfulness and affection. On the other hand, if they were perfection itself they would not have been so easily seduced. As a matter of fact, the narrator of *The Father and Daughter* seems more concerned with highlighting Agnes's virtues and making clear that her motives for abandoning her father were innocent, than with dwelling on her fatal mistakes. She is not presented as a degenerate who just wants to appease her desires and does not care about the harm she may inflict on others, especially on her father, but as the victim of a villain who knows perfectly well how to manipulate and convince her to abandon everything that is dear to her. As a matter of fact, as soon as Agnes becomes aware of the fact that Clifford has been deceiving her and has no intention of getting married but wants to keep her as his mistress, she takes the brave and hard decision to abandon him and return to the path of virtue. She admits her guilt and acknowledges the painful consequences of her actions: "there are few children so bad, so very bad as I am" (78). She decides to atone for her crimes by living in poverty, solitude and labour and fulfilling her duties as daughter and mother. Her devotion and dedication to her father are really admirable:

> It was a most painfully pleasing sight to behold the attention of Agnes to her father. She knew it was not in her power to repair the enormous injury she had done him, and that all she could now do, was but a poor amends; still it was affection to see how anxiously she watched his steps whenever he chose to wander alone

from home, and what pains she took to make him neat in his appearance, and cleanly in his person. Her child and herself were clothed in coarse apparel, but she bought for her father every thing of the best materials; and, altered as he was, Fitzhenry still looked like a gentleman. (146)

Agnes's exemplary industry and behaviour engage the sympathy and admiration of many of her neighbours. She becomes the perfect incarnation of Hanna More's penitent not only because she practises "the virtues of self-denial, patience, fortitude, and industry" (140), but because her whole body reflects the great suffering she is going through. Thus, as soon as the governors of the asylum, whom Agnes meets in order to convince them to allow her to look after her father, perceive "the ravages which remorse and anguish had made in her form", they give up their determination "to receive Agnes with that open disdain and detestation which her crime deserved; the sight of her disarmed them" (110).

This rather idealised and romantic view of Agnes's life should not mislead the reader to think that society has forgiven her after a long period of painful probation. Maybe she will be now received in many houses, but always as the fallen woman who has humbly acknowledged her offences and is still paying for them, and not as the virtuous, perfect Agnes she was considered to be before she broke the accepted rules. She will never be restored to her pedestal and become again the pride of her father and friends, but will always be the poor penitent who deserves the compassion of society because she has accepted suffering as the right path to redeem her sins. Fitzhenry is aware of the harshness of his everyday associates towards those who trespass the established boundaries and that is why he tries, in vain, to protect her from Clifford's advances: "and if you have not pride and resolution enough to be the guardian of your own dignity, I must guard it for you" (69-70). He is greatly shocked when he discovers that Agnes has eloped with her lover – "he sat for hours absorbed in a sort of dumb anguish, far more eloquent than words" (72) – but he still retains some hope for his daughter's future as a honourable woman, since he thinks that she is married. But when he learns about his daughter's disgrace, that is to say, about her living with Clifford as his mistress, "this was the death-stroke to his reason" (92). He knows that, socially speaking, his daughter is dead, that no matter how hard she tries to expiate her sins, society will never allow her to be fully restored to her former place. This explains why Fitzhenry repeats all the time that his daughter is dead and even draws the shape of a coffin and writes on the lid the name of Agnes. He is not so much hurt by his daughter being ungrateful to him, despite his having devoted his whole life to her, but overwhelmed by the consequences that Agnes's actions will have for her. He knows how much she is going to suffer for violating the father/daughter bond and losing her chastity. He is aware of the fact that they live in a society that is totally insensitive and unforgiving, and the idea of the whole ordeal his daughter will have to go through is just unbearable to him. He expresses it very clearly at the end of the novel when he recovers his sanity and recognises his daughter: "but how pale and thin you are! you have worked too much: - Had you no *friends*, my child?" (151). Agnes replies triumphantly that she has many friends who pity and respect her, but the truth is that she will never be on the same level with them, because the stigma of her offence will never disappear. Her death at the end of the book, like the death of many other fictional seduced maidens, is the logical outcome of her actions. Their physical death symbolises the social decay that awaits all those who challenge the *status quo*. Agnes herself, when she returns home, acknowledges the rejection and despise that her conduct will generate in those who not such a long time ago were her friends:

> Now, dread reverse! after a *long* absence, an absence of years, she was returning to the same place, inhabited by the same friends: but the voices that used to be loud in pronouncing her welcome, would now be loud in proclaiming indignation at her sight; the eyes that used to beam with gladness at her presence, would now be turned from her with disgust; (101)

The narrator does not dwell very deeply on the humiliations Agnes has to go through, but gives us a few hints. Thus, for example, Agnes goes to see the governors in the evening to avoid being insulted by the passers-by and has to leave Fanny's house after realising that her number of pupils has diminished because she has given shelter to a fallen woman. As a matter of fact, one of Fanny's children illustrates perfectly the general attitude of society towards those who have deviated from the path of virtue. When Agnes kisses an eight-year-old girl, she utters a loud scream and runs away from her because, "her mother had charged her never to touch or go near miss Fitzhenry, because she was the most wicked woman ever breathed" (126). Unfortunately, this mother, as well as the character of Mrs. Macfiendy, who with great malignity attacks Agnes for her past actions, affirming that "I do not expect when I go to another world to keep such company as Miss Fitzhenry" (122), represent not a minority, but a majority in English society at the end of the eighteenth century, and beginning of the nineteenth century, when, as we saw in the first part of the article, traditional values and customs were being reasserted. It is no coincidence that both these women are only able to feel sorry for Agnes when she dies, or, in other words, when she ceases to be a threat to the venerated patriarchal order.

Many eighteenth- and early nineteenth-century female writers used their novels to explore new alternatives to women's powerless and submissive situation in a patriarchal society. They created heroes who possess many of the traditional feminine virtues and were willing to grant their wives a degree of moral autonomy and authority unthinkable in the real world. These writers wanted to undermine the prevailing power relations between men and women, offering a model of courtship and marriage based on egalitarian principles. But, of course, as some critics have pointed out, these new alternatives belonged to the realm of fantasy and the ideal, since as long as there were no changes in the legal structure and social customs, women's oppressive condition could never change. Interestingly, in the adaptations of the tale to the stage, the tragic ending is replaced by a happy one. In *Agnes di Fitz-Henry* by Paër, *Smiles and Tears: or, The Widow's Strategem,* by Marie Therese Kemble, and *The Lear of Private Life! Or, Father and Daughter, a Domestic Drama* by William Moncrieff, father and daughter are reconciled after he is restored to sanity. In *Agnes di Fitz-Henry* and *The Lear of Private Life,* Agnes and Clifford do get married, whereas in *Smiles and Tears,* Agnes refuses to marry him, although she forgives him and assigns their child to his protection so that he can "teach him to shun the vices which have destroyed our happiness" (Kemble 292).

The great difference between Opie and many of her contemporaries is that she refuses to offer her female readers any fantasy of power that might lead them to believe that a change in their subservient condition is attainable. She wants women to become aware of the fact that no rebellion is possible in a conservative and reactionary society that sanctions the absolute authority and sovereignty of men over women. Women have no other option but to follow the path indicated by law and social customs if they do not want to become, like Agnes, "a wandering wretched outcast" (88). Opie does not live in a world of dreams but of reality, and it is precisely the harsh and bleak truth of women's predicament that she wants to portray in the novel.

References

Armstrong, Nancy. *Desire and Domestic Fiction: A Political History of the Novel.* New York: Oxford UP, 1989.

Bergen Brophy, Elizabeth. *Women's Lives and the Eighteenth Century English Novel.* Tampa: U of Southern Florida Press, 1991.

Eberle, Roxanne. "Amelia Opie's *Adeline Mowbray:* Diverting the Libertine Gaze; or, The Vindication of a Fallen Woman." *Studies in the Novel.* 26. 2 (Summer 1994).

Eger, Elizabeth, Charlotte Grant, Cliona Ó Gallchoir and Penny Warburton, eds. *Women, Writing and the Public Sphere 1700-1830.* Cambridge: Cambridge UP, 2001.

Gonda, Caroline. *Reading Daughters' Fictions 1709-1834: Novels and Society from Manley to Edgeworth.* Cambridge: Cambridge UP, 1996.

Hays, Mary. "Appeal to the Men of Great Britain on Behalf of the Women" in *Women in the Eighteenth Century.* Vivien Jones, ed. London: Routledge, 1991.

Howard, Susan K. "Amelia Opie" in *British Romantic Novelists, 1789-1832.* Bradford K Mudge, ed. *Dictionary of Literary Biography.* Vol. 116. Detroit: Bruccoli Clark Layman, 1992.

Johnson, Claudia L. *Jane Austen: Women, Politics and the Novel.* Chicago: U of Chicago Press, 1990.

Kelly, Gary. *Women, Writing and Revolution 1790-1827.* Oxford: Clarendon Press, 1997.

-----. "Revolutionary and Romantic Feminism: Women, Writing and Cultural Revolution" in *Revolution and English Romanticism: Politics and Rhetoric.* Keith Hanley and Raman Selden, eds. Hemel Hampstead: St Martin's Press, 1990.

-----. *English Fiction of the Romantic Period 1789-1830.* London: Longman, 1989.

-----. "Amelia Opie, Lady Caroline Lamb, and Maria Edgeworth: Official and Unofficial Ideology." *Ariel* 12. 4 (Oct. 1981): 3-24.

-----. "Discharging Debts: The Moral Economy of Amelia Opie's Fiction." *The Wordsworth Circle* 11 (1980): 198-203.

King, Shelley and John B. Pierce, eds. *The Father and Daughter with Dangers of Coquetry.* Toronto: Broadview Press, 2003.

Lowder Newton, Judith. *Women, Power and Subversion: Social Strategies in British Fiction 1778-1860.* Athens: U of Georgia Press, 1981.

Macaulay, Catherine. "Letters on Education" in *Women in the Eighteenth Century.* Vivien Jones, ed. London: Routledge, 1991.

More, Hannah. "Strictures on the Modern System of Female Education" in *Women in the Eighteenth Century.* Vivien Jones, ed. London: Routledge, 1991.

Opie, Amelia. *The Father and Daughter with Dangers of Coquetry.* Shelley King and John B Pierce, eds. Toronto: Broadview Press, 2003. All in-text references are to this edition.

Polwhele, Richard. "The Unsex'd Females: A Poem" in *The Origins of Modern Feminism: Women in Britain, France and the United States, 1780-1860.* Jane Rendall, ed. New York: Palgrave, 1985.

Rogers, Katharine M. *Feminisms in Eighteenth Century England.* Urbana: U of Illinois Press, 1982.

Schofield, Mary Anne. *Masking and Unmasking the Female Mind: Disguising Romances in Feminine Fiction, 1713-1799.* Newark: U of Delaware Press, 1990.

Shiner Wilson, Carol and Joel Haefner. *Re-Visioning Romanticism: British Women Writers 1776-1837.* Philadelphia: Philadelphia UP, 1994.

Spender, Jane. "'Of Use to her Daughter': Maternal Authority and Early Women Novelists" in *Living by the Pen: Early British Women Writers.* Dale Spender, ed. New York: Teachers College Press, 1992.

Staves, Susan. "British Seduced Maidens." *Eighteenth Century Studies.* 14. 2 (Winter 1980/81): 109-134.

Stone, Lawrence. *The Family, Sex and Marriage in England 1500-1800.* Harmondsworth: Penguin, 1990.

Todd, Janet. *The Sign of Angellica: Women, Writing and Fiction, 1660-1800.* New York: Columbia UP, 1989.

Ty, Eleanor. *Empowering the Feminine: The Narratives of Mary Robinson, Jane West, and Amelia Opie, 1796-1812.* (Toronto: University of Toronto Press, 1998.

West, Jane. "Tale of the Times" in *Jane Austen: Women, Politics and the Novel*. Claudia L Johnson, ed. Chicago: U of Chicago Press, 1990.

Wilkes, Wetenhall. "A Letter of Genteel and Moral Advice to a Young Lady" in *Women in the Eighteenth Century*. Vivien Jones, ed. London: Routledge, 1991.

Wikborg, Eleanor. *The Lover as Father Figure in Eighteen Century Women's Fiction*. Gainesville: U Press of Florida, 2002.

Wollstonecraft, Mary. *A Vindication of the Rights of Woman*. In *Political Writings*. Janet Todd, ed. Toronto: U of Toronto Press, 1993.

Yeazell, Ruth Bernard. *Fictions of Modesty: Women and Courtship in the English Novel*. Chicago: U of Chicago Press, 1984.

Disgusting Ventriloquism: The Short Story as a Site for Transgender Experiment in Narrative Voice

Mary O'Donoghue

In Hugo Hamilton's short story "The Compound Assembly of Evelyn Richter," Irish musician Frank shares an apartment in Berlin with German Evelyn and her boyfriend Werner. One evening, they take Frank out to a restaurant because Werner has "something important to discuss" (Hamilton, 93): he believes that Evelyn is in love with Frank. Frank is left in the invidious position of having to counter this as best he can, given that Evelyn has fallen into total silence:

> Frank is talking for Evelyn as if she has no mind. He becomes her mouthpiece. Frank can say what she wants to say. He can make her say what Werner wants to hear. He can make her say what he himself wants to hear. He can say what she never intended to say. He can make her say what she wants Werner to hear. He could make her say what she wants to say but doesn't want Werner to hear. He can say what she wants Frank to hear. He can also make her say what she doesn't want to hear herself say. He can provoke her. As long as she says nothing herself, she assents. (Hamilton, 99)

Hamilton's protagonist finds himself having to second-guess and speak for another character. Presented with the spectrum of what he can say, in Evelyn's stead, Frank blathers on and appears to draw on all ventriloquial possibilities for Evelyn's answer:

> Total fantasy! Any attraction that Evelyn has for me is entirely her love for Irish music. She also likes to speak English. Like everyone else, Evelyn enjoys the company of a foreigner. She loves the music and is fascinated by the way musicians live. In that way, I represent something new. Something carefree, maybe. But Evelyn has much more definite views about men. I don't fit into her scheme and never would, either. I'm not even her type of man. Evelyn thinks I'm too skinny. I'm too unhealthy. Evelyn would say I'm too much of a man's man. She thinks I'm too much in love

with beer and music and good crack. I wouldn't be her sort in a million years. (Hamilton, 100)

Hamilton's passage is both humorous for its scattershot response and critically appealing in terms of what it portrays of the phenomenon of ventriloquism. It speaks to the opportunities afforded for both power (making her say), and disempowerment, that risk of failure skirting round any attempt to speak for another: what to say?

I approach this topic as a fiction writer whose curiosity was considerably piqued by Lorrie Moore's parenthetically-posed question in her introduction to the anthology *Best American Short Stories* (2004). Noting patterns, making categories for the stories included, Moore writes of noticing "a number of the stories [she]'d chosen were written from the viewpoint of the opposite sex of the author" (xviii). She counts five writers who fit this bill (I count six) and asks, "(Is the short story especially hospitable to this kind of transgendered sympathy and ventriloquism?)" (xviii). What fuelled my curiosity was the question unanswered, in an introductory essay that turns many tricks in terms of explaining what the short story 'is' and 'does'; its whispered quality, marked by those parentheses; and the gendered consideration which I found most arresting. Isn't that "sympathy and ventriloquism" simply part and parcel of the creative act, which invites, expects even, entry into invented lives, other consciousnesses? In other words, what's the big deal? And, though undesignated by Moore, those writers whose "transgendered sympathy and ventriloquism" merits her mention are mainly women writers choosing male perspectives.

Interviewing Annie Proulx (herself one of Moore's six opposite-sex-choice authors) some years ago, I solicited her most important advice to beginning writers. She emphatically refuted the 'write what you know' dictum, and insisted that one should write as far away from it as possible. Moore's question engages reflection upon the transgender perspective, and posits the short story as a conduit for what suddenly, due to that sneaked-in question of Moore's, seems to be some sort of daring experiment. This paper will speak specifically to women writing through/about men as a narrative choice, addressing Moore's gendered question about such 'voice-throwing' within the ambit of short fiction and exploring the safe-risk element of the form that ought to make it a comfortable site for transgender experiment in narrative perspective. Yet, when tracking instances of such sympathy/ventriloquism in a number of short story anthologies of Irish women writers published in the past ten or fifteen years (notwithstanding that the anthology by its nature frequently presents a document written to a prescriptive 'agender') we see that the 'hospitality' of the short story form is frequently eschewed. This paper situates itself within wider theories of ventriloquism, both performative and literary. It studies short fiction by Mary Dorcey and Frances Molloy: stories that have hosted such experiment, and to arresting formal and thematic ventriloquial effect. Treating of ventriloquism on the nineteenth century stage, English diarist Henry Crabb Robinson proclaimed that:

> [v]entriloquism is disgusting when successful. The more successful he is, the more the ventriloquist risks revealing the fact that his power is not by any means the power that the audience wants him to have, but derives from the desire of the audience to be worked on. (cited in Connor, 306)

And, so, this paper evaluates how stories like those of Dorcey and Molloy present a transgressive, even 'disgusting', choice in perspective.

The short story ought to present a secure formal vessel for trying out narrative perspectives for size. In order of perspectival frequency: third-person, first-person, and the less-used (but compelling when skillfully employed) second-person. With respect, then, to writing from the perspective of the opposite gender, be it third-person (where viewpoint is limited to one character and perhaps less fraught with the anxieties of intimacy than first-person perspective), or first-person (with things happening to or being filtered through a central, but not necessarily panoptical, 'I', the most intimate mode of ventriloquism, that *yes, I said, yes*, of Joyce's Molly): what rewards are offered by the short story? In her pedagogic treatment of the short story, Janet Burroway writes that "[t]he virtue of the short story is its density. If it is tight, sharp, economic, well knit, and charged, then it is a good short story because it has exploited a central attribute of the form – that it is short" (42). So, with brevity as its central attribute, the short story affords a reduced risk of the failure of perspectival experiment that might dog the novel. At the same time, just as the writer might be breathing a sigh of relief at her choice of a lower-risk medium, she is pulled up short by that form's demand for compression, which enforces choice-making in terms of narrative inclusions, and demands close attention to authenticity and integrity of characterisation, be it male or female. Patrick O'Donnell, studying polyvocal ventriloquism and the multitude of voices in the work of Dickens, refers to the "authorial dream of omnipotence"(251), which strikes this author as a very necessary type of *chutzpah* when aiming for narrative control in the short story as much as the far more unruly novel form! Drawing on a study by Lewes, also on Dickens's ventriloquism, O'Donnell states that:

> while evidence of the 'phenomenon of hallucination' (that is, speaking or hearing in different voices) is a sign of insanity in most instances, for the artist it is a mark of creativity. [...] Lewes would say that Dickens is sane and brilliant [...] because he had mastery over the voices he hears, does not ultimately believe in their reality, and can successfully channel them into the rationally patterned work of art. (251-52)

Considering O'Donnell's pronouncement – guilty but insane – the short story form, then, seems the ideal place for temporary hallucinatory states. The voices can come in by the window, and leave by the door. And the smaller the crowd, the more interesting the party is likely to be!

Steven Connor's *Dumbstruck: A Cultural History of Ventriloquism* (2000) traces the phenomenon of ventriloquism from enigmatic 'because-I-told-you-so' oracles right up to contemporary horror films where frightening button-eyed dummies come alive. His ideas about the transgressive nature of ventriloquism *per se*, what he describes as "[t]he doubts and delights of the ventriloquial voice, of the voice speaking from some other place, reorganizing an economy of the senses, and embodying illegitimate forms of power" (43), prove useful to the act of writing fiction from the viewpoint of the opposite gender. It is Connor's contention that an audience is, in fact, conditioned to find the act of ventriloquism – be it literary or performative – flawed, incompetent, and deceitful (which, of course, it is; that is its very basis), but this raises interesting ramifications for the reception to short fiction that employs Moore's "transgendered sympathy."

Indeed, it may go some way towards explaining the polite refusal of the short story's hospitality as a site for transgender sympathy and ventriloquism. For, militating against such experiment is the threat of being 'found out' and booed at. In fact, the anxiety about being unmasked for some kind of fraudulence might well outweigh another apprehension: that of reader response and critique driven by speculation on a work's autobiographical underpinnings.

How, then, do findings from some anthologies of short stories by women measure up to Moore's "transgendered sympathy" and the sites for "embodying illegitimate power" as posited by Connor's understanding of ventriloquism? Running the numbers turns up a notable paucity in the publication of stories deploying the male perspective. In the 1989 *Territories of the Voice: Contemporary Stories by Irish Women Writers,* there are a total of twenty-seven stories; three are written from the male perspective; two are told through a third-person perspective. The third story, Jennifer Johnston's oblique and economical "Trio", is an intriguing blend of third person and interior monologue. The Introduction to *Territories of the Voice* delineates the editors' criteria for the inclusion of fiction by Irish women writers. They explicitly announce that they wanted it to be a "woman-centered collection"; the stories "represent the writer's oeuvre", depict "some significant feature about women's lives in Ireland that women elsewhere have also experienced", and "provide portraits of a variety of women's experience". The editors declare that "[v]irtually all the stories are about women, often narrated by first-person women narrators. But this is by no means a literature written on the margins of culture" (DeSalvo *et al*, xii). This makes for an anthology constructed upon the expectation that stories by Irish women must be about Irish women and told through Irish women's voices: a confluence that is a godsend for critical reception, yet straitjacketing for writers. It is a prescription refilled over and again in subsequent anthologies.

In the 1990 anthology *Stories by Contemporary Irish Women,* there are seventeen stories; two written from a male perspective, and both told through the third-person. In the 1993 anthology *Virgins and Hyacinths: Attic Book of Fiction*, there are thirteen stories; four written from a male perspective; two of those four are told through a first-person perspective. In the 2001 anthology *Cutting the Night in Two: Short Stories by Irish Women Writers*, there are thirty-four stories; six written from a male perspective; one of those six is told through the first-person. That one story is Frances Molloy's "Women are the Scourge of the Earth"; the other five are Emma Cooke's "The Greek Trip"; Lucile Redmond's "Love"; Blánaid McKinney's "Please"; Bridget O'Connor's "Bones"; and Mary Dorcey's "The Husband". It is worth noting that both Dorcey's and Molloy's stories also appear in Ailbhe Smyth's *Wildish Things: An Anthology of New Irish Women's Writing* – an anthology that does not precisely fit my criteria since it combines fiction and poetry. Rather, it is noted because indeed they do "wildish things" in their ventriloquism.

Regarding ventriloquism (of the performative variety) and gender, Connor informs us of an interesting balance:

> The desire to affirm and secure the masculine power of the voice amid the potentially emasculating play of dissimulation and mimesis surfaces frequently in writings about ventriloquism. From the late eighteenth century onwards, ventriloquist performers, as opposed to the possessed victims of ventriloquial speech, are nearly always male. Dugald Stewart remarks in passing that "[i]n the other [i.e. female] sex, the power of imitation is, I think, in general, greater than in ours", and women performers certainly got involved in multiple characterization. (Connor, 328-29)

Stewart's acknowledgement, though slightly grudging, is significant in its application to literary ventriloquism; it suggests a covert gift for imagining male consciousness. "The Husband", which first appeared in Mary Dorcey's 1989 collection *A Noise from the Woodshed* and has been anthologized many times since, sees the author ventriloquize the ire, trauma and abject confusion of a nameless character whose wife, Martina, is leaving him for her lover, Helen.

The story turns on his attempts to rationalise her decision; in doing so, he presumes to speak for her desire. If he can do this – not unlike Frank's predicament in Hamilton's story – then perhaps he can contain the situation: "He was tired of thinking, tired of the labour of anticipating her thoughts and concealing his own" (Dorcey, 234). Dorcey cleverly, but subtly, exploits the device of the mouthpiece in this story; the husband becomes a ventriloquist for stereotypes of same-sex relationships. Comically, he thinks he knows it all! "He knew every possible permutation, he had seen them all a dozen times on television and seventies' movies, but he never thought he might be expected to live out these banalities himself" (237). Through his blinkered perspective, we are shown Martina as a mouthpiece for newly-acquired feminist theories; according to her, "[d]ominance and submission were models women had consigned to the rubbish heap" (241). The story is lined with sympathy for his predicament, and one of the most moving moments in the story finds him observing Martina pack her belongings after they have made love for the last time:

> He watched her hands as they expertly folded blouses, jerseys, jeans, studying every movement so that he would be able to recapture it precisely when she was gone. It was impossible to believe that he would not be able to watch her like this the next day and the day after. That was what hurt the most. The thought that he would lose the sight of her – just that. […] He felt that if he could be allowed to watch her through glass, without speaking, like a child gazing through a shop window, he could have been content. (244-45)

Yet its tenderness is foiled by his continued attempts to ventriloquize for his wife: "He would not dare express it, needless to say. She would have sneered at him. Objectification, she would call it" (245). When we do get to hear from Martina in direct speech to her husband (beyond her awkward attempts at chat about coffee-making and bread-baking), it entirely disestablishes whatever control he has held over the situation:

> "Don't ring this weekend. We're going away for a while."He felt a flash of white heat pass in front of his brain and a popping sound like a light bulb exploding. He felt dizzy and his eyes for a moment seemed to cloud over. Then he realized what had happened. A flood of blind terror swept through him, unmanning him, because she had said something totally unexpected – something he had not planned for. He repeated the words carefully, hoping she would deny them, make sense of them. (249)

His blinding from sudden illumination, as well as the "blind terror" that "unman[s]" him, is fitting fall-out to the husband's over-reliance on his version of events. Martina's cool *précis* has completely blindsided him, and he must re-order the economy of his senses, relying on repetition of her words in one last attempt at ventriloquial control. But parroting her words – "Don't ring this weekend. We're going away for a while" – means that Martina is now speaking through him, and the ventriloquial relationship has been inverted.

However disgusting we may have found some of the husband's reactions throughout the story – and there are many instances of ugliness – Dorcey succeeds in forging a sympathetic character. The short story form, dealing as it does in particularities, allows her to present the particularities of this one break-up from the perspective of one party. It is through the husband's ears that we hear the mass bell toll outside the window after they have "made love then once more because she was leaving him" (234), and it is next to him that we are left in the kitchen, smelling the bread she has baked, standing "over the warmth of the stove, his head lowered, his hands clenched in his pockets, his eyes shut" (250-51).

The speaker in Frances Molloy's "Women are the Scourge of the Earth," believes himself cuckolded, and faces an inquest into the nature of his wife's death. Deploying the first-person perspective, which voice then addresses the reader as an interrogator/confessor, Molloy creates a story told with violent immediacy and negative capability: "I'm not a mug like your man next door. I kicked his teeth right down his throat and let her ladyship know that I would debollocks the bastard if he ever came snooking round my house again. I'll not be made a laughing stock of" (Molloy, 203). Molloy's story is a small miracle of narrative compression. Within the confines of a four-page story, she draws a character whose bluster compels us to listen right to the end, much as we are horrified by what is divulged:

> Women, they're all the same, after what they can get out of you. There's only one thing a woman is useful for and that's on her back. Nobody but a fool would marry a woman for that nowadays. There's plenty of it going free and no mistaking. I'm well rid of her. Women are the scourge of the earth. I've learnt my lesson. Once bitten, twice shy, as the man says. (206)

Unlike the husband in Dorcey's story, whose efforts at infiltrating female consciousness and sexuality are claustrophobically confined to one woman, Molloy's husband's irrational rage at his wife drives him to direct his rage outwards, towards 'women', presuming that "they're all the same." If not necessarily a 'sympathetic' portrait, it is to Molloy's credit that she chooses the first-person as the intimate (and unnerving) means for her ventriloquism. Her character fairly much damns himself in front of us. And he is oddly pitiable for his repeated insistence that he is "not going to be made a fool of."

In her introduction to *Wildish Things*, Ailbhe Smyth asks, "[w]hat is imagination if we may never look into our wildest depths?" (7). I contend that contemporary short story writers, such as Dorcey and Molloy, in their adoption of transgendered ventriloquism, have sought their narratives in just such risky depths. Describing the elasticity of the human voice, Connor writes: "My voice can bray and buffet only because it can flinch and wince. My voice can be a glove, or a wall, or a bruise, a patch of inflammation, a scar, a wound" (5), which flexibility is encouraged by the supple short story form, and should perforce flow into narrative choice and fictional voice.

References

Brown, Elund, ed. *The London Theatre 1811-1866: Selections from the Diary of Henry Crabb Robinson.* London: Society for Theatre Research, 1996.

Burroway, Janet. *Writing Fiction.* 4th Edition. New York: Harper Collins, 1996.

Casey, Daniel and Linda Casey. *Stories by Contemporary Irish Women.* New York: Syracuse UP, 1990.

Conlon, Evelyn and Hans-Christian Oeser, eds. *Cutting the Night in Two: Short Stories by Irish Women Writers.* Dublin: New Island, 2001.

Connor, Steven. *Dumbstruck: A Cultural History of Ventriloquism.* Oxford: Oxford UP, 2000.

DeSalvo, Louise, Kathleen Walsh and Katherine Hogan, eds. *Territories of the Voice: Contemporary Stories by Irish Women Writers.* London: Beacon Press, 1989.

Dorcey, Mary. "The Husband" in Conlon and Oeser, *Cutting the Night in Two.*

Hamilton, Hugo. "The Compound Assembly of Evelyn Richter." *Dublin Where the Palm Trees Grow.* London: Faber, 1996.

Molloy, Frances. "Women Are the Scourge of the Eart" in Conlon and Oeser, *Cutting the Night in Two.*

Moore, Lorrie, ed. *Best American Short Stories.* Katrina Kenison, ed. Boston: Houghton Mifflin, 2004.

O'Donnell, Patrick. "'A Speeches of Chaff': Ventriloquy and Expression in *Our Mutual Friend.*" *Dickens Studies Annual: Essays on Victorian Fiction.* 19 (1990).

O'Donoghue, Mary. Interview with Annie Proulx. *Sunday Business Post.* (Dublin) 20 May 2001.

Smyth, Ailbhe, ed. *Wildish Things: An Anthology of New Irish Women's Writing.* Dublin: Attic Press, 1989.

Walsh, Caroline, ed. *Virgins and Hyacinths: Attic Book of Fiction.* Dublin: Attic Press, 1993.

Nuala O'Faolain's *My Dream of You* and the Feminist Panoramic Novel

Mary Power

Nuala O'Faolain's *My Dream of You* is a significant feminist, post-modern novel. It is a step forward in a tradition that includes George Eliot's *Middlemarch* (1871), Virginia Woolf's *The Years* (1937) and Doris Lessing's *The Golden Notebook* (1962). Like these novels, *My Dream of You* examines the condition of intellectual women, their level of satisfaction with life, and their response to an increasingly fast-paced world. Kathleen de Burca, the main character in O'Faolain's novel, has recently retired from her job as a specialised journalist – a travel writer. As the novel begins, she is starting a new project as well as a new phase in her career. She is returning to her native Ireland from which she has long been estranged.

Kathleen has held what many would consider an enviable job, flying to tourist destinations around the world and writing them up in an always fresh and up-beat manner for publication by a London travel company. She has worked for the firm 'Travel/Write' for twenty years, and has become attached to her co-workers, who she regards as her family. She is assigned to visit a rich array of places from western Europe, the United States, and the Philippines, to Thailand, Sri Lanka, Senegal, Jerusalem, China, and Korea. Though Kathleen is aware of poverty and injustice in her travels, her assignment is to write about each location in an appealing up-beat way. There seems to be something in her personality that thrives on the glibness she must practice as a travel writer. On an early pleasure trip to Greece, passing through Thebes, she recalls, "This was where Oedipus himself really lived – just there – where there's a petrol station at the crossroads" (O'Faolain 230). Kathleen has been driven by the demands of her work, and is so busy that she has failed to see that her career has hampered her personal development. At the age of forty-nine, she is dealt a severe blow when her friend and colleague, Jimmy, dies of a heart attack. Kathleen re-examines her own priorities, and decides that it is time to leave 'Travel/Write', go back to Ireland, and research a nineteenth century divorce case which has long fascinated her. In other words, Kathleen has decided to work in-depth on a historical problem, and plans to write about it.

Kathleen de Burca is both versatile and highly serious. In this paper, I would like to suggest that her quest for her own identity, her search for a serious love relationship, her increasing knowledge of Irish history, and her acquaintance with a congenial group of Irish people, put her at the centre of a multi-faceted, far-reaching novel. At the age of forty-nine, Kathleen is interested in asking questions, and developing and changing her life. She left rural Ireland (fictionalised as Kilcrennan), and a depressing home at twenty years old. She went to London and, for a while, worked at prosaic entry-level jobs. Unlike Edna O'Brien's Cait and Baba in *The Country Girls*, however, Kathleen never loses sight of her need for a good education. Having abruptly left Trinity College, Dublin, she talks her way into a journalism programme at a London Poly.

The constant trips to beautiful places have left Kathleen urbane, fashionable, sophisticated, yet, often, emotionally numb and sometimes detached and isolated. Though she has had casual sexual encounters with men during her travels, she has not really had a partner since she lived with Hugo, an English law student, when both were in their twenties. Although she is close friends with her co-worker Jimmy Beck at 'Travel/Write', he is gay, and the two make a point of not knowing where the other lives. Between assignments, Kathleen camps out in a basement flat in London, but has no regard for her surroundings, and never entertains there. She feels that she is still a foreigner in London after more than twenty years. When Jimmy dies, Kathleen faces her own mortality, and sees the need to change. Her project is a nineteenth century Irish divorce case which reconnects her with her intellectual self in pre-'Travel /Write' days: her first lover, Hugo, had given her the copy of the divorce decree, Talbot vs. Talbot, many years before.

Kathleen's desire to delve into the nineteenth century Talbot divorce case challenges her abilities as a writer and scholar. The return to Ireland also gives her new perspectives on her own identity. Apart from being born Irish, Kathleen's qualifications for the legal and historical research she is about to undertake are non-existent. She does, like any Irish person, have decided feelings about the 1840s and the Great Hunger, though some of her feelings are naïve, even if deeply ingrained. She recalls that, as a child, she once had a part in a school pageant about the Famine. Ruefully, she remembers the stage pageantry in which she and her friends participated. She also recalls, ironically, that they wore spotless old-fashioned clothing and rode on the back of a lorry. On an existential level, Kathleen is convinced that the Famine knocked the happiness out of the Irish people, especially her immediate family. For example, her father saw the Famine politically, rather than compassionately. He told her, again in her childhood, that Queen Victoria once wrote a check for ten pounds to the Dogs' Home, and then one for five pounds to aid Irish famine sufferers. She considers the Famine as "the trauma deep in the genetic material of which I am made" (O'Faolain 73). Kathleen has to be reminded of the larger issue as she proceeds with her research – that the Famine is, of course, a survival story.

The divorce case Kathleen researches, the Talbots' story, is, in some ways, the opposite of Kathleen's: Richard and Marianne Talbot are a young married couple, English and well-born, with a precocious little daughter, Mab. They come to Ireland to live on family property – the Mount Talbot estate, in the West of Ireland – an inversion of Kathleen's own journey from Ireland to England. The Talbots are members of the gentry, while Kathleen is Catholic and makes her own way economically and socially. Kathleen – to an excessive degree – refuses to be concerned with questions of property: she refuses to 'settle in'.

The Talbots' story, which Kathleen has known from the divorce papers, begins in the worst year of the Famine. For a while, the Talbots' marriage had progressed well enough, but Richard becomes increasingly concerned about the necessity of producing a male heir in order to own Mount Talbot free and clear. Marianne, as a bride, is naïve and shy. She defers to the housekeeper as well as her husband, and dotes on her little daughter Mab. She sees a few of the local Anglo -Irish socially, and is unconcerned about her own tenants or people in the area dying. When she sees dead bodies over a wall near where she and some friends are picnicking, her impulse is to turn away, and to say and do absolutely nothing about the ghastly sight.

Marianne is rumored to have had an affair with William Mullan, an Irish groom and coachman on the estate. Mullan, in many ways, is privileged among the servants. In the version of the divorce proceedings Kathleen has long been familiar with, other servants had been ready to testify that they had seen their mistress and the coachman together in the stables, that Marianne had entered William's room and had given him gifts, including bottles of her husband's good wine. Related documents that Kathleen sees for the first time in her visit to the village library near Mount Talbot suggest there may be a conspiracy afoot in which Richard Talbot has convinced some of the servants to perjure themselves. Richard has no mercy on his tenants and is anxious to remove them from his land, tear down the wretched hovels in which they had lived, and sell the property to commercial interests.

Kathleen, in reading the documents available to her in Ballygall, has to wonder whether Richard has become frustrated and thwarted over the passage of time by the lack of a son, and wants to replace his wife for reasons of infertility alone, or if Marianne has actually committed adultery. In either case, the new documents attest that Marianne is treated brutally. She is unable to defend herself, and may have, on some levels, sadly decided she must be guilty, even if she isn't. Richard declares Marianne will never see Mab again, and rips the rings off her hand. She is then sequestered in a hotel/nursing home in Dublin, and later confined in a similar place in England, near Windsor. From the agony of her grief without her daughter, Marianne goes mad. This part of the narrative, fraught with loneliness and alienation, is reminiscent of Charlotte Perkins Gilman's, *The Yellow Wallpaper*. It was documented that William Mullan tried to see Marianne in Dublin, but was turned away. In yet a third document, it is stated that Richard Talbot sought a divorce settlement against Mullan, and legal proceedings would leave the latter penniless if he were to stay in Ireland. However, Mullan sees what lies ahead for him and goes to America, eventually finding work with horses in Saratoga Springs, New York

Kathleen's conscientious research, with its contradictions and uncertainties, leaves her in a dilemma about retelling what she has discovered factually, or of working against verifiable history and filling in the gaps by turning it into fiction. In other words, she does not as yet know how to give form to the results of her research. She questions the genre of the historical novel because Henry James was not keen on it. She also gets an earful in terms of relations of ordinary late twentieth century Irish people to the Famine. Some comment unaccountably that they didn't know people in Ireland had sex during the Famine. A few old people Kathleen meets in Ballygall go out of their way to deny there ever was a famine – presumably because the memories of what they have heard long ago are too terrible to face. Her former boss at 'Travel/Write' teases her in a 'phone conversation about the similarity between this story and Lady Chatterley. Members of Kathleen's family try to assess the financial outcome of Kathleen's work and prophesise that the result will be a sizzling bestseller and Kathleen will grow rich.

The heroines of the earlier feminist novels mentioned all lack guides or mentors. For example, in *Middlemarch*, Dorothea Brooke's mother dies early, and she must look after her sister. Eleanor Partiger in *The Years* is in a similar family situation and, as the oldest daughter, dutifully assumes the maternal role after her mother dies. Kathleen's mother often was depressed during Kathleen's formative years, and she early on declares that she and her brother and sister were victims of her mother's victimhood. By contrast, Kathleen is fortunate: *My Dream of You* presents Ballygall's seventy-five year old librarian, Nan Leech, as a phenomenon. She is a countrywoman, and an extremely competent professional, who challenges Kathleen's assumptions, making her at first uncomfortable, then amazing her by her generosity and expertise. Nan knows how to obtain materials and make them available to patrons in, as Yeats would say, 'the best modern way' ("Among School Children" in Finneran). She is thoroughly computer literate and has been in charge of a recent library display on the Great Famine. She has also involved school children in the project by having them check the workhouse records for relatives during and slightly after the Famine years. The children are also asked to interview their grandparents about their earliest memories in that regard. Nan is unmarried and lives alone, but has strong life-long friends in Ballygall. She also tells Kathleen that she never married because to do so in the earlier days of her career would have meant losing her job. In just one week, Kathleen makes significant contact with the older woman. They match wits, but Nan seems to ration her time at the library, and is not always available to help the impatient Kathleen recover documents relating to the Talbot project. The reason is devastating: Nan is dying of cancer.

Nan completes her mentorship of Kathleen as well as saying good-bye to her and lifetime friends at a small party in her honor. She prepares to die by slipping away to a hospice without fanfare or emotion. Nan has it all planned, right down to finding care for her cat.

At the impromptu gathering, Nan is still very busy – suggesting to Kathleen some of the architectural details of the Talbot estate which Kathleen must take into consideration for her research. But this is also a way of avoiding tears at the party. Nan does not have a shred of sentimentality about her, and she proves to Kathleen that older unmarried women in small Irish towns can live happily and fully as professionals. Perhaps it is even more interesting that Kathleen quickly sees that Nan has a lot to teach her, not only in guiding her through the Talbot materials, but also in much more intimate issues about how to proceed with her life. The creation of Nan Leech adds sparkle and dimension to O'Faolain's novel. Though one might reply that Anna Wulf in *The Golden Notebook* has a similar resource with her psychiatrist, Mother Sugar, the portrait of Nan Leech stands in the foreground of *My Dream of You* as fully realised and absolutely compelling. It was a wise step on O'Faolain's part to distance Kathleen's counterparts – her sister, Nora, and her English friend, Caro. This strategy meant that Kathleen had to act independently without the endless conversations, reminiscences and comparing of notes which occur in *The Golden Notebook* between Anna Wulf and her friend Molly in the former's kitchen. Kathleen was also free to meet a number of other people in the West of Ireland who treated her warmly and helped her on her way.

Another aspect of Kathleen's self-discovery in Ireland involves her becoming re-acquainted with her younger brother, Danny, his wife and daughter, who still live modestly in Kilcrennan, where Kathleen had grown up. Danny is a mechanic and Annie runs the family dry cleaning business. Kathleen has prided herself on escaping her father's desire to control the family and his oppressive and punishing Catholicism, as well as the depression and lassitude of her mother, whom she never understood: her mother, who liked books and libraries, once told Kathleen that she knew why Anna Karenina had thrown herself in front of a train. Kathleen, like her sister, ran off and abandoned Danny and left him a legacy of family troubles. On this visit, she comes to realise that her regular postcards from exotic locations and generous financial gifts are not enough to forge connectedness with members of the family she would now like to know and love better.

My Dream of You excels in its portrayal of middle-aged romance. In London, Kathleen has first lived with a rich English law student, but felt she was too young to settle down. She acts out her confusion promiscuously – thereby losing Hugo, whom she really cared about. She may, however, have distrusted him for a perceived prejudice against the Irish. While she has numerous brief desultory romances or one night stands on her business travels to exotic countries, they lead nowhere. Kathleen is in so much of a hurry to catch planes and meet deadlines at 'Travel/Write' that she puts her feelings and personal life on hold.

Her friendship with her American co-worker, Jimmy, at 'TravelWrite' is incomplete because he is gay. She and Jimmy were really compatible, but each protected a core of privacy and never ventured too far into each other's lives. They knew each other on the job, and talked a lot in local pubs as well as in exotic foreign watering holes. Yet what seemed most important was their ability to share daily trials and tribulations of 'Travel/Write' and joke about them.

A day or two into her working holiday in Ireland, Kathleen meets a man who is also just back from England, in his case, to visit his father. His name is Shay (for Seamus) Murphy and he and Kathleen enjoy several leisured romantic encounters. Shay runs a landscaping business in England and the relationship works out well sexually as well as emotionally. Kathleen views this as the first real romantic relationship she has had since Hugo – more than twenty years before. Shay and Kathleen buy groceries, prepare meals, and dine together in a cottage Kathleen has been loaned. Theirs is a successful and pleasurable adventure in playing house, and it suggests compatibility. Shay seems protective of Kathleen and treats her as if she were very young. He sings 'I'll take you home again, Kathleen' to her and tells her, "You are Ireland to me" (O'Faolain 271), and she is, at least momentarily, awe struck by his comment.

Shay is not perfect, however. He mysteriously disappears on Kathleen when he says he is going on a short errand in the village. On the other hand, he expects she'll be waiting for him days later when he returns. He admits to Kathleen that he's contentedly married in England. He and his English wife have two married daughters who live nearby, and together they delight in their grandchildren. Shay pictures Kathleen as a modernised, Irish colleen with her curly red hair and streak of wild independence. Paradoxically, Kathleen never contradicts this image of herself, nor does she try to convince Shay to visit her in London and to appreciate how much more she is than his construction of her. In other words, his dream of her is Irish sweet talk, verging on blarney. At the end of the novel, as Kathleen prepares to return to England, she leaves Shay what seems to be her reply to the 'I'll Take You Home Again Kathleen' overture. On the telephone answering machine she sets up a tape of 'September Song' on the lines, "And I haven't got time for a waiting game" (487).

While Kathleen warms to the affection and attention Shay provides, she stops short of idealising him or constructing images around him. She manages such adjectives as "middle-aged" (135), "ordinary-looking" (140), and "nondescript" (135) in describing him, but does see a redeeming similarity between Shay and Paul Newman around the eyes, and she shares a revealing and intimate aside with readers about Shay's false teeth and love-making. Shay suggests that Kathleen might rent a cottage and stay in the West of Ireland, and pledges to visit her whenever he comes over to see his father near Sligo. There are problems with the relationship, but Kathleen seriously considers the idea of it because it is palpable, real, and satisfying. At some points, Kathleen is flattered that Shay sees her as his image of Ireland, but the vision is severely limiting. If Shay lives in England near Chester, why doesn't one of them suggest that if Kathleen returns to London they will meet halfway – perhaps in Wolverhampton, Coventry or Birmingham? Would all the romance escape from their relationship if they continued to see each other in England? Would the affair, given a sea change, become ordinary – even sordid?

If Shay sees Kathleen as his idealised Irish woman, Kathleen's vision is another matter entirely. When she envisions a man in her dreams it is not Shay, but William Mullan, the coachman who figured prominently in the Talbot story. This idealisation or dream accounts for the title of the novel and provides a link between the main narrative and sub-text. Kathleen, in her impatience to get something of her most recent work down on paper, writes a highly mythologised, beautifully realised picture of Mullan's life after he leaves Ireland. Having studied the Talbot vs Talbot papers again, as well as the 'new' papers from the ecclesiastical courts and, finally, the Paget pamphlet which Nan Leech has found for her, Kathleen decides she cannot finish a historical study, given all the contradictory evidence about Marianne's character. Kathleen first sees William Mullan and Marianne Talbot as two people who have really loved each other for three years and even after Mullan has left Ireland and the Talbots.

Kathleen still envisions Mullan as a good person and a romantic figure, no matter how much she has doubts about Marianne and the destructive turns in her life. After all, Mullan's conduct toward Marianne, whether or not they had ever been lovers, was entirely honorable and compassionate. In addition, he consistently showed kindness and solicitude toward little Mab, and took very good care of his dog, and the horses that were entrusted to him. Kathleen idealises William and romanticises his going on alone to an independent life in harmony with nature, far from Ireland. She imagines a very beautiful end for him – in which he is united beyond the grave with Marianne. His death, as Kathleen pictures it, suggests transcendence:

> William Mullan was not alone when he died. He did fall back on the path through the clearing, very early one autumn morning. But the deer came to feed where he had fallen, as the mists dissolved slowly in the low sun. They were all around him and he knew it, when life was draining from him. When the men from the stable found his body, it did look lonely. But he had seen her dolphin body above him – the white torso and turning in a most beautiful way – at the very end. And the deer did not move until he was dead. (O'Faolain 500)

This passage suggests the purity and innocence of William Mullan in the natural beauty and wilderness of New York State. It also suggests Mullan's connection with Irish mythology. In the Celtic tradition, James MacKillop suggests that, "deer commonly entice heroes into the realm of the gods" (117). It is also well known that deer, or images of deer, once protected St Patrick from his enemies during his journey. Other, more general, studies state that deer can show people how to love unconditionally and be more alert and patient (http). This passage is not only Kathleen's tribute to William Mullan – it is, I think, the dream of the novel's title, and a point at which she declares that she cannot complete a full manuscript. The significance of the dream for Kathleen may be that she is, from a Jungian perspective, a counterpart of Mullan's as she goes on in a foreign country alone.

In terms of the form of the novel, Kathleen's decision to end her work with Mullan's death on such a transcendent and imaginative note is highly creative. While many modern novels are about characters writing novels, Nuala O'Faolain states at the beginning of *My Dream of You* that the Talbot documents are part of an authentic historical record. On top of that, her character, Kathleen the journalist, is scrupulously concerned about the boundaries between fiction and history, or perhaps she is invoking the disdain of her master, Henry James, toward historical novels. In terms of crafting the novel, it is important to see the distinction between the running time of the main narrative, which takes little more than a week, and the materials which comprise the intertext which develop over a period of about five years. The imbalance of time frames in the two stories creates a pronounced tension, and gives momentum to O'Faolain's novel as a whole. The indeterminacy of the ending, as well as what Kathleen comes to write about Mullan, show her impatience to complete a project which is part of her training as a journalist. Her finished work, whatever its genre may be, given time, reflection and future research, may be changed entirely. Novels and historical projects of any length usually take more than a week to complete. Nan Leech has astutely commented on the development of Kathleen's project in observing that, as more information is added, the project changes its shape. Readers can only anticipate what the outcome of the Talbot story will be.

Kathleen has experienced a great deal of what Henry James would call "felt life" (x) in her week or so in Ireland. It seems unlikely that she will become Shay's Irish colleen, but possible that she will be able to devote time and openness to a future romantic relationship in which her heart and intellect will both be recognised. Though the novel's text is framed by predictable and familiar scenes of the din at Shannon Airport, similar to the pattern of Kathleen's comings and goings with 'Travel/Write', it now seems as if she has accomplished something with both her research, and her ability to continue her journey through life in a positive and friendly way.

Finally, I want to emphasise that Nuala O'Faolain's *My Dream of You* should join the exclusive company of novels like *Middlemarch*, *The Years* and *The Golden Notebook*. I would like to call these novels feminist panoramic novels since they emphasise what intelligent and sensitive women strive for, as well as presenting the obstacles they must face and try to overcome in order to reach self-fulfilment. These novels, in my reckoning, should enjoy a bookshelf across from *Dombey and Son* or *Bleak House, Vanity Fair, Buddenbrooks* and *Ulysses*. All of these novels present a broad spectrum of characters portrayed on a distinct and detailed sociological and historical canvas, and who make memorable efforts to come to terms with complicated questions of their own time and identity.

O'Faolain's *My Dream of You*, like the novels of Eliot, Woolf, and Lessing, has a special resonance. Each presents a heroine who is sensitive to the demands of the era in which she lives, and each is given time to develop, travel, and recreate herself according to life's experiences and broadening horizons. *Middlemarch's* Dorothea Brooke has to deal with compromises in the development of her life. Her political and sociological understanding of her milieu is acute and, in her case, the honeymoon trip to Rome and Vatican City reveal only how completely devoted her husband is to his work, while she is left to be a tourist in the Eternal City in the company of her sister. Her later relationship with Will shows her maturity and ability to love someone for himself rather than for his intellectual accomplishments,

In *The Years*, Eleanor's father, Colonel Abel Partiger, and her brothers, dominate the action, and this emphasises the truth that social institutions were all on the men's side in the last decades of the nineteenth century, when women played supporting roles. Yet Virginia Woolf portrays the battle for women's suffrage in her novel directly, and shows how women like Eleanor gradually come into their own. Eleanor capably manages the family household after her mother's death and also maintains other properties she later inherits from her father's estate. By this time, she is a middle-aged woman, and she seizes her freedom pleasurably. She enjoys the advantages of being able to travel, and adventurously goes to China and India on her own. Though Eleanor never marries, she is in regular touch with her sisters and brothers and their families. She is enriched by coming to know her wide circle of neices and nephews, particularly Peggy who becomes a medical doctor. Eleanor relishes the progress a later generation of women have made. *The Years* ends with a party in which Eleanor's generation is aging and some even doze off, but Eleanor, looking back, seems to have few regrets about the way she has conducted her life.

Doris Lessing's *The Golden Notebook* chronicles Anna Wulf's personal life, her involvement with the Communist Party, day by day news bulletins of the Korean War, her early life in Rhodesia, and the 'soft' melodramatic and romantic novel she is writing. *The Golden Notebook* shows the demands of Anna's compartmentalised life, including her friendship with Molly, and the difficulties of being a single mother. The novel shows Anna with different men, some of whom she loves. With Saul Green, she shares her special 'golden notebook', and after she writes the first sentence he goes on to write a novel about Algeria which does quite well. At the end of *The Golden Notebook*, Molly marries and Anna goes on alone. The compartmentalised life Lessing depicts has become embedded in the consciousness of a later generation of feminists like no other book has. O'Faolain's Kathleen mentions reading *The Golden Notebook* as a young woman, and intimates that she has learned from it.

The reader hopes Kathleen De Burca has learned something important, existentially, on her trip to Ireland. Yet at Shannon Airport, she is busy amidst the usual noise and pandemonium trying to 'phone her former boss. Does this mean she will return to her old haunts and 'Travel/Write', or has the trip to Ireland fundamentally changed her ideas about both life and writing? It may mean simply that both Kathleen's life and the narrative she is researching are works in progress.

References

http://tentpegs.blogspot.com/2005/08/st-patricks-prayer-or-deers-cry.html

http://www.dierinbeeld.nl/animal_files/mammals/deer/

Finneran, Richard J., ed. *W.B. Yeats: The Poems.* New York: Scribners, 1997.

James, Henry. Preface to *Portrait of a Lady.* Vol. 1. New York: Scribners, 1936 (New York Edition, Vols. 1-IV).

McKillop, James. *Dictionary of Irish Mythology.* New York: Oxford UP, 1998).

O'Faolain, Nuala. *My Dream of You.* New York: Riverhead Press, 2001. All references to the novel in the paper are to this edition.

Adapting the Gaze: From *Lolita* and *A Clockwork Orange* to *The English Patient*

Tara Prescott

The second wave of women's liberation in the United States in the early 1970s acted as a catalyst for new ways of interpreting, understanding, and discussing how women are represented in media, society, art, and film. In the 1970s, feminism "challenged sacred movie industry canons about the nature of sexuality and the family," forcing Hollywood to "pay attention to the changes in women's consciousness" (Quart 109). British filmmaker and critic Laura Mulvey's groundbreaking 1975 essay, 'Visual Pleasure and Narrative Cinema,' published in *Screen*, became a crucial milestone in feminist film criticism. In this essay, Mulvey defines the 'male gaze' as a gendered camera or narrative viewpoint, an ideal target audience for a film, and the way male characters look at female characters in film. By applying Mulvey's framework for the male gaze to film adaptations of popular novels, one can see interesting patterns. There are different ways to adapt the male gaze from one medium to the other. The film adaptations of *Lolita*, *A Clockwork Orange*, and *The English Patient* are good examples of three types of the male gaze; the Gaze as Vicarious Voyeurism, the Gaze as Punishment, and the Gaze as Possession.

"The place of the look defines cinema, the possibility of varying it and exposing it," notes Mulvey. She categorises the "three different looks associated with cinema: that of the camera as it records the pro-filmic event, that of the audience as it watches the final product, and that of the characters at each other within the screen illusion" (47). These categories are extremely useful in discussing the reflexive meta-terrain of film. Although many critics have analysed the male and female gaze in narrative cinema, most have focused on the camera's view (as gendered and masculine) or the ideal spectator (assumed to be male). This essay will focus primarily on the last category, the ways in which male characters gaze upon female characters, both in the parent text and in the film adaptation.

In "Visual Pleasure and Narrative Cinema" Mulvey applies principles of psychoanalysis to the study of women in film as well as the personal experience of watching film. According to Mulvey, traditional narrative film incorporates "the actual image of woman as (passive) raw material for the (active) gaze of man" (46). Although the trend is slowly changing, in mainstream film "men act and women appear. Men look at women. Women watch themselves being looked at" (Berger 47). Mulvey also states that the pleasure gained from cinema is derived from voyeuristic and fetishistic forms of gazing. In some ways, her essay is a call to arms, demanding an end to traditional film techniques that, though pleasurable for the 'invisible guest' audience member, are harmful to the overall status of women. The passive/female/being seen and active/male/seeing dichotomy was refined by many critics, including Mulvey. Within structuralist and post-colonial theory, the gaze was broadened to include consideration of homosexual versus heterosexual, minority groups versus caucasians, and colonised groups versus the colonisers. As Kaplan notes, "the gaze is not necessarily male (literally), but to own and activate the gaze, given our language and the structure of the unconscious, is to be in the masculine position" (130). For clarity, this essay will focus primarily on Mulvey's original designations of passive/female and active/male.

The camera's gaze is usually male due to the fact that most directors are male (Kaplan 121). Although female directors are making great progress in independent film, they are still under-represented in mainstream cinema, especially Hollywood films meant for a mass audience. Even Sophia Coppola's extraordinary directorial achievement, *Lost in Translation* (2003), was overshadowed by the fact that Coppola was related to a famous male director. Coppola's *Virgin Suicides* (1999) and Marlene Gorris' *Mrs. Dalloway* (1997) are just two recent film adaptations directed by women. Many of the film adaptations usually discussed in film criticism, including *The Rocking Horse Winner* (Anthony Pelissier, 1950), *A Place in the Sun* (George Stevens, 1951), *One Flew Over the Cuckoo's Nest* (Milos Forman, 1975), *Ragtime* (Forman, 1981), *Passage to India* (David Lean, 1984), *The Hours* (Stephen Daldry, 2002), and *House of Sand and Fog* (Vadim Perelman, 2003) were directed by men. The films discussed in this essay, *Lolita* (Stanley Kubrick, 1962; Adrian Lyne, 1997), *A Clockwork Orange* (Kubrick, 1971), and *The English Patient* (Anthony Minghella, 1996), were also directed by men.

The Gaze as Vicarious Voyeurism: Lolita

When discussing voyeurism, fetishism, gazing, and forbidden passion, the consummate fictional example is Vladimir Nabokov's *Lolita*. For a novel replete with cheesy pop culture, convincing roadside relics, and gum-cracking teenage slang, it is astonishing that the writer himself was not American. However, *Lolita* was the "product of fourteen years of observation, assimilation, and apprenticeship", observes critic Alfred Appel (86). It is not surprising, then, that Nabokov, a careful observer and lepidopterist, crafted a novel about a character notorious for meticulous observation who studies a little girl as if she were a rare butterfly.

Lolita is the tale of "the wayward child, the egotistic mother, [and] the panting maniac" (5). It is also a story about the connections between love, lust, and sight. As the narrator, Humbert Humbert suggests that, "there are two kinds of visual memory: one when you skillfully recreate an image in the laboratory of your mind, with eyes open...the other when you instantly evoke, with shut eyes...the objective, absolutely optical replica of a beloved face" (11). Humbert successfully utilises both types of visual memory throughout the novel: "I loved her. It was love at first sight, at last sight, at ever and ever sight" (11). One challenge of adapting *Lolita* to the screen is to transfer the enduring love-at-first-sight to the audience and to create the sense of "ever and ever sight" (11).

In the novel, Nabokov uses sunglasses to draw attention to Humbert's gaze. The sunglasses represent the hidden view, the desire or ability to safely gaze from a distance, without being caught. When the young Humbert finally possesses his beloved Annabel, "somebody's lost pair of sunglasses [is the] only witness" (13). This moment in the novel introduces the glasses-gaze, a technique made famous by Alfred Hitchcock in *Strangers on a Train* (1951). It is a shame that neither film version of *Lolita* showed the initial scene with Annabel because filming the act as reflected in the sunglasses would have been an excellent adaptation from the novel.

While scheming about ways of isolating Lolita from her mother at a picnic, Humbert imagines hunting for a pair of lost sunglasses, with "the Quest for the Glasses turn[ing] into a quiet little orgy" (54). He later uses sunglasses as a method to escape from Charlotte (83). The sunglasses return again when Humbert first sees Lolita, a vivid passage that not only connects Lolita with Humbert's lost love

Annabel, but also makes the new nymphet so incredibly vivid that the reader cannot help but stare in wonder at her as well:

> [A]nd then, without the least warning, a blue sea-wave swelled under my heart and, from a mat in a pool of sun, half-naked, kneeling, turning about on her knees, there was my Riviera love peering at me over dark glasses...It was the same child – the same frail, honey-hued shoulders, the same silky supple bare back, the same chestnut head of hair...The twenty-five years I have lived since then, tapered to a palpitating point, and vanished. (39)

The richness of Humbert's language in this section and, indeed, throughout the novel, seduces the reader. The images he describes are so lovely that the reader enjoys them vicariously through Humbert. This moment is arguably the most important scene in the novel, and establishes for the reader/viewer Lolita's innocent, near-mythical power over Humbert. Throughout the novel, Humbert's language is the primary vehicle for attaining the reader's sympathy. Language, however, is not easily adapted to film. So directors, Stanley Kubrick and Adrian Lyne, had to find cinematic ways of adapting the gaze and beauty of this scene. To have sympathy for a wife-beating, child-molesting, murdering character as loathsome as Humbert, the reader must be able to understand his motives, to slip into his psyche and feel his own tortured desires. It is crucial when depicting Humbert's first gaze of Lolita to make the viewer feel that "palpitating point" (39), that initial moment of pure rapture.

Adrian Lyne's *Lolita* (1997) is particularly skilful in winning the viewer's sympathy. Humbert (Jeremy Irons) is portrayed as so gentlemanly, so earnest in his love for Lolita (Dominique Swain) that he is easy to sympathise with. Although Lyne is a male director and focuses on Humbert's male gaze upon a female subject, the introductory scenes with Lolita are so beautifully filmed that the men as well as women in the audience fall in love with her too. Perhaps for women, Lolita's sprawling limbs, delighted obsession with the telephone, and tempestuous moods are reminders of their own girlhoods. Although Humbert's obsession is mostly sexual, it is also a love of fleeting adolescence, a carefree time most viewers will remember. Kaplan asks, "women are in fact present in audiences:

what is happening to them as they watch a cinematic apparatus that constructs a male viewer?" (122). In the case of Lyne's *Lolita*, one could argue that the film is carefully constructed so that what 'happens' to the female spectator is very similar to what happens to the male spectator. Despite their moral judgement, despite their age or sexual preference, even despite themselves, the viewers feel drawn to Lolita and, therefore, to Humbert's plight: "I think that what the audience maybe will find disturbing is that they don't hate Humbert," notes Lyne (Commentary).

Lyne's recreation of the first scene between Humbert and Lolita is so powerful, so pure and breathtakingly beautiful, that the viewer full-heartedly participates in the pleasure of viewing Lolita. The sun-drenched little girl, lying belly-down, surrounded by soft green grass, absorbed in a book and oblivious to the haloes of sunlight and sprinklers all around her, just glistens. The image is far from disturbing, in fact, it is so pleasurable that it was used for the title menu on the DVD release (the DVD edition of the Kubrick version also used the corresponding scene for its main menu): "Every movement she made in the dappled sun plucked at the most secret and sensitive chord of my abject body," Humbert confesses in voice-over, and the viewers agree with him, because they feel it as well. Even in the novel, Humbert's view of Lolita is all in close-focus. His microscopic observation includes the "glistening tracery of down on her forearm" (41).

As in the novel, sunglasses appear several times in Lyne's *Lolita*. For example, when Humbert and Lolita begin their automobile journey, Humbert's sunglasses are strapped to the driver's side sunshade. The scene after he pulls the car over to let Lolita kiss him is filmed from the back seat so that the sunglasses are easily visible behind Lolita's head, peering down at her as she kisses Humbert. She wears sunglasses while enjoying the 'Magic Fingers' bed and kicks sunglasses off Humbert's face as he is driving. The most poignant sunglasses scene, however, occurs at a roadside shop. While Humbert is inside trying on a pair of sunglasses, Quilty approaches Lolita outside. Humbert, wearing the new sunglasses with the price tag dangling from the nosepiece, suddenly sees the strange man talking to Lolita and runs out of the store in a blind panic. However, the mysterious man is suddenly gone.

Although sunglasses do not appear in the Humbert/Lolita introduction scene, the Lyne movie posters included heart-shaped sunglasses to pay homage to advertising for the famous Stanley Kubrick version. In Kubrick's *Lolita* (1962), when Humbert (James Mason) first gazes upon Lolita (Sue Lyon), his lips part and he stands as if stunned. Lo pulls off her sunglasses and returns his gaze unflinchingly. An interesting side note is that these are not the sunglasses made famous by the movie posters. The heart-shaped glasses, which have attained a near cult-like status, actually do not appear in the film at all. Immediately after seeing Lo, Humbert accepts the room Charlotte is offering: "What was the decisive factor? The garden?" asks the over-eager and oblivious Charlotte (Shelley Winters). "I think it was your cherry pie," Humbert replies before the camera cuts to a close-up of Lolita.

As a voyeur, Humbert is obsessed with viewing nymphets and maintaining a cool, impassive front. Perversely, however, he is also an exhibitionist, often imagining starring in a film version of his life. When Humbert speaks in the novel, Nabokov provides the "prose equivalent of deep-focus" (Appel 195). There are several self-reflexive cinematic moments throughout the text, which could either be a blessing or a curse to someone actually adapting the novel. Humbert imagines gazing at Lolita as "a cinematographic still" and later remarks "pity no film had recorded the curious pattern" of flirting with Lolita (44, 58). After describing a series of wanted posters at a post office, Humbert advises, "if you want to make a movie out of my book, have one of these faces gently melt into my own, while I look" (222). Although neither Kubrick nor Lyne took Humbert up on this particular offer, both made movies out of his book which focused on him while he looked.

In the novel, Lolita is a vociferous consumer of mass-media and pop-culture, reading magazines such as *Glance and Gulp* and being "an expert in dream-slow close-ups" (47, 49). Lo also enjoys being the object of the gaze, and "would do her utmost to draw as many potential witnesses into her orbit as she could" (164). This makes her the stereotypical female in the film who enjoys being the object of attention. However, after her girlish fantasies of Humbert turn into horror, Lolita's desire to be viewed becomes less of a vanity and more of a cry for help. She threatens to draw attention from a policeman, teachers, friends, and even strangers, not because she wants to be the centre of attention, but because she is desperate to escape her situation.

Unfortunately, the attention she attracts is from Quilty. In the Kubrick version of the film, Peter Sellers wears distinctive, black-rimmed Beatnik glasses for his portrayal of Quilty. Sellers also plays the role of Dr. Zempf, Beardsley High School Psychologist (or Quilty impersonating Dr. Zempf, the exact nature of Dr. Zempf is somewhat ambiguous). As Dr. Zempf, Sellers wears ridiculously comic Coke-bottle glasses. He looks so foolish, and is so obviously the same man as the playwright Quilty, that the audience wonders why Humbert doesn't recognise him. It is as if the thick glasses are symbolic of Humbert's myopic gaze; he is so focused on Lolita that he cannot see the threat sitting right in front of him.

During his first night with Lolita at 'The Enchanted Hunters', Humbert notes "I seemed to have shed my clothes and slipped into pajamas with the kind of fantastic instantaneousness which is implied when in a cinematographic scene the process of changing is cut" (128). Lyne, in fact, adapts this section of the novel exactly, cutting the scene in such a way that the fully dressed Humbert enters the bathroom, closes the door, then immediately opens the door again in pajamas. Lyne's direct adaptation of the narrator's directions would likely have pleased Humbert greatly.

For the first part of *Lolita*, the male gaze, even the gaze of a pedophile, is acceptable without much criticism, and is, in fact, made safe enough for the reader/viewer to share, regardless of gender. Reading or watching *Lolita*, we become co-conspirators up to a certain point. The male gaze, Humbert's obsessed gaze, is sanctioned by the narrative. It is not until Humbert goes beyond the gaze to physical touch that the tone of the story changes. The reader gets the sense that if Humbert had remained only a voyeur, he would not have deserved or received punishment. The novel and films punish Humbert, not for gazing, but for acting on the gaze.

"I knew exactly what I wanted to do, and how to do it, without impinging on a child's chastity; after all, I had some experience in my life of pederosis" Humbert brags (55). He takes pains to tell the reader how harmless his gaze is, he even refers to himself and men of his kind as "dog-eyed gentlemen" (88). In the end, however, the gaze isn't enough, and Humbert does far more than 'impinge' on Lolita's chastity. Although the reader/viewer doesn't see it, Humbert is arrested and later addresses the jury members who will pass judgement on him. By saying "gentlewomen of the jury" (123), and "winged gentlemen of the jury" (125). Humbert shows he is aware of being the object of someone else's gaze and judgement.

The one person in the way of Humbert's gaze, who tries to obscure her own daughter, is the aptly named Charlotte Haze. Charlotte gazes as adoringly at Humbert as Humbert does at Lolita. However, unlike her quaint 'old-world' lodger, Charlotte cannot hide her passion. Charlotte's view of her only surviving child is extremely negative: "You see," she tells Humbert, "she sees herself as a starlet; I see her as a sturdy, healthy, but decidedly homely kid" (65). In this line, the conflict between Charlotte's view of Lolita and Lo's view of herself is evident. Charlotte's hazy gaze is indicative of her status as an indifferent mother who "simply hated her daughter" (80). It also points to a power struggle between Lo and Charlotte for Humbert's attention. As Kaplan notes, "motherhood can be seen as narcissistic" in film, and Charlotte is the prime example of Kaplan's designation of "The Silly, Weak, or Vain Mother" (133).

The person with the ability to gaze, or control how others gaze, has significant power. Even before the reader meets Charlotte, and well after she is dead, the text supplies a "haze of stars" (15), "a hazy view" (26), a "platinum haze" (152), and "Mrs. Hays" (239). This wordplay also helps maintain the problem of vision in the text. In "one of those dazzling coincidences that logicians loathe and poets love," history put a final 'haze' into the life of Lolita; censorship, similar to the 1930 Hays Code, greatly restricted Kubrick's version of the film (Appel 31).

The end of the novel, as well as both films, returns to the use of glasses as a symbol for vision. The 'grown-up' Lolita in the novel wears "pink-rimmed glasses" (269). In both the Kubrick and Lyne versions, there is something bookish, matronly even, about glasses on the heavily pregnant girl, contributing to the sadness of the scene and the change in Lolita. The novel's description of Humbert's final gaze on his lost love is humorous and painful:

> There she was (my Lolita!), hopelessly worn at seventeen, with that baby, dreaming already in her of becoming a big shot and retiring around 2020 A.D. – and I looked and looked at her, and knew as clearly as I know I am to die,

that I loved her more than anything I had ever imagined on earth. (277)

The repetition of "looked and looked" puts emphasis on Humbert's gaze, implying that he knows he will never have the chance to gaze at her again. In Kubrick's version, when Humbert goes to see Lolita for the last time, she answers the door wearing the signature black frame glasses worn by Quilty (Peter Sellers). The black frames are too large and harsh for Lolita's face, making her look even more frumpy and less nymphet-like. Even more torturous for Humbert, Lolita is now gazing at him through the eyes of the man who stole her away.

The Gaze as Punishment: A Clockwork Orange

In another Kubrick film adaptation – of Anthony Burgess' *A Clockwork Orange* – the novel's point of view is overwhelmingly evident from the first page, where "Your Humble Narrator" Alex barrages the reader with his distinctive nadsat, Russian and cockney-based neologisms that form his everyday slang. A reader new to *Clockwork* will struggle with Alex's diction until about halfway through the book, when the reader simply succumbs and the language starts making sense.

From the opening scene of the film adaptation, Kubrick lets the audience know whoever viddies, whoever controls the gaze, has the power. The film begins with a closeup of Alex (Malcolm McDowell), head tilted downwards so that he is staring off the top of his eyeballs, which practically bore through the camera into the audience. The wide, bulging, unblinking eyes lock onto the camera, unmoving, holding the gaze throughout the scene as the camera slowly pulls back. In addition to the intensity of Alex's gaze, one eye is highlighted with large false eyelashes. This is another mechanism for drawing the audience's attention to Alex's eyesight. Finally, Alex and his droogs' white street clothes are adorned with eyeballs on the cuffs, which function as talismans of the violent power of their gaze.

The creepy, foreboding music, the penetrating, possessive eyes, and the sadomasochistic setting of the Korova Milkbar in the first scene all contribute to the audience's conclusion that Alex's gaze is powerful and one should avoid being the object of that gaze at all costs. The use of nude female mannequins in the Milkbar also sets the tone for the society Alex lives in; here is a place where women are used as furniture, so as viewers, we can expect that women will be objectified, sexualised, and likely brutalised throughout the film. According to Kaplan, the objectification of women is "designed to annihilate the threat that woman (as castrated, and possessing a sinister genital organ) poses" (121). To view women as 'castrated' and therefore threatening is an interesting concept, especially given that Alex is 'castrated' by the Ludovico treatment, and is consequently reduced to a woman's role, passive, objectified, unable to defend himself, and at the mercy of violent men.

The subsequent scenes in which Alex attacks various victims who catch his eye further enforces the sinister power of his gaze. Like Humbert Humbert, Alex is a loathsome character who does terrible things, so the writer and director must work to make him sympathetic to the audience. In Burgess' novel, the use of Alex's strange language distances the reader from the graphic violence he commits; the worst acts are at the beginning of the book, when the reader is still learning the language. When adapting the violent scenes to film, Kubrick used highly stylised sets, costumes, cutaways, and voice-overs to achieve a similar idea of separation. In both the novel and the film adaptation, the descriptions of sexual acts are translated as pure violence. In Kubrick's vision, "sex has almost nothing to do with erotic pleasure and everything to do with chilling cynicism about the human condition" (Quart 206). The mechanical, clockwork nature of sex is summed up by Alex's nadsat term for it, "the old in-out" (Burgess 103).

The society in Burgess' novel decides an adequate treatment for a criminal such as Alex is to condition him by forcibly controlling his gaze. In *Ways of Seeing*, John Berger notes, "to look is an act of choice" (8). Part of the horror of the Ludovico treatment is that it removes an individual's choice of sight in order to remove the choice of moral action. The parallel between choice and sight is strongly evident throughout the film.

In the novel, Alex notes, "where I was wheeled to, brothers, was like no sinny I had ever viddied before" (100). As the doctors transfer Alex from wheelchair to viewing chair, strapping his body in place, he describes their actions, "they put like clips on the skin of my forehead, so that my top glaz-lids were pulled up and up and up and I could not shut my glazzies no matter how I tried" (101). At first Alex doesn't realise the films are for conditioning and he examines them as if they were for entertainment. When the scenes become increasingly more violent and his discomfort intensifies, Alex assumes the films aren't 'real' and focuses on their construction, making comments such as "a very good like professional piece of cinny," and "so it must have been very clever what they call cutting or editing or some such veshch" (102-3). Subconsciously, Alex is trying to achieve the effect that the novel creates for the audience; a separation from horror by highlighting the fact that what is being viewed is a constructed entity. This is a technique advocated in Mulvey's 'Visual Pleasure and Narrative Cinema', when she suggests that calling the viewer's attention to the fact that a film is a deliberate construction will help break the seamless acceptance of the male gaze.

"But I could not shut my glazzies, and even if I tried to move my glazballs about I still could not get like out of the line of fire of this picture" notes Alex (104). In *A Clockwork Orange* the character's gaze is completely, forcibly controlled by another character or group of characters, to horrific effect. Alex's phrasing is appropriate; he is in 'the line of fire' of the film, literally; the film is a weapon with the power to kill him.

"It's funny how the colours of the like real world only seem really real when you viddy them on the screen" Alex notes (103). His inability to separate real from cinema could be indicative of his moral inability to choose right from wrong: "A dream or nightmare is really only like a film inside your gulliver," he later mentions (111). In fact, many of the nightmarish acts that Alex performs are under the influence of "milk with knives in it," drugs to induce a state of ultraviolence (1).

Although considered a 'treatment,' it becomes obvious to the reader and audience that the Ludovico is punishment: "A man who cannot choose ceases to be a man," one character declares. However, the book and film also show that a man who cannot choose his gaze also ceases to be a man. In a film heavily imbued with phallic and yarbles imagery, the threat of castration is closely linked with the loss of gaze control.

The Gaze as Possession: The English Patient

In Michael Ondaatje's novel, *The English Patient*, the narration is shared among several characters, both male and female. When asked about his ability to create multiple perspectives, Ondaatje answers, "I can't write a letter. But I could if I was the character of x in the novel.

Once I have that mask, I can reveal more" (UCLAlive). One of the primary masks Ondaatje uses in *The English Patient* is that of Hana, a female character. The other main characters, however, are all men.

A crucial point in the book is intricately tied to the problem of the male gaze and the ownership of women associated with it. One night, as Katherine, her husband Clifton, Count Almásy, and the other members of their expedition tell stories around a campfire, Katherine recalls a tale from Herodotus: "Perhaps she was just reading it to him. Perhaps there was no ulterior motive in the selection ... But a path suddenly revealed itself in real life" Almásy states (233). Almásy questions the 'ulterior motive,' because the story, about a forbidden male gaze and its consequences, is so closely paralleled to his own situation with Katharine:

> [King Candaules] said to Gyges: "Gyges, I think that you do not believe me when I tell you of the beauty of my wife, for it happens that men's ears are less apt to believe than their eyes... I will contrive [means by which you may look upon her naked] so from the first that she shall not perceive that she has been seen by you...you will be able to gaze at her at full leisure. (232-3)

In this section, Ondaatje achieves many feats. On one level, he introduces the idea that men trust and rely on what they see rather than what they hear. The importance of sight and appearance figures throughout the story, where a Hungarian man is captured by the British for being German, shot down by the Germans for appearing to be British (flying a British plane), and then, finally, assumed to be English by his rescuers. The Herodotus story also introduces the concept of the ownership of women, especially wives; that a man of power can own a woman while still gaining pleasure from showing off his property, for exchanging his wife's body (visually or physically) with another man. As Kaplan notes, "many male fantasies focus on the man's excitement arranging for his woman to expose herself (or even give herself) to other men, while he watches" (127). The primary difference between the romantic triangle in the Herodotus story and the romantic triangle in *The English Patient* is that Clifton does not want to share his wife with anyone and his mounting jealousy and possession of her will end in a murder/suicide.

In adapting the Herodotus scene to film, director Anthony Minghella showed what the novel could not; the tentative, gentle way Katherine (Kristin Scott Thomas) looks at Almásy (Ralph Fiennes) across the fire as she speaks, the shameful, fearful way he looks away from her, and the growing recognition on her husband's (Colin Firth) face. Minghella layers the gazes of the actors with the described gazes in the Herodotus story. As the scene progresses, Almásy steals looks at his unrequited love in the romantic, flickering light.

"She takes off her clothes... until she is standing, naked, in full view of Gyges," Katherine recites, while she herself is standing in full view of Almásy. The camera has Katherine framed just off centre, in flickering firelight, and Almásy's profile, blurry and hidden, at lower left. Immediately after Katherine says, "and indeed she was more lovely than he could have imagined," the blurry profile of Almásy comes into sharp focus and he bows his head away from her, eyes blinking, perhaps in shame or recognition, perhaps because he himself cannot bear to look upon a married woman "more lovely than he could have imagined."

"But then the Queen looked up and saw Gyges concealed in the shadows," Katherine continues and suddenly she looks directly at Almásy, who is indeed concealed in shadow, and as she begins her next line, "and although she said nothing, she shuddered," the camera shifts focus again, blurring Almásy and returning the focus to Katherine.

"Men do not simply look," Kaplan notes, "their gaze carries with it the power of action and of possession" (121). By watching the way Almásy and Clifton look at Katherine in the Herodotus scene, the viewer can gauge who is winning the battle for possession. Recalling the Queen's ultimatum to Gyges, Katherine says, "either you must submit to death for gazing on that which you should not, or else kill my husband who has shamed me." At this point, the camera cuts to Clifton, who is smiling, oblivious, and rocking back and forth casually. His gaze has no power because he accepts that Katherine is his and doesn't feel threatened. However, as Katherine's story comes to its conclusion, his face quickly changes. When she says, "and become king in his place," suddenly the full relevance of her story becomes obvious and Clifton stops moving and his smile fades.

The Herodotus story in *The English Patient* perfectly illustrates a central problem for the characters. To gaze on a woman is to own her in some way, to take possession of her even if she legally belongs to another. 'Gazing on that which you should not' will have consequences. As the Queen in the Herodotus story predicted, one of the men must die, and in *The English Patient* it is the King who dies and the challenger who wins the Queen, even if only briefly (she dies soon after they are reunited).

Lolita, A Clockwork Orange, and *The English Patient* are all films that closely adapt the male gaze from their original texts and successfully translate it into a visual medium. Each of the novels has a male narrator and each of the films has a male director and male narrator. Yet the manners in which the gazes are used, both in the novels and films, is different. *Lolita's* male gaze is startlingly sympathetic for female as well as male spectators and the use of sunglasses and film references keeps the gaze forefront in the audience's mind. *A Clockwork Orange* provides an example of a violent male gaze and how society can reverse that gaze and use it as punishment. *The English Patient's* male gaze does not address the viewers as openly, but, instead, focuses on the possessive qualities of the gaze, illustrating its power and ultimately presenting a warning. In addition to successfully adapting the original gaze from the novels, these films are also commercially and artistically successful. As UCLA Professor of Screenwriting and author, Hal Ackerman, observes, successful screenplay adaptations are like bumblebees; even though physicists have mathematically proven that a bumblebee shouldn't be able to fly, they do. The film adaptations of *Lolita, A Clockwork Orange,* and *The English Patient* are remarkable creations that, in their own unique ways and despite all odds, take flight.

References

Ackerman, Hal. Guest Lecture. Claremont Graduate University, Claremont. 17 Dec. 2004.

Appel, Alfred. *Nabokov's Dark Cinema*. New York: Oxford UP, 1974.

Berger, John. *Ways of Seeing*. New York: Penguin Books, 1977.

Burgess, Anthony. *A Clockwork Orange*. New York: WW Norton, 1986. All in-text references are to this edition.

A Clockwork Orange. Dir. Stanley Kubrick. Perf. Malcolm McDowell. Warner, 1971.

The English Patient. Dir. Anthony Minghella. Perf. Ralph Fiennes, Juliette Binoche, Willem Dafoe, and Kristin Scott Thomas. Miramax, 1996.

Kaplan, Ann E. *Feminism and Film*. New York: Oxford UP, 2004.

Lolita. Dir. Stanley Kubrick. Perf. James Mason, Sue Lyon, Shelley Winters, and Peter Sellars. MGM, 1962.

Lolita. Dir. Adrian Lyne. Perf. Jeremy Irons, Dominique Swain, Melanie Griffith, and Frank Langella. Showtime, 1997.

Mulvey, Laura. "Visual Pleasure and Narrative Cinema." in Kaplan, *Feminism and Film*.

Nabokov, Vladimir. *Lolita*. New York: Vintage International, 1989. All in-text references are to this edition.

Ondaatje, Michael. *The English Patient*. New York: Vintage International, 1992. All in-text references are to this edition.

Ondaatje, Michael and Russell Banks. In conversation with Willem Dafoe. "Film & Fiction: Russell Banks & Michael Ondaatje." UCLAlive. UCLA, Los Angeles. 7 Nov. 2004.

Quart, Leonard and Albert Auster. *American Film and Society Since 1945*. Westport: Praeger Publishers, 2002.

Language and Masculinity Studies: 'Within' or 'Without' Feminist Linguistics?

Eduardo de Gregorio-Godeo

In a classical definition of Language and Gender Studies, David Graddol and Joan Swann (1989) demarcate the object of this discipline as the analysis of "the role of language in establishing and regulating gender divisions" in society (3). Since the 1990s, a new direction of research within the study of language and gender has started to explore the relations that men and masculinity have with language. An increasing number of works (Kuiper 1991; Henton 1992; Jahr 1992; Herring *et al*. 1995; Adams *et al*. 1995; Kiesling 1996; Mackenzie 1996; Harvey 1997; Johnson and Meinhof 1997; Gough and Edwards 1998; Baron and Kotthoff 2001; Coates 2003) have striven to individualise the study of men and masculinity outside what many have regarded as an overbearing influence of feminist linguistics upon the field of language and gender until the early 1990s, where most of the attention to the masculine had been previously situated. In 1973 Robin Lakoff published "Language and Woman's Place," an article that inaugurated the new direction of research on language and gender in English. In a footnote, which has gone significantly unnoticed to later investigations on language and masculinity, Dell Hymes, editor of the journal where the paper was published, pointed out at the time that, "'men's language' needs study too".

The publication of Sally Johnson and Ulrike Meinhof's collection of essays in their co-edited volume *Language and Masculinity* (1997) was to become a turning point in the attempts to constitute a consolidated sphere of research revolving around the relations between masculinity and language in English. In a review of this pioneering volume, Paul McIlvenny echoes the fundamental purpose of this type of study, undertaking "the task of painstakingly and critically uncovering how masculinities are performed in and through discursive practices" (117). As another review added some time later, the publication of this explanatory volume made plain "the urgent need for further empirical work that [could] contribute to a fuller theory of masculinity within language and gender studies" (Bucholtz 312). Recent best-selling works like Jennifer Coates' *Men Talk. Stories in the Making of Masculinities* (2003), account for the deep interest raised by this direction of research on language and gender.

Nonetheless, what initially aimed to become an autonomous domain within Language and Gender Studies may only be possibly understood within the broader research tradition of feminist linguistics. As it is, language and masculinity studies may be claimed to have come into being only through the foundational effect exerted by feminist linguistics upon this new area of research, both epistemologically and methodologically. As discussed throughout this contribution, feminist attempts to call into question the traditional silencing of the feminine within linguistic inquiry have led researchers on language and masculinity to challenge the likewise historically taken-for-granted character of men and masculinity as an assumingly implicit and universal category in language. Moreover, feminist linguistics' self-criticism regarding the 'essentialist' constructions of gender, formerly characterising the so-called 'dominance' and 'difference' perspectives in Language and Gender Studies, has similarly served language and masculinity analyses to adopt methodological approaches conceptualising masculinity and femininity as mutually dependent upon, and constitutive of, each other, which is consistent with current approaches to gender as a complex and fluid construct. By focusing on such major questions throughout a revision of the literature on language and masculinity since the 1990s to date, this paper intends to shed light on the impossibility of understanding contemporary research on language and masculinity without considering the remarkable contribution of feminist linguistics to the study of language and gender.

In an attempt to accomplish this task, I will start by investigating the part played by the longer-lasting tradition of feminist linguistics within the constitution of this 'new' area in Gender Studies. In order to fully comprehend the emergence of language and gender research – and its primary objective of disentangling the role of language in the representation and construction of gender – it is necessary to highlight the influential role of second-wave feminism during the late 1960s and early '70s in Britain and America, including that which took place within the academy.

In *Talking Difference: On Gender and Language* (1995), Crawford maintains that:

With the re-emergence of the women's movement in the 1970s, scholars in psychology, linguistics, speech communication, anthropology, and other disciplines began to search for relationships between language and sex, and to think about how cultural gender roles influence speech style. (xi)

Since the 1970s, feminist linguistics has taken pains to challenge the concealment of feminine universes within western canons of knowledge, which have implicitly taken for granted the assumingly masculine verbal patterns as a universal dimension in language. As Cameron (1992) puts it, early work in feminist linguistics was mainly concerned with revealing and fighting against any sexist and androcentric usage of language:

Not surprisingly the sexism of many conventional usages was challenged by feminists early on ... usages were thought to be in need of reform if they were blatantly offensive ([e.g.] 'Blonde in fatal car crash'; 'bitches wear furs') or else androcentric, implying that the norm of humanity is male ([e.g.] 'Man', 'mankind', 'man in the street', and so on). (6)

Although earlier in the twentieth century there had been some vague experiments to examine the relations between the speaker's sex and the choice of linguistic features (Jespersen 1927), the actual study of language and gender resulted from second-wave feminist linguistic enquiry in the 1970s. Nowadays it proves somewhat difficult to delineate a clear boundary between – let alone separate – feminist linguistics and Language and Gender Studies. Indeed, although research in feminist linguistics has continued steadily to date, this initial investigation of the role played by language in the perpetuation of gender differences and women's oppression soon made it clear that more ample analyses were necessary to decipher how language contributes to our perception of gender. Therefore, it is not surprising, as Cameron states, that a great deal of recent work on gender and language has come into being without actual reference to feminism, as either a political movement or an analytical approach:

In practice the two [i.e. feminist linguistics and language and gender *per se*] overlap significantly – most contemporary language and gender research is also feminist in orientation – but in principle the subject-matter can be treated without reference to feminism, either as a political movement or as a body of theory. Indeed, it can be treated from an overtly anti-feminist perspective. What distinguishes a feminist approach is not merely concern with the behaviour of women and men (or of women alone): it is distinguished, rather, by having a critical view of the arrangement between the sexes. (1997: 21)

At any rate, we can but admit that the work undertaken by feminist linguistics has not often been accompanied by an explicit examination of the relation that men and masculinity hold with language. In trying to theorise masculinity and language from a feminist perspective, scholars like Sally Johnson (1997) have stressed what may be regarded as two outstanding deficiencies within the fundamental analytical perspectives dominating feminist linguistics research over past decades, namely the so-called 'difference' and 'dominance' approaches (10-11). On the one hand, the 'dominance' approach tends to examine how language actually reflects women's oppression in society: "the DOMINANCE explanations that arose in the 1970s linked [...] negative evaluations of women's language to their social domination by men" (Bergvall 277). On the other hand, throughout much of the 1980s, the 'difference' approach tried to unravel the function of language in the articulation of the realm of femininity and women's social identities by assuming that "women and men 'come from different sociolinguistic subcultures'" (Ushida 547), so that from an early age "women and men [would] 'learn to do different things with words in conversations' [and in their use of language on the whole]" (*ibid*). In addition to concentrating on women and femininity almost exclusively, both approaches did end up conceptualising gender in an essentialist and binarist manner. As a result, hardly any attention to the interactional practices of men and masculinity was drawn by both of these perspectives of linguistic enquiry throughout the late 1970s and '80s.

However, in spite of this deficient attention to the world of men and masculinity, this renovated interest in femininity on the part of feminist linguistics – certainly a traditionally silenced category within linguistic research – served as a starting point to justify the need to delve into the relations between men, masculinity and language. Language and masculinity studies have consequently come to pay full attention to the masculine *per se*, rather than as an implicit, universal, unmarked and taken-for-granted category in language. From an epistemological point of view, feminist linguistics has turned out to be most influential for delineating the object of language and masculinity studies. For, as a result of the patriarchal and androcentric ideologies prevailing in western canons of knowledge, the study of masculinity has been historically unattended, due to the same silencing practices imposed on femininity in scholarship, which did not even contemplate the actual need of examining men and masculinities as an independent analytical variable.

Furthermore, feminist linguistics has been highly self-critical regarding the extremely essentialist methodologies followed by 'dominance' and 'difference' approaches within previous work on language and gender. This has led to the establishment of current perspectives within the discipline conceptualising gender as a complex construct, where masculinity and femininity come to be seen as mutually dependent upon and constitutive of each other within a so-called "continuum of variability" (Romaine 49). Language and masculinity studies, accordingly, mean to leave behind any binarist association of distinctive linguistic features with the speech of men or women. In fact, this new area of work may be located within a research paradigm investigating the role of language in the constitution of gender identities in society, since there is an underlying approach to gender, which assumes that, if gender is a social and cultural construction, then one should be able to find evidence that this is so, including evidence of the process of its creation. In particular, one should be able to find linguistic evidence, since language is the primary means by which we create the categories that subsequently come to organise our lives (Poynton 4).

As Romaine underlines, the conventional approach to meaning in latter-day linguistics is that we use language not only to describe the world, but also to do much more than that:

> With language we bring different worlds into being [...] language plays an active role in the symbolic positioning

of women as inferior to men. It both constructs and perpetuates that reality, often in obvious ways, but at other times in subtle and invisible ones. The verbally represented world is gendered. (15)

By the late 1990s, all the essays in such an influential and pioneering collection as Johnson and Meinhof's, *Language and Masculinity* (1997) happened to be most innovative in this regard, since such a volume – and, also, all the subsequent work which it has generated – has come to be seen as part of an overall re-evaluation of theoretical and methodological issues in language and gender research these days:

> In particular there is a keen avoidance [...] of essentialist accounts of differences in language resources, form or use by men and women; [...] [shifting the issue instead] from adding up the apparent differences to determining how 'difference' is accomplished locally with largely shared linguistic and interactional resources (McIlvenny 108).

At this point, it is imperative to add that one of the main contributions of feminist linguistics to the conceptualisation of gender pervading contemporary research on language and gender lies in the premise that, given the multiplicity of interactional and social practices where gender is performed (cf. Butler 1990), there is no single version of masculinity or femininity, but rather multiple constructions of the masculine or the feminine. This means that masculinities and femininities constantly shift, and are redefined on the basis of various social, cultural and personal variables. According to Lazar:

> feminist debates and theorization since the late 1980s have shown that speaking of 'women' and 'men' in universal, totalizing terms is problematic longer tenable. Gender as a category intersects with, and is shot through by, other categories of social identity such as sexuality, ethnicity, social position and geography. (1)

Much of the research on masculinity and language since the 1990s, has been loyal to this tenet by trying to disentangle the role of language in the articulation of different types of 'masculinities' in a variety of social and cultural settings. Following this re-evaluation, the great majority of research conducted on masculinity and language these days has come to draw upon, and fully implement, methodologies disregarding any essentialist constructions of masculinity and the language of men. This is the case in different contributions analysing masculinity from methodological approaches, such as conversation analysis (Coates 1997, 2003), critical discourse analysis (Talbot 1997), or narrative analysis (Meinhof 1997). All of these instrumental tools are widely applied in many other fields of linguistic research nowadays for analysing, not only gender, but also other social and cultural dimensions such as, class, age, ethnicity or environment.

In short, bearing in mind the broad epistemological and methodological context surrounding the emergence of language and masculinity studies in the 1990s, and the parallel activity of feminist linguistics since the late 1970s, we can conclude that recent work on masculinity and language is to be acknowledged as being totally indebted to the feminist linguistics tradition of the past three decades. In addition to analysing the specificity of women's worlds and femininity for a long time, the feminisms have been trying to cast light on the oppressive effects of patriarchal social orders upon women. Thus, an insight into the mechanisms whereby the realm of men and masculinity contributes to excluding and discriminating women in society seems to be consistent with the feminist agenda, so that it does not seem to be very appropriate to separate the study of masculinity from the major goals of feminist research and enquiry. As advocated by Sally Johnson (1997), "a focus on the highly variable ways in which masculine identities are formed, and in particular the role of language in the construction of those identities, is a worthwhile feminist project" (25). All in all, feminist-oriented work on language and gender has lately exerted a vital influence upon the very articulation of language and masculinity studies. We can predict that, in all probability, the work and advances in this new direction of research will be highly enriching for the longer-standing and fully consolidated feminist tradition within Language and Gender Studies, both in English and, without a doubt, in other languages as well.

References

Adams, Peter J. *et al.* "Dominance and Entitlement: The Rhetoric Men Use to Discuss Their Violence Towards Women". *Discourse and Society* 6 (3) 1995: 387-406.

Baron, Bettina and Helga Kotthoff, eds. *Gender in Interaction: Perspectives on Femininity and Masculinity in Ethnography and Discourse.* Amsterdam: John Benjamins, 2001.

Bergvall, Victoria L. "Toward a Comprehensive Theory of Language and Gender." *Language in Society* 28 (2) 1999: 273-293.

Bucholtz, Mary. "Language and Masculinity Reviewed." *Language in Society* 28 (2) 1999: 308-312.

Butler, Judith. *Gender Trouble. Feminism and the Subversion of Identity.* London: Routledge, 1990.

Cameron, Deborah. *Feminism and Linguistic Theory*, 2nd ed. London: Macmillan Press, 1992 [1985].

----. *The Feminist Critique of Language: A Reader.* London: Routledge, 1990.

----. "Theoretical Debates in Feminist Linguistics: Questions of Sex and Gender" in Ruth Wodak, ed. *Gender and Discourse.* London: Sage Publications, 1997: 21-35.

Coates, Jennifer. *Women, Men and Language.* London: Longman, 1986.

-----. "One-at-a-time: The Organization of Men's Talk" in Sally Johnson and Ulrike Hanna Meinhof, eds. *Language and Masculinity.* Oxford: Blackwell, 1997: 107-129.

-----. ed. *Language and Gender. A Reader.* Oxford: Blackwell, 1998.

-----. *Men Talk. Stories in the Making of Masculinities.* Oxford: Blackwell, 2003.

Coates, Jennifer and Deborah Cameron, eds. *Women in their Speech Communities.* London: Longman, 1989.

Crawford, Mary. *Talking Difference. On Gender and Language.* London: Sage Publications, 1995.

Gough, Brendan and Gareth Edwards. "The Beer Talking: Four Lads, a Carry Out and the Reproduction of Masculinities." *Sociological Review.* 46(3) 1998: 409-435.

Graddol, David and Joan Swann. *Gender Voices.* Oxford: Blackwell, 1989.

Harvey, Keith. "'Everybody Loves a Lover'. Gay Men, Straight Men and a Problem of Lexical Choice" in Keith Herring and Celia Shalom, eds. *Language and Desire: Encoding Sex, Romance and Intimacy.* London: Routledge, 1997: 60-82.

Henton, Caroline. "The abnormality of Male Speech" in George Wolf (ed.) *New Departures in Linguistics*. New York: Garland Publishing, 1992: 27-55.

Herring, Susan *et al*. "'This Discussion is Going Too Far!' Male Resistance to Female Participation on the Internet" in Kira Hall and Mary Bucholtz (eds.) *Gender Articulated. Language and the Socially Constructed Self*. London: Routledge, 1995: 67-96.

Jahr, Erns Håkon. "Middle-Age Male Syntax." *International Journal of the Sociology of Language*. 94 (1992): 123-34.

Jespersen, Otto. *Language: Its Nature, Origin and Development*. London: George Allen & Unwin, 1920.

Johnson, Sally. "Theorizing Language and Masculinity: A Feminist Perspective" in Sally Johnson and Ulrike Hanna Meinhof, eds. *Language and Masculinity*. Oxford: Blackwell, 1997: 12-22.

Johnson, Sally and Ulrike Hanna Meinhof, eds. *Language and Masculinity*. Oxford: Blackwell, 1997.

Kiesling, Scott Fabius. "Cultural Models and Alignment Roles in Fraternity Men's Discourse" in Natasha Warner *et al*. eds. *Gender and Belief Systems. Proceedings of the 4th Berkeley Women and Language Conference*. Berkeley, California: Berkeley Women and Language Group, 1996: 363-373.

Kuiper, Koenraad. "Sporting Formulae in New Zealand English: Two Models of Male Solidarity" in Jenny Cheshire, ed. *English Around the World*. Cambridge: Cambridge UP, 1991: 200-209.

Lakoff, Robin. "Language and Woman's Place." *Language in Society* 2. (1973): 45-80.

Lazar, Michelle M. "Politicizing Gender in Discourse: Feminist Critical Discourse Analysis as Political Perspective and Praxis" in Michelle M. Lazar, ed. *Feminist Critical Discourse Analysis. Gender, Power and Ideology in Discourse*. Houndmills: Palgrave, 2005: 1-28.

Mackenzie, Adrian. "A Troubled Materiality: Masculinism and Computation." *Discourse*. 18(3) (1996): 89-112.

McIlvenny, Paul. "Book Review: Sally Johnson and Ulrike Hanna Meinhof (eds.) *Language and Masculinity*". *Discourse & Society* 9(1) (1988): 107-109.

Meinhof, Ulrike Hanna. "'The Most Important Event of My Life!' A Comparison of Male and Female Written Narratives" in Sally Johnson and Ulrike Hanna Meinhof, eds. *Language and Masculinity*. Oxford: Blackwell, 1997: 208-228.

Poynton, Cate. *Language and Gender: Making the Difference*. Oxford: Oxford UP, 1989.

Romaine, Suzanne. *Communicating Gender*. London: Lawrence Erlbaum Associates Publishers, 1999.

Talbot, Mary M. "'Randy Fish Boss Branded a Stinker': Coherence and the Construction of Masculinities in a British Tabloid Newspaper" in Sally Johnson and Ulrike Hanna Meinhof, eds. *Language and Masculinity*. Oxford: Blackwell, 1997: 173-187.

-----. *Language and Gender. An Introduction*. Oxford: Polity Press, 1998.

Ushida, Aki. "When 'Difference' is Dominance: A Critique of the 'Anti-power-based' Cultural Approach to Sex Differences." *Language in Society* 21 (1992): 547-568.

The Art of Women's Moral Agency

Devin Kuhn

Traditional theories about moral agency, or one's capacity for making moral judgments, generally focus on rationality and impartiality as requisites for making informed moral decisions. For instance, according to Aristotle, one had to be free from any constraints in order to make a rational moral choice. For Kant, one had to act solely out of universal d[1]uty for one's actions to be considered moral. Feminist ethicists challenge these traditional standards of moral virtue and ethical behavior, arguing that such codes do not resonate with many women's, and even many people's, lived experiences of moral virtue and agency. For instance, we are all constrained by our relationships and obligations to other people, and impartiality – hiding behind what John Rawls' calls a "veil of ignorance" (136 *passim*) – is impossible. A major contention of feminist ethics is, thus, that women's experiences and perspectives have been excluded from traditional moral theories.

Feminist ethics argues, instead, that the traits some women value, while often considered amoral or even immoral, in fact provide a foundation for an alternative sense of moral agency. Womanist[2] ethicist Katie Geneva Cannon argues this point:

> how Black women live out a moral wisdom in their real-lived context...does not appeal to the fixed rules or absolute principles of the white-oriented, male-structured society... Black women's analysis and appraisal of what is right or wrong and good or bad develop out of the various coping mechanisms related to the conditions of their circumstances. (60-61)

---

[1] For further information on the traditional ethicists named, please see Aristotle, *Nichomachean Ethics*; Immanuel Kant, *Critique of Practical Reason* and *Critique of Pure Reason*; and John Rawls, *A Theory of Justice* and *Justice as Fairness*.

[2] Cannon self-identifies as a 'womanist' in Alice Walker's sense of the term and the Womanist movement. Womanism grew out of a critique of feminism's early lack of attention to race and class, and is predominantly an African American women's movement, though it is also distinct from Black feminism.

Geneva Cannon highlights the ways in which traditional ethicists, those very ethicists who hold impartiality as the mark of moral agency, have in fact constructed a sense of virtue that is located in very specific historical locations and cultural understandings. Social location is, thus, a significant component of even these traditional theories, and Geneva Cannon's work explores the ways in which African American women's social location influences the traits valorised as moral qualities in that cultural context. Although her work focuses on African American women, the foundation of Geneva Cannon's argument might apply for any marginalised group.

But how does one determine women's concepts of moral behavior, if they have been so long excluded from mainstream ethics? Geneva Cannon suggests that one way is through literature, which, she claims, is an adequate indicator of moral agency because "as recorders of the Black experience, Black women writers convey the community's consciousness of values that enables them to find meaning in spite of social degradation, economic exploitation, and political oppression" (61). Thus, as sources of women's own analyses that both reflect and construct women's particular cultural contexts and values, women's literature, narratives, and art are useful indicators for determining different senses of women's moral agency.

In this paper, I will use Geneva Cannon's methodology to explore women's moral agency by examining how it is portrayed in the poetry of Parvin E'tessami, an Iranian poet of the early 20th century; of Suheir Hammad, a contemporary Palestinian poet living in Brooklyn; and of Sinead Morrissey, a contemporary poet from Northern Ireland. This paper examines how these writers demonstrate agency not only through their characters and narratives, but through themselves in their very act of creating art: the acts of writing and storytelling become sites of women's moral agency, as well.

These women come from a variety of backgrounds and represent different classes, ethnic groups and religious affiliations. It would be too simplistic to draw wide-ranging conclusions about women's moral agency from these pieces to apply to women in general across such broad spectrums of identity and situation. Thus, the purpose of this paper is not to impose an ethic for all women, but rather to show that women's ethics and values may differ from those esteemed by traditional ethicists (and even other feminists) and yet also to establish some of the virtues that may be valuable to women's experience. Instead of impartiality, rationality, and universality, these women demonstrate celebration, relationality, and subversiveness as qualities important to moral agency.

Parvin E'tessami, "God's Weaver"

Parvin E'tessami was an Iranian poet born in 1907 and raised by a well-to-do, liberal family who encouraged her in her writing and sent her to the best schools available to women at that time. Because of her liberal parents, she led a life far from typical for a woman in the first half of the 20th century (Milani 102). E'tessami was a groundbreaking poet, and at age fourteen became the first woman ever to publish a book of poetry in Iran. Her writing was so strong and eloquent, in fact, that she has even been accused by a number of critics, both in her own time and posthumously, of not having actually written the poems. Instead, many people believe a man actually wrote them, believing that no woman – let alone a fourteen-year-old – would be capable of such achievement. Ironically, then, this denial of her authorship has occasionally been interpreted as a compliment, because it demonstrates just how much her work exceeds the expectations of women's talent. Thus, just by the act of writing, E'tessami challenged dominant expectations.

In the poem, "God's Weaver," E'tessami portrays a "lazy laggard" observing a spider hard at work weaving and spinning a web. Though the laggard criticises the action he deems worthless, E'tessami pays homage to the delicate, intricate and important work the spider is achieving, challenging the notion that there is but one standard by which to judge value. As critic Farzaneh Milani describes in her commentary on E'tessami:

> The spider, assured its art would eventually triumph in mysterious ways, insists that one worldview – that of the man – is not enough to provide full understanding of the world. It is too narrow, too limited, too one-sided. It leaves out the perspectives of those behind walls and curtains who do not exercise institutional power; those immured in silence and allegedly unworthy of attention and recognition. (116)

At the surface level, E'tessami's poem is about valuing the choices and work that society often makes invisible or dismisses as not real work because they are such a part of the everyday they have become mundane. But the poem is much more nuanced – E'tessami uses the metaphors of weaving and spinning, which are traditionally associated with women's work, to raise the arts of women – arts that are often not considered art at all, because they also serve everyday, mundane purposes. The spider asserts: "I've been a weaver from the beginning,/ and this I'll be as long as I live... This is my calling, important or not" (67). Thus, the spider's creation stands in for women's folk art – and for all the other jobs and roles that predominantly women perform, such as child-rearing and running a household – that are often not considered 'real' jobs or work (Milani 117).

The emphasis on weaving in this poem, and in these lines specifically, can also be a metaphor for story-telling traditions; thus, E'tessami is highlighting her own art, and women's (or, at the very least, her own) ability to craft stories and weave their own oral histories. Writing, and even more unusual for her time, publishing her poetry allowed her a voice she likely would have otherwise been denied. E'tessami spoke out on subjects that affected Iranian women, such as poverty and gender inequality, and she demanded education for women – both in her poems and in her public speaking appointments. She further established her own agency by breaking with conventional writing and asserting her own style and rules. She chose subjects that appeared innocent, ensuring her poems would be overlooked by the censors, but which, in reality, were metaphors for her social commentaries (119). In this sense, writing was very much a form of resistance for E'tessami, through which she used her talent and her agency to craft unique and creative forms of resistance.

Finally, the spider's insistence that "this is my calling, important or not" (67) is a powerful assertion of women's space and of a woman's right to simply be – of her own accord, regardless of the role others may prescribe for her. It is also E'tessami's way of saying that critics, and even popular cultural convention, will not deter her.

Suheir Hammad, "Mama Sweet Baklava"
Suheir Hammad is the granddaughter of Palestinian refugees. She was born in 1973 in Ammad, Jordan, and moved to Brooklyn, NY with her family when she was five. Her Brooklyn childhood was set against an urban, multi-racial, multi-ethnic background, and the important

influence this has had in her life is apparent in her writing with regard to marginality, identity, and issues of oppression. Hammad incorporates musical rhythms, particularly jazz, hip-hop and traditional Arabic music, into her performance poetry. She is socially and politically active on a variety of issues, particularly in relation to Palestinian self-determination, violence against women, and anti-war movements. Though all three poets are from spaces of contested lands, this is reflected most explicitly in Hammad's work.

In her poem, "Mama Sweet Baklava," Hammad describes the traditional Middle Eastern dessert as made of "layers thousand layers/upon each other" (www.cafearabica). As a metaphor for women, this describes the oppression which results from being both a woman and an Arab, in Arabic and American cultures. Hammad addresses these levels of hybridity, describing: "more layers infinite/upon each other pressed/into steel children marriage/nation woman" (*ibid.*). She outlines various layers of womanhood and the gendered roles women are expected to play, in familial and domestic, as well as state and nation capacities, and the intersectionality and conflicting allegiances these identities create.

Hammad also describes, "years of rough pounded heart/ hear her crunch in/the mouths of men who barely taste blood" (*ibid.*). This portrays oppression experienced specifically as a woman, and alludes to domestic violence and sexual assault, while a few stanzas later, she addresses oppression experienced specifically as an Arab: "this woman called arab/alien to jaw breaker children/of flan and chocolate bars" (*ibid.*). Hammad – herself a Palestinian woman born in Jordan and raised in Brooklyn – is describing the "alien" perception of Arabs that many western, and particularly American, people have. "Jaw breaker children" represents these western, American children, as jawbreakers are a common candy in the US. Yet Hammad's choice of "jaw breaker" to modify children, rather than chocolate (which she mentions later) or other typically western sweets, also underscores the violence between these cultures, and reveals a literal meaning of "jaw breaker," as well. These images portray a disturbing reality of the oppression faced by Arab and Arab -American women, when their hybrid identities are not accepted or acknowledged by the various cultures within which they interact.

Yet within these descriptions, Hammad's baklava is not a metaphor of mere passivity. Among its intricate layers, Hammad portrays subversive capability as well, and the baklava becomes a site for strength and agency.

The lines "toothsome and full too much /of her aches stomachs but/…" (*ibid.*) highlights the pain such violence can bring, as "too much of her aches," too much of her is in pain. Yet as the line continues, it creates a space for agency, as well: because baklava is "toothsome and full," eating too much of it causes stomachaches. The word "toothsome" also indicates speaking out; this woman causes problems for those who would abuse her by and through her resistance, which for Hammad is located particularly in her writing. The multiple meanings in these lines not only describe oppression, but also create an even stronger space to subvert such oppression.

The lines "her recipe old and passed/down through word of/hand creating and sustaining/substantial delicious" (*ibid.*), celebrate women's traditions and rituals in a manner similar to E'tessami's celebration of weaving and spinning. As with E'tessami, these traditions become other sites for moral agency. The pause created by breaking up "word of/hand" into two lines calls attention to Hammad's appropriation of a cliché, "word of mouth," and makes it a tool for communication and agency. It is with their hands, their own hard work, that women assert their space and identity. By enjambing the next phrase on the same line, "hand creating and sustaining/substantial delicious," Hammad further emphasises that notion, as the hand creates and sustains the life of these women. There is also a sense of connection to ancestors and survival, like recipes, becomes a tradition passed down through generations.

For Hammad, the act of making baklava is an act of moral agency. She portrays it as a subversive and celebratory act of preserving a ritual unique to the women in her family. Similarly, writing is an act of agency for Hammad. She describes her need to write as follows:

> Language is power, politics…. Why do I write? 'Cause I have to. 'Cause my voice, in all its dialects, has been silenced too long. 'Cause women are still abused as naturally as breath. Peoples are still without land. Slavery still exists, hunger persists and mothers cry. My mother cries. Those are reasons enough, but there are so many more. (Hammad 1996, ix)

Through writing, she acts, she struggles, and she perseveres.

Sinead Morrissey, "My Grandmother through Glass"

Like Hammad, Sinead Morrissey is a contemporary poet. She is often considered an emerging poet, but, in fact, she has been recognised for her writing for some time now, including winning the Patrick Kavanaugh Award for poetry in 1990, becoming the youngest person to do so. She was born in 1972 in Portadown, Northern Ireland, but she has spent much of her life traveling abroad, living and working in both Japan and New Zealand. In recent years she has settled back in Ireland and Northern Ireland, earning a degree from Trinity College in Dublin and currently working as the Writer-in-Residence at Queen's University Belfast.

In Morrissey's poem "My Grandmother through Glass," the narrator stands in her grandmother's house after her grandmother's death and sifts through the memories of three generations of women in her family. As she moves between the heartache, frustration, jealousy, caring and love that unite the women, she is at once inheriting a legacy and creating her own, as memory involves choosing what to include, even if some is painful. Her act of remembering, then, becomes both eulogy to her grandmother and a reconstruction of her past, and, thus, of herself. It is through this reconstruction that Morrissey's narrator and the women of the poem achieve moral agency.

Whereas in life, the grandmother and great-aunt were adversaries, the narrator describes how her already-deceased great-aunt Sarah helped birth her, and as she sent the narrator into the world, "Sarah saw me off with a message of love - / to give you [the grandmother] all the kindness she never could" (44). Thus, the narrator uses her constructed, imaginative memory, as well as the literal space of her poetic narrative, to recreate the relationship between grandmother and great-aunt and heal past wounds.

The poem also portrays the art and skill of midwifery as another place for agency. Sections II and IV of the poem describe Sarah as a midwife, a profession traditionally associated with women that is often used as a symbol of women's powerful skills and ability to generate life. Sarah's ability to midwife, even from "the other side" (44) is what connects Sarah to the narrator and, thus, in many ways helps to heal the fractured relations between grandmother and sister-in-law, as well as grandmother and daughter, the narrator's mother. The narrator herself then inherits this talent for midwifery as part of her familial legacy, but in her it takes the shape of poetry.

In his review of the poem, critic Tom Herron describes the poet's role here: "There is the fantastic sense of the poet holding the weight of history in her mind: this history has resulted in the poet who now retraces it, gives it form, brings it back into the light" (www.carcanet). The image of bringing it back to the light echoes the language Morrissey uses in the poem to describe the passages both of birth and of death. Thus, the narrator delivers her family's history through her words and through her memory in the act of writing, and, like both E'tessami and Hammad, the act of writing becomes the site of agency for the self.

As with Hammad, Morrissey suggests the relational importance of connectedness with ancestors. Morrissey emphasises the power in preserving one's history but not being bound by it. Both she and the narrator retell stories, but they are also taking part in their creation, and it is through this active authorship that space for agency is created.

These poems represent different forms of moral agency exercised in a variety of ways. The spider in E'tessami's poem finds strength and beauty in her action, and she defends it to those who would mock her. E'tessami also elevates the spider's work, giving praise to that which is typically overlooked. Likewise, the woman/baklava of Hammad's poem, and the midwifery of Morrissey's poem symbolises the traditionally feminine, which in these poems, rather than be stereotyped, become instead celebrated valorised as subversive sites of agency.

The characters in these poems, thus, reflect varieties of women's moral agency. The writers themselves also demonstrate means of agency, through their various art forms. The act of storytelling through a poem is a powerful assertion of one's existence, and allows control over the way in which one interprets her experience, thus becoming location for agency as well as preserving traditions and histories that are often overlooked by mainstream historians. It is a way for women to claim their space and acknowledge their worth. It gives voice to those who might otherwise go unheard.

It is not a coincidence that these narratives pay homage to art itself in their pieces. The act of creating, of giving life, has long been associated with women. These pieces demonstrate some of the many ways in which women create and give life – both literally and artistically – and the ways in which doing so can be an act of moral agency for women.

References

Cannon, Katie. Katie's Canon. New York: Continuum, 1996.

E'tessami, Parvin. *A Nightingale's Lament: Selections from the Poems and Fables of Parvin E'tessami* (1907-1941). Trans. Heshmat Moayyad. KY: Mazda Publishers, 1985.

Hammad, Suheir. *Born Palestinian, Born Black.* New York: Harlem River Press, 1996.

-----. "Mama Sweet Bakalava."
www.cafearabica.com/culture/cultureold/articles/culsuh10x1.html

Handal, Nathalie "Drops of Suheir Hammad: A Talk With a Palestinian Poet Born Black." *Al Jadid* (Summer 1997), vol. 3 no.2.
www.alajadid.com/interviews/DropsofSuheirHammad.html

Herron, Tom. "Reviews of *There Was a Fire in Vancouver* by Sinead Morrissey."
www.carcanet.co.uk/cgiin/reframe.cgi?app=scribe&author=morris seys

Milani, Farzaneh., *Veils and Words: the Emerging Voices of Iranian Women Writers.* New York: Syracuse UP, 1992.

Morrissey, Sinead. *There Was Fire in Vancouver,* Manchester: Carcanet, 1996.

Feminist Writing for Performance: The Images that Speak to Us

Georgia Rhoades

> To move beyond isolation is the writer's constant goal . . .
> we all need to essay our lives. In doing so, we never arrive
> at the end of things but agree to linger thoughtfully,
> painfully, ecstatically, along the way, in the company of
> others, in the agency of our words.
>
> Wendy Bishop (267)

I'm rewriting this introduction in bed: the email portal is on the other side of the house with the promise of breakfast bewteen. As I get older, I (who always felt a nap to be in order) wake earlier, and there seems to be a new space in early morning (or even earlier, in Molly Bloom time) to do the writing that matters. Once I put on underwear and move in the direction of the computer, writing will be different. I can hear a drip from the eaves and bird-chirp. I found wild clematis in the woods and planted it by this window just before I left for Galway this summer, and now it has run across the window and is hung with white stars. In the North Carolina mountains I plant seeds early and they come to flower late if they germinate at all: here at the far end of August, the morning glories have just begun to bloom, so late that I had forgotten what colors to expect. I love gardens. They help me with my mourning. They inspire me to move, to do some work. I find it hard to read in the garden, though I can read at any ballgame and always wanted to read in church. A garden makes me look and think. Later I will take the laptop into the garden to type these sentences, which may take a place in the piece I'm writing with you in mind — other women, in Galway, Dublin, London, Siler City, and Todd. But first I want you to have this quiet, sleepy image of the writer, older than I have ever been, writing inside while looking out into the garden, impatient and content, growing but dying, within and without.

When I write in this way – in the ways that link what I think about with what resonates, the images that seem to speak to me – I come closest to believing in something sacred. When the storyteller comes back round to the image that was hidden early in the story, we are surprised and delighted and know that in that symmetry there is meaning. In their study of the rhetoric of discovery, Young, *et al.* wrote that:

> the task of the writer is to set in motion a process that will result in a particular change in the reader's image. This change may be one of three kinds: (l) a change that results in reconstruction of the image or some part of it, (2) a change that expands the image or some part of it, or (3) a change that alters the clarity or the certainty with which some part of the image is held. (217)

When an image calls, the writer is unlikely to know the scope of its possibilities: the writing itself either creates or uncovers them.

Writing oneself, for women academics especially, can often mean reconnecting with what we have kept within. For me, feminist conferences are likely to provide that possibility, especially international conferences that allow me to talk with women whose experiences might appear very different from mine. The validation from finding our common conclusions has led me to design writing workshops that lead to connections. In July 2005 I led a workshop called "Feminist Writing for Performance: The Images that Speak to Us" for the NUI-Galway conference "Feminisms: Within and Without" and, in July 2004, I led a similar workshop for the WERRC Dublin conference "Feminism Contesting Globalisation." In this essay I am also offering the background for these workshops and sharing the writing of the women who agreed to be included.

The July 2005 'Feminisms: Within and Without' theme resonates for those of us who came to Women's Studies after traditional educations: reading women writers, we rediscovered what we valued as girls and revisited some aspects of our formal learning that rarely included our knowledge and experience. At the opening of the NUI-Galway conference, Rebecca Pelan invited us to have experiences that would "confirm everything you believe to be true." For academic feminists that confirmation is what keeps us in spirit, the unexpected gift of illumination and community when we are slipping under.

For me, the challenge to bring my experience to my writing and education came when, after fourteen years of teaching writing and literature, I began teaching Women's Studies and reading some landmark texts for the first time. As a writing teacher with a degree in

Rhetoric and Composition Studies, discouraged from writing creatively by teachers who were literary critics, I learned to turn my poems into love letters and my impulse to write into academic models. I taught writing with a focus on rhetorical and composing theory within a feminist community in Composition Studies and Women's Studies and, with the encouragement of the best in my field, I helped students learn to ignore early educational advice to avoid first and second person and to use their experiences and observations to support their conclusions. The shift to process writing called on us to create spaces in which students could write with authority, which meant that they were encouraged to write about what they knew and turn to research when they needed to know more, an approach that invited more confusion and messiness into the classroom, mirroring real-world writing lives.

Wendy Bishop encouraged us to find "writeable experience" (270). For me, after years of teacher writing, I was able to bring my creative writing expression to performance. In the early 1990s, working with Mary Anne Maier and Dennis Bohr, I formed 'Black Sheep Theatre', primarily because Mary Anne was a director and Dennis a playwright. The academic, I was to serve as feminist researcher, grant writer, and managing director. But at their encouragement, I began also to perform and to write for performance, and the world of images reopened to me, just at the time when I felt called to risk.

In performances of our writing since 1995 and in classes and performance since 2001 at The Playhouse in Derry, Northern Ireland, we have premiered political plays in Derry and collaborated with Derry and Donegal artists in writing and performance. Using Augusto Boal's ideas of dialogue and image theatre in our classes in Derry we offer adult learners opportunities to create and perform theatre pieces from their own experiences. I have written about the witchcraze in Ireland, England, and the U.S., about U.S. and Irish women accused of child-murder, and about Mother Shipton and Grace O'Malley. I have performed in plays about Pope Joan and other historical and imaginary women, all based on research, but stretching imaginatively toward the lives these women might have lived. This endeavor, which gave me writing, performance, learning, and travel opportunities I could never have envisioned, has changed me as a writer and a teacher of writing.

Though I teach process writing, which privileges the invention stage of text creation and allows for different learning and writing styles, I have found that the rhetoric of performance, especially for political theater, requires me to return to images. The development of my writing for academia usually depends on format, chronology, or the formula of establishing a context, presenting the thesis, and elaborating upon it. In this essay, for example, I frame with an image that I hope will illuminate the logic. I establish the main idea and then go into the background of how and why my writing for performance is different from my other writing, and in doing so, I tell personal history. I will offer an extended example as well as the writing of the women who participated in my workshops in Galway and Dublin.

When I write for performance, which is different from the rhetoric of my academic writing, I usually begin with an idea to write about and a symbol or image that occurs to me as a way to tell the story. In *Feminist Rhetorical Theories*, Foss *et al.* define rhetoric as "associated strictly with human symbolic efforts to discern truth" (6), either as truth that we can discover, as truth we make as members of a community, or as the truth we inherit from a culture we may wish to distinguish ourselves from (6). As a writer for political theatre, I find that the image has become the medium for telling the argument, not as indirection but as a way for me to discover the depths of the truth that I want to write about.

As a student of literature and rhetoric, I learned to appreciate the image or symbol in the writing of others and to analyse it: one of the most common moves for the student of literature is to identify the vehicle and tenor of a metaphor (the thing carrying the meaning and the idea itself) and the ways in which each enrich the other. Foss *et al.* refer to rhetors (a term feminists may be drawn to more than 'rhetoricians') as "individuals who struggle to eradicate oppression and domination" (81). When I came to writing for performance as a rhetor, more aware of the relationships between message, writer, and reader, I learned about this symbiosis from the other side, not as a reader, but as a writer. This relationship between image and idea is often inexplicable, though it promises to be rich and logical. In using the image to explain the idea, we discover associations between the two that explode in their appropriateness to bring both elements into new meaning. The writer finds herself writing not to record what she has articulated already in her mind to herself, but to discover.

One of the first times I wrote in this way was in creating "Waterwoman," a piece that I needed to write in order to come out as a white U. S. Southerner whose family had owned slaves. As a result of teaching Women's Studies courses, as well as noting the mermaids in Irish church decoration (and reading Jim Higgins' *Irish Mermaids*), I recovered a symbol that in my girlhood had meant a lot to me. As a child I was always drawing mermaids, but as an adolescent I found them slightly embarrassing, since they were most often depicted barebreasted, luring sailors to their deaths and wishing they had legs. The poet Kelly Ellis and I discussed mermaids and how we were surprised that they were so potent as symbols to us, since we were feminists who wanted no truck with patriarchal representations of the female. But as I read about mermaids in older contexts (suggested by Moira Quinn's essay "Sea, Symbolism and Women of the Waves"), I began to realise that there were sound reasons that we were drawn to the mermaid as a rich and strong image of women.

In developing the piece, I wrote a remembered story about my paternal ancestors losing money belts in the Green River in Kentucky as they capsized on their way to buy slaves. The water context allowed me to talk about water and to introduce mermaids I had recently read about: Oshun, Lyserine, Oya, Yemana. In putting together mermaids and slavery, I found ways to tell the stories that were new to me (in writing about the Satterfield plantation, I described the rows of slave cabins as facing the river, which gave me a reason to talk about connections between the people who lived there and water, especially to imagine what the sight of the river might have meant to them). In part, the analogy between the story and the image worked because I kept it in mind and found ways to use water references to enrich the original stories. One intersection occurred when I was talking about growing up in the 1960s and race relations: when I asked Dennis for a song from that time, he suggested "Rescue Me," which came to evoke the mermaids singing to sailors from the rocks and resonated throughout the finished piece, though I didn't realise that possibility initially. But the connection itself between slavery and mermaids was something I couldn't explain, except that it captured me.

One night, Kelly called to tell me that she knew why I was writing about mermaids and slavery. In her research into voodoo and hoodoo, she had found Mami Wata (or Mammy Water), the huge mermaid who had swum up to the slave ships and called the Africans to jump and hold onto her hair so she could swim them back to home. Kelly had found the truth out there to be discovered in the folklore of the Africans enslaved in the U. S.: as a community, we were investing the mermaid with significance we had felt, but had had no cultural corroboration for; as feminists we were rejecting the Disney-fication and patriarchal reading of the mermaid as only interested in transformation for the male or in diabolically plotting his enslavement (another intersection).

In the workshops I offer at feminist conferences, I ask participants to write for performance, not because I have an interest in converting all of us to performance art or asking that everyone abandon the kind of clear, compelling political argument of our session speakers. But as a way of writing political truth, since sometimes the indirect offers the opportunity for discovery. And for many of us, talking our politics too quickly becomes ineffective argument. I find that I rarely convince those not inclined to agree with me when I tell them what I think. The rhetorical situation offered by performance, though, gives us audience members seduced into the role of participant in the creation of a character, colluding with us in hopes of avoiding the embarrassment of all of us if the piece doesn't work. They listen and watch with sympathy if we have done our job of reaching them at all. For those in these workshops who might not perform but look to writing as a way to order our thoughts, I also hoped we might create or discover some truth through writing.

To prepare for the performance and workshop aspects of the sessions, I asked participants to make notes in answer to these prompts: an image you are drawn to; a process you are very familiar with; the name of a woman whose voice you want to hear; and an issue that you care deeply about and see as a focus for your activism. Women from Ireland, New Zealand, Australia, England, the U. S., Croatia, South Africa, and Indonesia participated in these workshops, and some shared their writing with the groups at the conferences. Those who have allowed me to use their writing and reflect about it in this account are talented writers who may or may not develop these notes for performance or publication: it's tempting, when sharing notes we have written for ourselves, to polish and revise, but most of these writers were especially generous in sharing what they wrote in just a few minutes at the conferences. So, some of the notes are elliptical and written primarily for the writers: in a few cases, I've added slashes to separate ideas and changed spellings for clarity. These notes reveal different ways in which these women responded to the prompts and how they connected visually and emotionally to the work of the session. Their responses are surprising and intriguing: for example, in answer to the directions, Amy Brust wrote "Julie Andrews" as the woman she wanted to hear speak. For the image, she chose "a pig going to the slaughter with squealing in the background (because pigs, unlike other animals, know that they are going to be killed—and they scream out loud before death)."

Allowing this first writing to steep, I performed some of my short pieces: "Ask Me What I Think," a monologue about place and patriotism from a series I am writing in the voice of Mary; "The Banshee Talks to the Yanks," a monologue in Northern Ireland voice; "The Sheela-na-gig," about the icon and my mother's Alzheimer's; and "Divorcing George," in which a woman from the States decides to divorce George W. Bush. I felt that the riskiest piece for me to perform was "The Banshee Talks to the Yanks," which requires a Northern Ireland accent and perspective. Particularly in light of the tradition of U. S. filmmakers and playwrights appropriating Irish voices and viewpoints, I am wary of sentimentality and colonisation as aspects of the relationship between the States and Ireland, particularly the North, and the dangers of anyone speaking as someone else.

I chose the banshee as an image initially for a play I am writing about Cecily Jackson, a Derry cook who was burned at the Bishopquay Gate in 1725. I had had the banshee on my mind since seeing "Darby O'Gill and the Little People" in the 1950s, as one who knows all, even death and back, more than witch, immortal and wise. But as I was working on this play and thinking about the banshee, the U. S. invaded Iraq, and I found myself thinking about her in this contemporary context. As someone from the States with strong objections to the policies of George W. Bush's administration, I wanted to be clearly critical. I also wanted to apologise for how the U. S. acts in the world and to satirise it, but my own voice didn't feel adequate. Using the banshee, identified as Irish in my mind, as the speaker, I had the chance to show U. S. audiences how they are seen by the rest of the world. I decided I wanted the speaker to be Irish because of the deep knowledge the Irish have of U. S. culture and their fondness for some aspects of it, along with their ability to satirise it. This voice, it seemed to me, had the authority of a cousin— a family member with the right to criticise from within and yet enough distance to call us on our shit. I was fortunate to be helped by Pat Mulkeen, Teresa Cunningham, and Bridie Canning in revising the voice.

The Banshee Talks to the Yanks

I am the Banshee, the woman of the faeries, who comes to wail to those whose deaths are imminent, and I follow the children of the North wherever they go, to tell them when their time has come. And you hear me in the most still minute of the night, when you wake and wonder: was that a cat yammin? Or a dog barking? Sure it was just a car passing. But that was me. I have no comfort to give you, unless you are comforted by the truth. Hear me and beware.

So they called me in here to give you Yanks a bit of advice now in your time of trouble, trouble not being exactly alien to us where I'm from. Weren't we waiting for the invaders when Finn was not yet a giant and when the Hag of Beara and her sister Cailleach flew in the thick twilight and some thought their sisterly conversation to be the thunder.

And haven't a fair number of us come across to you, the families staging a wake there in Ireland before we left, knowing in the old days that you would never see their faces again and not wishing to be robbed of the funeral, though these days you're flying thick and fast into Shannon and Dublin and even Belfast and Derry airports, coming back to nostalgia and the smell of turf you all say you love.

But I've been watching you, not just when you come over and talk about your roots and buy the tin whistles and sweaters and go home and tell them all that you found yourself in Ireland. It isn't just your money that's lovable: it's your innocence; it's your belief that you're the chosen ones to whom war will never come and that you have the occasional bit of responsibility to tell the rest of the world where to go. You're endearing like a puppy, but tiring as well, especially when it shits all over the place and doesn't have a clue it's done it or how to clean it up. Or the actor in the family who always has the centre of the stage and doesn't even consider that the movie being made in this family could ever be about somebody else. And don't we all know those people.

Part of the shining dream of the movies is that some places are safe; once for us it may have been Tir na nog and for you it's the end of the movies, when you go out for a pint or an ice cream, and some are dead but not the major stars unless it's like Mel Gibson in Braveheart and that was OK, him being Mel Gibson and already shooting some ten hour movie about Jesus or something. And isn't it OK for some of the heroes to die, especially if they've made love to a French princess whose son will now be the new hero. We all know that will set up the sequel.

But now that you've had a taste of it, I think it'll be harder for you. Maybe, you're thinking, there is no safe place, and that's weighing on your minds. Though some of you older ones may remember hiding under your wooden desks in school from Khruschev in 1962, whose country is now your ally: does that tell us something about how the world works? But you're used to simpler stories, and you're used to the hero coming in at the end of the movie on his horse or motorcycle and sorting out all the bad guys. And at the end of the movie there's no worry, it's the end of the movie, and if there were people run over when the cars crashed into each other during the chase scene, you don't see their mammy or wains at the funeral or follow the sad wife on the bus to the prison in another county on the off Saturday when they let her visit. That's the leftovers, always messy to clean up and not that appetising, not cinematic moments, you might say. Do you remember that movie with Harrison Ford and your man Brad Pitt, and Brad Pitt is gunrunning out of Boston and he says to Harrison Ford, "This story won't have a happy ending, because it's an Irish story." And, of course, it didn't have a happy ending if you were Brad Pitt, being the Irish lad, but didn't it end well for Harrison Ford, being the Irish American hero who's still standing at the end.

Now I'm not saying you're simple, but just that the world isn't simple, if you see what I mean. And I think for you it has been, everybody now in the world speaking English and hoping to be on CNN. You offer to the world what you call freedom, and isn't it lovely, but it's the movies and blue jeans and music you have a right to be proudest of, I'd say. To be American is to be sitting there in your Levi's drinking your wee Diet Coke (and looking good, I'll grant you that) and Cindy Crawford does drive up and gets her own drink out of the machine, and that's a fair enough vision if it's what you have. And doubtless it's what most of those in the world would settle for, leisure and a chance to see a celebrity, but they sent for a banshee, and you don't expect to hear too much about sunshine from the likes of me. The banshee cries as a warning. The question is whether it's an omen or a fire drill.

War is noble, as those shite John Wayne films told us, and exciting if you're Tom Cruise flying airplanes and getting Kelly Gillis in the end, an Irish girl after all.

Are you thinking that females always shy away from war? You'll be noticing that if it's a Charles Bronson or Clint Eastwood film the wife and probably the kids are dead at the beginning and then the hero is not only free but he has a mission, to do revenge on those that killed them, though you can be sure there will be a pliant and pleasing young woman around somewhere before the film is over. It isn't that the female is not suited to war. We have had our firebrands who could turn a crowd of holidaymakers. The great Queen Maeve once stood on a hill outnumbered and exposed her woman's parts to the enemy, who knew they had seen a sacred moment and went home to their mammies, afraid of women's power. That's a bit harder to do today when showing the genitals is a click of a mouse away or served up on the same platter as the drink. And you may not believe that there was ever a moment when the female was more than a slave in the firepit or a sweet beleagured wee woman futilely trying to keep together the hearth and home by pleasing the priests and cooking the supper.

Women may be caught up by the idea of war and freedom, even with greed and exhilaration from taking what isn't theirs to have, always wishing to be considered as tough as the men and playing their game as well as men; there's Margaret Thatcher for example, and there's revenge for what has been taken, and there's Queen

Boadicea, her daughters raped and her determination to tear the limbs from those that did it and those who ordered it. And isn't that always the way, that the old men in their castles and offices, with the trappings of wealth and power, make the decisions that send the beautiful young men to die. For them it's always a choice of the two things, war or peace. But at home in the houses big and small there are lots of ways to settle a fight, and seldom do we condone violence if we want to keep the family together under one roof. And someone sometimes moves away and never speaks again, and sometimes someone dies away and is never spoken of, but most likely there's somebody that mourns and never forgets.

We're the ones who dream that the dead are back and wanting their breakfast, the one running from the winners and wishing for our own deaths to be quick. It's women tonight that are wondering if the war comes here how will I get the medicine for the boy's asthma and how will I ever make granny understand what's happening and how can I hide the girl from the soldiers, and how can I comfort the wains when they're not as afraid as I am and where was my boy sent and what if everyone I love dies tonight and leaves me living?

You see, in this world we have made between us, I have no rest. From the beginning of time I see the circle of the planets and the way of the water through the rock. Now that lass in *The Lord of the Rings*, slender as a willow with her dream of being a noble soldier, and Frodo himself walking into the fire with the ring, now that's a war I could go for. Then after we could all go out for a pint and sing a song with ten verses in it and cry a few tears   together. All's I'm saying is maybe we need a few new stories here.

Along with these pieces, I explained how they evolved. For my writing about Mary in her series of monologues, it helped me to consider how I would alter her story if I were able to see her as a real woman, a strategy which also helped me in writing "Divorcing George." One could also approach this writing assignment of creating a monologue for a woman by empowering her beyond the real, as well: the banshee, as an omniscient figure with knowledge of the whole world, could know about movies as well, I reasoned, since she spans all time (a comprehensive study of the banshee is Patricia Lysaght's *The Banshee*).

Returning to our earlier writing, I asked participants to choose the woman or the political idea to write about and to use the image or the process to write about the first: either by listing or freewriting. Ailbhe Smyth's writing, which she performed at the Galway workshop, immediately claimed a character, voice, and image (boxes):

> Sides squares circles lids covers. Opening shut tight squeezing rattling. Base boundaries edges. Empty spacious crammed full. Airless useful practical pointless dangerous. All sizes stackable sensible serviceable on the shelf in the corner. Crying out to be diverted from their true purpose, torn apart with bare hands. Blue ones are best, but only with their lids off.

And in the voice of another person/character, Ailbhe wrote this monologue:

The De-Boxing of Hortense
They call me Hortense which is not exactly the coolest name for a person like me, or for any person really. But of course that's part of the problem – always problems, more and more problems, morning, noon and night problems – the other part being that I'm not sure I'm a person at all. Well maybe I'm not, seeing as I'm more of a persona, when you look at me up close and personal, so to speak. But the moment comes – must come – in any sort of life (or at least you'd expect it to, wouldn't you?) when you have to stand up and say 'No, no, no. Whoever you think I am, and whatever I may be,' (not usually the same thing in my experience and probably not in yours either however different we are), 'you've got it all wrong! I'm a different kettle of fish entirely and I'm not going to sit inside this silly box any more just so you can lid and unlid me whenever you fancy. No, definitively' (education being a wonderful thing), 'I've had enough impermeability and airtightness to do me for ever and ever'. (After all, who can predict the volatilely vital longevity of a persona?) 'I'm

finished, once and for all, with boxes. So I'm just going to jump up and out, right now this very minute in the 'hic et nunc', simple and agile as you please, all ready-made and grown-up, and do the 'moi' performance of my life. Stand by (for a long and continuing time) for the DE-BOXING OF HORTENSE!'

Hortense emerged with her own voice and, when Ailbhe performed her, we all responded to the jubilation of her speech, which we recognised in our own best moments. The feeling of the piece is of a jack-in-the-box bursting from her prison not to be crammed back in again, and in its first workshop shape the piece was already a performance script.

For Tonya Hassell, who had chosen as her image "Stonewall, and also suffocation/the destruction of a wall (ie. the walls that block consciousness); .... standing on my head/a compilation of stones stacking together," the freewriting built on her recent academic life as graduate student and teacher with a sci-fi quality:

> there are many people who've been looking for me recently, traipsing through bars, down into people's basement/they even went to my first grade teacher's house, interrogated her, but she didn't even remember my name/they call me dangerous — they said ('a lecherous wench' disrupting the grand design: an invariant and neutral country. You see, they've been designing a new educational system, working on it since the 30s, I heard. It was a plan to refashion the human brain, slow it down a bit, and train it to 1. speak only when spoken to; 2. think, when told to think, but only about the things they've read in their textbooks (aha! Textbooks, we will come back to that later); 3. keep/do what you are told (and nothing more) refrain from resistance — resistance is bad; a form of manual. . .the book. Then, they would reiterate and reform the information (consult sources only from their books. . .) and compose a list of questions that, more than likely, no one would know the answers, and this was the trick: there would be a wrong and right, which would place people here and there, some people would be out, while others would be in the creation of the grade as a mind controlling device as a way to enforce power.

Tonya's writing goes from the personal, the hunted, to the abstract academic, the walls that block consciousness in the institution of education, and though she doesn't appear to write literally about the stone wall itself or the Stonewall of 1969, she allows the image to speak through a character in a society that recognises her as a danger and is constructed to perpetuate itself at the cost of learning or individuality. I was surprised and moved by the parallels and differences between Ailbhe's box image and Tonya's wall. Ailbhe's call to consider the end of usefulness of a persona is echoed in Tonya's search toward an alternative to the persona society wants to force us to create.

Sarah Zurhellen's list from the workshop is interesting because she says that the woman she wants to hear is "the statue by the Oscar Wilde memorial" in Dublin and that the issue she's most interested in focusing on is "poverty/abortion." Sara speculates about what the image meant to the artist ("she sort of looks accusing as well as despairing, yet she is so perfectly beautiful/birthing words/Oscar's mother/birthday something so genuinely beautiful only to later see him scorned" and "her hair is pulled back so tightly ... with perfect ringlets around a haunting face/expression/she looks more like she belongs in a fancy dress at a ball than naked, pregnant, on her knees").

Sarah notes that the process she knows well is "riding a Dressage test," a process that is precise and ritualised and hints of the kind of contrast that she has written about in her questions about the statue: beside the impeccable ritual of society that is presented in the fancy dress ball, she seems to suggest that we look at the reality of the women in the ballgowns dying as they gave birth; beside the rules of the society Oscar Wilde and his mother lived in were the ways that Oscar lived; beside the beauty and order of his work and life before the trials are his imprisonment and early death; beside his lionisation by society before is the shunning of him after. So, in her ideas, are sets of contrasts that are rich for investigation. I can easily imagine her performing a series of monologues for the Dublin statues of women who fascinate her, and all of us would like to hear what they would say.

Kay wanted to write "through the voice of Frida Kahlo on the evening that she was taken to her exhibition opening in Mexico on her bed. I used her voice to talk about disability and creativity, although of course it is all my own agenda." Kay was able to compose this poem as her freewrite during the workshop session. As audience members, we can easily see why she wanted this woman to speak directly about an issue she addressed through painting: Kay gives Kahlo another medium and allows her to extrapolate on the themes of the visual art. Though Kay says that these words represent her "own agenda," they fit with what we know of Kahlo and are reasonable suggestions for what she might have said, which help to make her real to us in the body she lived in.

> On a bed
> Lifted roughly through the streets
> limbs jarring,
> pain and fatigue scour my bones
> so fragile now i dare not lift my waist.
>
> As they used to laugh and jive and point
> refigure my body into humiliation,
> maybe today they see me,
> who i am,
> not what my body screams within their minds.
>
> Even so they cannot see the connection
> this body creates,
> it lives, and shapes, and flows,
> it is the stem from which my colours grow.
> My body is not the wounded vehicle for my soul
> it IS my soul.

jac s. m. kee's writing underscores women writers' need to honor women who give us permission to write ourselves. Jac wanted to hear more from Gloria Anzaldua and created a scene that allowed for dialogue:

> Gloria, she is alive. She is strong. She has wings. She can fly and speak to women in their dreams. And she knows when you need some spirit. She knows if you need some reminders about your own magic and energy. But she comes with a sharp tongue and the flicking of a cigarette. Steaming cup of coffee. When you forget who you are. When you are bloated with other people's words of flattery,

codes that you don't question, when your shadow stops the grass from growing, the tree from sprouting. I was in between. And she could feel my uncertainty and the pain hidden by layers of porcelain, clear plastic and wool.

She was waiting for me with a smile that quirks and two steaming cups of coffee at the green dining table with worn out wooden stools. We sat. It was empty, no one was about, so I rolled a cigarette and lit hers. We smoked in silence for some moments, watching the smoke curled up, then she asked me, why do I hate? Why am I feeling so suffocated by everything that reminds me of USA? Why do I get so choked up by black that I could no longer listen, stay still or stop my snarl from narrowing my eyes?

Gloria, don't you know? You spoke about what it means to be in close proximity, so intimate yet be invisible, like ants. Gloria, I don't know. I cannot see redemption from the self-centred aplomb that snakes from the 'American' flesh, blood, until you cannot separate what is legend and what shares your oxygen. The pus from the wounds is poisoning every single part of me, I am drowning in its poison. Before I learnt how to swim.

She looked at me and I saw she understood.

We sat in silence, smoked and sipped our coffee.

It lasts forever. Suspension.

Jac. You do know. Unlayer what you ought to and remember. Separate the. . . .

Ivana Radacic wrote for this article about the emotional impact of the workshop after she had reflected on it:

> It's a bit hard now to put in words the feelings I had during Georgia's workshop. It was much less hard to put my emotions in words during the workshop. Actually it was even easy, it felt so releasing. So releasing that I even cried. The words were just bursting out from me, and with them all my longings, pains, and fears.

This is the piece Ivana wrote at the workshop, part of the passage originally in Croatian:

Peggy was shivering. How could it be that she can just now finally see? Would it last? She cannot go blind again. Not now when she finally sees. The feeling of possibilities made her body shiver. This is possible? There is a world in this chaos we live in. There is this feeling of sheer happiness that she felt when she was in a womb, and that she still feels when she looks at her mum. There is SHE! She exists!!!! But, how scared she is! Would it go away? Would it disappear, shrink. . . .

So, this is being a woman. This is how it feels. Peggy cried. Her father will never know this woman. Would her mum? And sister? Would she? Is she this woman? Was she born this woman, or she is only to become? Would she be brave enough?

Sometimes we must say what we mean directly, writing as ourselves without images to carry the meaning, and when those words are effective they are most likely to be grounded in our own experience (or in what we as witnesses know to be the real experience, as of Kahlo, in Kay's poem). For some of us, politics is more often shaped by the expression art allows us. Instead of the thing itself, we are taken by the image that is drenched in feeling and shaped by the idea. We can describe the process and analyse its result, but when it works it is magic, and it bridges our lives within and without.

Our Black Sheep Theatre director, Mary Anne Maier, brought me plants from her garden when I returned from Ireland last year. Because we recently moved house, I had to leave behind plants that weren't yet up in March, and in some cases the next year would have been the time they were likely to spread and make their presence clear in the garden. Mary Anne told me to be patient with some of the new plant slips, saying: "first they sleep, then they creep, then they leap." We try to define ourselves daily in our conversations, speeches, and writing for work. But we are also activist artists, rhetors, storytellers, and performers who are constantly exploring what we may mean. I am thankful to have been reminded that we can say ourselves (and the characters and real people who capture our imaginations) into a wider reality, where shapes, colors, sounds, and feelings burst from rich images like Hortense from the blue box. We can tell and listen to stories, to imagine how another woman's experience gives her a certain kind of voice, how growing up in one landscape gives us appreciation for the effects of another, and how talk and research can take us so far. Then, like the garden, we leap.

Thanks to Ailbhe, Kay, Amy, Tonya, Sarah, Ivana, and jac for allowing me to quote them and speculate upon their workshop writing.

References

Bishop, Wendy. "Suddenly Sexy: Creative Nonfiction Rear-ends Composition." *College English.* 65 (2003): 257-275.

Foss, Karen A., Sonja K. Foss, and Cindy L. Griffin. *Feminist Rhetorical Theories.* Thousand Oaks, CA: SAGE Publications, 1999.

Higgins, Jim. *Irish Mermaids.* Galway: The Crow's Press, 1995.

Lysaght, Patricia. *The Banshee: The Irish Supernatural Death-Messenger.* Rev. Ed. Dublin: The O'Brien Press, 1996.

Quinn, Moira. "Sea, Symbolism and Women of the Waves," *Ms.chief* 12 (1996): 5-6.

Schutzman, Mady and Jan Cohen-Cruz. *Playing Boal: Theatre, Therapy, Activism.*London: Routledge, 1994.

Young, Richard E., Alton L. Becker, and Kenneth L. Pike. *Rhetoric: Discovery and Change.* New York: Harcourt, Brace & World, 1970.

Feminism in Divergent Lights: Mary Wollstonecraft vs. Godwin's *Memoirs* of Mary Wollstonecraft

Eva M. Perez

Before Godwin's presentation of Wollstonecraft in the *Memoirs*, the literary critics and public at large had known little of her. The *British Critic* reviewer of *Letters from Sweden* had assumed that she was married to Imlay, and Godwin himself admitted that before their first meeting in 1791 he had expected to see "a sturdy, muscular, raw-boned virago", and had judged her *Vindication of the Rights of Men* as filled with sentiments of a "masculine description" (Philp 109-10).

However, in the course of this paper I intend to show that Godwin, in his biography of Wollstonecraft, *Memoirs of the Author of A Vindication of the Rights of Woman* (1798), reverted, in most cases, to the sentimental clichés of the time as, for example, when he presents Wollstonecraft as endowed with a frame of mind full of "exquisite and delicious sensibility" (Philp 118). That was merely one of the contradictions that he incurred; alternatively, in spite of his criticisms of her style, he often appropriated her words when he quoted from her *Letters*; and, finally, at other times, he simply fell into contradiction between his intentions and his disappointing wording. The result is often an unfair and patronising account of Wollstonecraft's literary achievements and personal worth, in spite of Godwin's prior avowal of admiration. For example, Godwin's vindication of Wollstonecraft's character in the *Memoirs* is one of his most unsuccessful passages:

> There are no circumstances of her life that, in the judgement of honour and reason, could brand her with disgrace. [She had errors; but her errors, which were not those of a sordid mind, were connected and interwoven with the qualities most characteristic of her disposition and genius.] Never did there exist a human being that needed, with less fear, expose all her actions, and call upon the universe to judge them. (Philp & Clemit 127. Brackets enclose second edition amendments. Philp, Variants, 155)

Out of four sentences, three contain understatement or double negatives. The paragraph unfortunately raises doubts about Godwin's faith in the integrity of his wife's acts, whatever philosophical standard one applied to them. Unfortunately, his mention of her "disposition and genius" could be interpreted at the time as a reference to sensibility. In the aftermath of the French Revolution, and following the tide of criticism against Gothic and Sensibility novels, sentimental women could be interpreted in different lights, but always negatively: if they were taken for revolutionary Rousseauists, they were considered mindless and lustful; if, on the other hand, they were considered tough-minded, they were labelled as "unsex'd" (Barker-Benfield 377). The Anti-Jacobin, too, equated sensibility with un-Christian sexual licence in women. And although Wollstonecraft had criticised the excesses of sensibility on the grounds that it subjected women to a state of dependence on men (McCalman 112-114) she, too, eventually became the target of the anti-sensibility critics.

Another example of Godwin's inability to portray Wollstonecraft successfully comes at the end of the *Memoirs*, where he draws a comparison between his mental features and hers, but it is so unsatisfactory that he had to rewrite it. He failed again, because the passage disagrees with his previous judgement of her as a woman of literary worth, and because it reads as patronising and chauvinistic. For example, Godwin assures his readers that "in the strict sense of the term" Wollstonecraft "reasoned little" in view of which, "it is surprising what a degree of soundness is to be found in her determinations" (Philp 140). The amendment in the revision was rather ineffective: "In the strict sense of the term, she had reasoned comparatively little" (Philp, Variants 157).

Worse still, Godwin appropriated the use of associative language to draw a line between men and women's mental dispositions. But his own displeasure with this description of the "leading traits of [Wollstonecraft's] intellectual character" (Philp 140) led him to rephrase the whole final section, only to make it worse:

> A circumstance by which the two sexes are particularly distinguished from each other is, that the one is accustomed more to the exercise of its reasoning powers, and the other of its feelings. Women have a frame of body more delicate and susceptible of impression than men, and

in proportion as they receive a less intellectual education, are more unreservedly under the empire of feeling. (Philp, Variants, 156)

This comes as a shocking comparison since Godwin himself, in his account of Wollstonecraft's *Vindication of the Rights of Woman* had complained that men had "degraded" women "from the station of rational beings, and almost sunk them to the level of the brutes" (Philp 108). And, more relevantly still, his private notes say he acknowledged Wollstonecraft's unique endowments, as he asserts in one of his letters written days after her death that, "I firmly believe she has left no equal in her sex" (Abinger MS).[1]

One of Godwin's constant drawbacks as a biographer is his taste for the language of rationality, which explains why he was called 'the Philosopher' after the publication of *Political Justice* in 1793. For example, although the following is a relatively touching excerpt on his loss of Wollstonecraft, the vocabulary is mainly philosophical:

> The improvement I had reason to promise myself, was however yet in its commencement, when a fatal event, hostile to the moral interests of mankind, ravished from me the light of my steps, and left to me nothing but the consciousness of what I had possessed, and must now possess no more! (Philp, Variants, 157)

The mention of 'improvement,' 'reason,' the 'moral interest of mankind,' or the 'consciousness' in the expression of his pain, indicate that Godwin is never far removed from his rational pursuits, even when in mourning.

Fuseli and Imlay

On those occasions when Godwin praised Wollstonecraft without reserve, it was his readership that found fault with her behaviour and his candour. On the occasion of Wollstonecraft inviting herself to join Mr and Mrs Fuseli's household, Godwin says nothing, except to praise her integrity, as he maintains that:

---

[1] I would like to thank Lord Abinger and, on his behalf, Dr Bruce Barker-Benfield, for permission to consult and quote from the papers.

> Superior at the same time to the idleness of romance, and the pretense of an ideal philosophy, no one knew more perfectly how to assign to the enjoyments of affection their respective rank, or to maintain in virgin and unsullied purity the chasteness of her mind. (Philp, Variants, 152)

Fuseli's biographer, John Knowles, offers a radically different version of Wollstonecraft's gesture, which was, in his opinion, a "temerity" (cited in Tims 167). In such passages, Godwin, as a striving Romantic biographer, requires skills he does not possess. In the Variants to the first edition, Wollstonecraft was "chearfully submitting to the empire of circumstances" (Philp, Variants, 152), an optimistic use of words which, again, recalls the jargon of *Political Justice*. But, originally, "she repined when she reflected, that the best years of her life were spent in this comfortless solitude" a "source of perpetual torment" (Philp 113-14).

In the section of the *Memoirs* that deals with the affair between Wollstonecraft and the American dealer Gilbert Imlay, Godwin originally included ample quotations from Wollstonecraft's letters to the American:

> She nourished an individual affection, which she saw no necessity of subjecting to restraint; and a heart like hers was not formed to nourish affection by halves. Her conception of Mr Imlay's 'tenderness and worth, had twisted him closely around her heart'; ... This was 'talking a new language to her'; but, 'conscious that she was not a parasite-plant', she was willing to encourage and foster the luxuriancies of affection. Her confidence was entire; her love was unbounded. Now, for the first time in her life, she gave a loose to all the sensibilities of her nature. (Philp 118)

In the second edition, most of the paragraph was deleted and replaced by Godwin's rather unattractive psychological account of Wollstonecraft's move. In it he explains that she overreacted to Fuseli's rejection by falling for Imlay, a "very unequal" connection (Philp 118). Still worse, is Godwin's attribution of this mistake to her poor use of reason:

The mistake of Mary in this instance is easy of detection. She did not give full play to her judgement in this most important choice of her life. She was too much under the influence of the melancholy and disappointment which had driven her from her native land; and, gratified with the first gleam of promised relief, she ventured not to examine with too curious a research into the soundness of her expectation. (Philp, Variants, 153)

Marriage

One of the reasons for the severity of the public attacks against Godwin was his initial rejection of the institution of marriage in *Political Justice*. In Godwin's apologetic account of his and Wollstonecraft's decision to marry, he assures his readers that he would not have complied, had it not been for "accurate morality" and the necessity that Wollstonecraft, pregnant at the time, could gain "a surer footing in the calendar of polished society" (Philp 131). It is obvious that, for all his convictions, there may be a conflict between Godwin's sense of public duty and private affection. An undated note in Don Locke's biography of Godwin reveals how he related the onset of public animadversion to his marriage to Wollstonecraft:

> It was at that time my purpose to live and die a bachelor. I resolutely applied myself to the producing the mature fruits of my intellect unshackled by my superogatory impediments to the attainment of my object. That done, I had leisure to feel the burthen of a solitary life and I married. What was the moral offence I committed in this, I know not; nor do I know how much less of evil would have attended the decline of my life, if I had not married. (Locke 156-57)

In general, the accepted critical opinion of this period is that, as the cultural and political atmosphere changed, so did the contemporary views on Godwin, his philosophy and, by association, his wife. Of course, the reaction against Godwin's *Memoirs* was only part of a broader movement against sensibility that seized England from the mid 1790s onwards. As a result, all sorts of productions, from prints to novels, poems to pamphlets, were devoted to the slander of both Godwin and Wollstonecraft. The attacks hurt Godwin because they came from intellectuals who had previously sought him, or at least respected him if they did not agree with his ideas. Dr. Samuel Parr and James Mackintosh were two of those former friends and fellow radicals, but they later turned coats. With good judgement, Godwin asks of Dr Parr, "what crime I am chargeable with, now in 1800, of which I had not been guilty in 1794, when with so much kindness and zeal you sought my acquaintance" (Abinger MS). In addition to insults, attacks and criticism, Godwin was made to face demands for the settlement of Wollstonecraft's businesses:

> The answer I have to make to [the] letter is simply this: that I have surrendered the whole property of Mrs Godwin's posthumous works, without deriving a penny advantage from them; that I have paid and undertaken to pay her small debts, in addition to this, to the amount of about fifty pounds; that I was married to her five months; and that I have taken upon myself the care and support of her two children. More than this, under my circumstances, cannot, I think, be expected from me. (Abinger MS)

The heavy presence of financial terms in such a small paragraph is indicative of Godwin's preoccupation with money. Specifically, the mention to the "advantage" he could have derived from Wollstonecraft's "posthumous works" reveals his pragmatism in embarking on such a project. Godwin appears here as discharging himself from the obligation to fully pay off Wollstonecraft's debts on the grounds that their marriage was of a few months' standing. Such a careless denial of the marriage, together with the dubbing of little Fanny and Mary as only Wollstonecraft's children makes one flinch at the petulant businessman Godwin could become when he wanted.

Godwin as Editor of Wollstonecraft's Works
Daniel O'Quinn has done some very interesting work on Godwin's clumsiness as the mediator in Wollstonecraft's story. In an interpretation that merges Wollstonecraft's literary and political purposes in *Maria, or The Wrongs of Woman*, O'Quinn affirms that Godwin's intervention "significantly weakens not only Wollstonecraft's critique of the effects of literature, but also her analysis of the historical contingency of women's social confinement"

(778). In *Maria*, Godwin interferes with her creativity, chooses endings and variations, and closes the volume, which, today, could be considered post-modern by virtue of its multiple potential endings. In the following editorial comment Godwin excuses himself for interfering with Wollstonecraft's work:

> In revising these sheets for the press, it was necessary for the editor, in some places, to connect the more finished parts with the pages of an older copy, and a line or two in addition sometimes appeared requisite for that purpose. Wherever such a liberty has been taken, the additional phrases will be found inclosed in brackets; it being the editor's earnest desire, to intrude nothing of himself into the work, but to give to the public the words, as well as ideas, of the real author. (Kelly 81-82)

The reader is thankful to Godwin for his honesty as an editor. It is particularly interesting to read of both the words and ideas of his wife. He here shows his awareness that they wrote and thought differently. But, in reality, Godwin did not comply with his promise to "intrude nothing of himself" (Kelly 81-82).

The post-modern use of parenthetic additions poses a clear example of editorial intercession. Godwin found himself polishing what he considered the rough ends of *Maria*, whose radical and social themes were very similar to those of Godwin's *Caleb Williams*, published following the success of *Political Justice*. However, Wollstonecraft and Godwin's concerns were mostly different, and he maintains that her end was the presentation of "the misery and oppression, peculiar to women, that arise out of the partial laws and customs of society" (Kelly 184). In Godwin's own fiction, however, readers rarely find ex-prostitutes and women on the run from their brutish husbands. When they do appear, it is marginally, and always with mentions of their dissolute past. Bad women are not Godwin's forte. As a matter of fact, neither are good women, as he persistently tends to idealisation.

Godwin's most outstanding interference with textual annotations is in Wollstonecraft's 'Letters to Gilbert Imlay.' As the expression of love between the American and Wollstonecraft, the letters should have been left untouched – and unpublished. However,

Godwin was carried away by his publishing enthusiasm, and even these most personal of documents were dissected, expurgated, annotated and, eventually, given to the readership. One can only think of Godwin's prospects of the proceeds when accounting for his candour. But, as noted, Godwin was in the search for "the language of sentiment and passion", and he no doubt thought the correspondence some of "the finest examples", so much so that they are deemed superior to "the fiction of Goethe" (Todd 1989b: 367).

One of Godwin's unforgivable and rather tasteless confidences is the mention of Fanny Imlay as the "barrier girl" (Todd 1989b: 370), in an explanatory note that says she was conceived at the tollgate outside Paris where Imlay and Wollstonecraft met. The fact that Godwin omitted fragments from the original letters reveals his preoccupation about disclosing too much of his late wife's affair with Imlay. In particular, Godwin seems intent on hiding Imlay's financial dealings, which not even Wollstonecraft approved of (Todd 1989b: 388).

Rather uncharacteristically, Godwin breaks off some of the sentences he expurgates in mid-course, making no editorial apologies. It is through the latest editors of Wollstonecraft's works, Todd and Butler (1989), that we learn where Godwin cuts the text, and how many lines were removed (Todd 1989b: 395, 399, 407 *passim*). All in all, the letters to Imlay reveal more of Wollstonecraft's anxieties, desperation, dependence and, when she gave in, irrationality, than the *Memoirs*. They are amazingly sensitive, the reflection of a woman on the verge of extreme sentiment, whether destructive or loving. But they are also frank. Godwin, once more, in attempting to benefit from Wollstonecraft's exceptional use of sentiment, ignored that her feelings, and her letters, had better been kept within their envelopes.

References

Abinger MS. Godwin and Shelley Papers. Shelfmark Dep. b. 227/8 (a). Bodleian Library, Oxford. Uncatalogued.

Barker-Benfield, G. J. *The Culture of Sensibility. Sex and Society in Eighteenth Century Britain.* London: U of Chicago Press, 1992.

Kelly, G. ed., *Mary Wollstonecraft. Mary, A Fiction [1788] and The Wrongs of Woman [1798].* London: Oxford UP, 1976.

Locke, D. *A Fantasy of Reason: The Life and Thought of William Godwin.* London: Routledge & Kegan Paul, 1980.

Mc Calman, I. ed., *An Oxford Companion to the Romantic Age. British Culture 1776-1832*. Oxford: Oxford UP, 1999.

O'Quinn, D. "Trembling: Wollstonecraft, Godwin and the Resistance to Literature." *Journal of English Literary History*, Vol. 3 (1997): 761-88.

Philp, M. & P. Clemit, eds. *Memoir of the Author of A Vindication of the Rights of Woman* (1798). Vol. 1. *Collected Novels and Memoirs of William Godwin*. 8 Vols. London: William Pickering, 1992.

Tims, M. *Mary Wollstonecraft; A Social Pioneer*. London: Millington, 1976.

Todd, J. & Butler, M. eds., *Vindication of the Rights of Woman* (1792). Vol. 5. *Works by Mary Wollstonecraft*. London: William Pickering, 1989a.

Todd, J. & Butler, M. eds.,. "Letters to Gilbert Imlay" (1879). Vol. 6. *Works by Mary Wollstonecraft*. London: William Pickering, 1989b.

Looking Over My Shoulder – From a Work in Progress

Colleen Z. Burke

Born and bred
at Bondi under the smell
of surging surf, sewerage
scent of lonely Sundays
and trams hurtling to the
cluttered sea. Asphalt days.
Pools of summer shadows,
gullies, ferns, coral trees,
billy cart corners.
Tadpoles
changing shape and leaping away.

Days of shyness – clinging to my mother's dress – sitting beneath the dining/lounge room table, covered with a thick grey blanket, intent on biting the feet of mum, her sister, women friends who played cards endlessly.
How ya going love – you look lovely today.
Drinking, smoking – leaving the door of the toilet open – smell of piddle, perfume – hugging, kissing me deeply on the cheek – bright red lips imprinted forever.

A warren of relatives – Burkes, O'Briens, O'Connors, Lees, Ryans, Shaws, Tierneys, Collins, Fitzpatricks – next door, across the road, around the corner, in my school class.

Friday night tea – fish and chips from the Greek fish shop on Bondi Road. Mum's one night of respite from cooking, which was usually revolting – overcooked cabbage, cauliflower, tasteless curries, lank squishy tripe, giblet soup, chokos. Sunday ritual – a baked dinner. Every Sunday I gagged at soggy cabbage and Dad locked me in the bathroom until I'd eat it cold, but I never could.

Mum's culinary successes – wonderful apple pies and stewed white peaches from our backyard peach tree.

An occasional breakfast treat – Weetbix smothered in plum, apricot or strawberry jam, preferable to mum's winter glug of inedible porridge.

. . .
> Sometimes
> after the factory
> the 6 o'clock swill
> on winning streaks
> from card games
> dad would bring home
> two long jars of seaplucked oysters.
> My parents relished
> slippery slide dunked
> in Worcestershire sauce.
> A luxury.
> I gagged at slimy texture
> squishing down
> Oystertime. Quiet time.
> A week's wages still intact . . .

Both my parents gambled, but Mum mainly backed horses with Irish names. On Saturdays I'd go to the Chinese bookmaker chanting her instructions – *a 1/- each way 'Danny Boy' and 'Irish Eyes' for mum please.* Sometimes, the house would be shut up – the Police on the prowl, so I'd know to go to their other house in the next street.

One of the great occasions of my mother's life was backing, before I was born, 'Old Rowley' in the Melbourne Cup at 100 to 1. One of the names of my brother, born soon after.

St Patrick's day – a joyous day – my mother's day and I her *Irish Colleen*. It was as though my tiny vivacious mother, in passed-me-down bright silk frocks, from the Jewish families she cleaned houses for, had been re-born.

Smiling, singing, chasing radio stations for popular/sentimental Irish songs, Mum pinned green ribbons on us all. For us kids, after early mass, fervently belting out – *Hail glorious St. Patrick*, the day was ours.

Aunty Matt, a close friend of mum's, who lived a couple of doors down from us in an old weatherboard house, always had a stall at the Easter show. She dressed plastic dolls in scarlet, purple, pink and blue tulle, sprinkled with silver glitter. Their gold wavy hair, red lips and bright smiles shone through the gloom. They balanced on cane sticks like the fluffy monkeys. Every year her house was transformed. Magical.

Good Friday was our family day at the Easter show. My dad came as well. Different to our usual outings of mum plus kids. At school, just before Easter, the nuns would ask us what day we were going to the show. I was the only one who always said Good Friday. Sister Oleander would scream at me saying it was a mortal sin and we would burn in everlasting hellfire – couldn't we make a sacrifice – look at Christ, he died for you – I did look at Christ – he was my special friend. I constantly wept for the nails, thorns, blood. Every year I told mum what Sister Oleander said, and every year we went to the show on Good Friday. My enthusiasm was dampened by the nuns' curses. I worried about mum and dad roasting in hell, while I looked down from the safety of heaven.

The show was hot and crowded, but we loved it all – the showbags, smells, dirt, animals and displays of fruit and vegetables. We always wanted the Northern Rivers district in New South Wales, where my mother had grown up, to win. Her childhood memories of Lismore were our only link to the country. My brother and I had never left the city. Holidays were unheard of, we couldn't afford them, but as mum said – *we didn't need holidays because we lived by the sea.*

Every year I got a new doll and monkey from Aunty Matt's stall. During the Easter Show Aunty Matt was sober as a judge. At other times she would have a jar or two but, unlike my mum, held it well. When I came home from school and heard the crooked singing coming from our house, I would run and get Aunty Matt. She'd come with me, hug my mother saying – *Oh, my darling.* They'd cry and sing together – *When Irish eyes are smiling all the world is bright and gay, but when Irish eyes are laughing sure t'would steal your heart away.* I'd sit in a corner with my doll and monkey. Watch them dancing together. Stumbling, but never falling, laughing and crying – *oh, my darling.*

My family was Labor and mum was always sorry for the underdog. Dad, a trade unionist, was staunch to the Australian Labor Party (ALP) when it split apart in the 1950s, decimated by the fanatical anti-communism of the Democratic Labor Party (DLP). The DLP was Catholic-based, as was the ALP, which was largely founded on Irish Catholic working class Australia. From the pulpit the Priest preached allegiance to the DLP. It was the days of 'reds under the beds'. Dad was fired from the Kellogg's factory where he worked in the early 1950s, because he spoke to presumed communist workers after he was directed not to. Our endless supply of cornflakes came to an end.

I borrowed books from the penny dreadful library – *mum wants a juicy book with lots of murders please*. I escaped into the world of *Anne of Green Gables*, *What Katie Did*, *The Magic Faraway Tree*, *The Secret Seven*, *Famous Five*, the *Abbey* and *Billabong Books* – all so remote from my life. In little green notebooks I wrote stories in pencil about picnics in the bush with lavish meat, salad sandwiches, fruitcake and drinks as though I was starving to death. I wasn't.

When I was thirteen, mum gave me *Jane Eyre*, which I read and re-read.

For days after I started kindergarten at St. Patrick's Home Science and Commercial School, I'd cry and cry, try and escape, and run home in playtime. The school was run by the Sisters of St. Josephs, an Australian order – a picture of Mother Mary MacKillop, the founder, on every classroom wall. On special occasions we sang *Advance Australia Fair* not *God Save the Queen* – our allegiance to the Church, not the State. I attended St. Pat's until I left at fifteen, after the Intermediate, and thank the nuns for my total lack of domestic skills – can't cook or sew. But with appropriate use of terror – the cane – I did learn to type and did pass final exams.

For external exams we put topics in a hat, said a prayer to Our Lady and selected pieces of paper – we were lucky with topics the year I did my final exams, but I hedged my bets and studied as well.

Most of the priests at St. Patrick's Presbytery, in the same street we lived in, were Irish. In school concerts we sang – *Galway Bay, The Days of the Kerry Dancing, The Isle of Innisfree. Sure a little bit of heaven fell from out the sky one day* – our school entry in the annual Eisteddfod. My mother rented this lovely dress for me with layers of pale green tulle. I appeared at the end of the song holding a big shamrock – the only part of me visible – my feet.

At school or home we were always under surveillance. Someone always reported us to the nuns for not wearing hats, gloves, for being high-spirited, rowdy and, as teenagers, for wearing shorts to the beach on the weekend or loitering outside milkbars where the bodgies/widgies hung out, listening to rock n' roll – 'the devil's' music' – on the juke box.

When I was ten I said I wanted to marry a Burke and have ten children. But then thank god, or whoever, I grew up.

I was going to be called Maureen, but a cousin, born just before me, took the name and I used it for the heroine of my poem "To whom it may concern". The following extract highlights Catholic schooldays:

> We have known Maureen Ryan
> all her school life. We do not
> hesitate to say she will give you
> every satisfaction. At all times
> we have found her to be an
> obedient girl. *Maureen was scared of the*
> > *convent of the silence of*
> > *grass growing dead of nuns*
> > *drifting down concrete paths*
> > *whispering rosaries obscenities to god*
> > *their long robes rustling*
> > > *afraid of the*
> > > *thin mad fingers of sister oleander*
> > > *twisting girls around the classroom*
> > > *twisting their lives leasing*
> > > *them out on holidays watching*

through the open spaces
                in the
still gullies watching through
fingers groping deep in orangeclay
for shapes and
                Maureen was obedient

. . .

We do not hesitate to
recommend Maureen to you
protestant or catholic preferably
catholic   she is a girl with
a conscience who liked to go
                to early morning mass
                meeting the milkman
                with his horse and cart
                wellworn working men and women
                who went to church
                to pray in the warmth
                of the calm high colours
                and the bright sound
                of early morning slipping
                through stained glass windows

                Maureen
wore a white veil, red cloak on first Fridays
working a parole system against
purgatory for herself   others
a girl with a conscience whose
footsteps they followed saying
to think a bad thought was the same
as doing it so they slipped through
her dreams arranged her nightmares/her
guilt the voice in her head censoring
the devil while her guardian angel sat
on her left shoulder and watched
over her at night slaying dragons
devils men women while she dreamed a young
girl's dream and woke to the sound
of his pastel smile
                & a guilty conscience

Maureen was a good
pupil in secondary school
she came second in the class
and sang with feeling *faith of our fathers* and *o jesu me*
> *absorbed in the warmth of ritualised*
> *images oblivious to the dragging sound*
> *of their gowns across the floor the mad*
> *hooded eyes of sister oleander watching*
> *kneading her to shape because*
> *she didn't know the answers*

. . .

We do not hesitate to recommend
Maureen to you. She was always a good
pupil. Solitary at times alone on the asphalt yard
beneath the moreton bay fig tree alone in the girls
groups   sometimes stalking sister oleander
down the dead corridors mostly playing basketball
co-operatively
> everyone else playing competitively
> for the school to win
> for the girls to win
> > for the nuns

to win
> the girls

. . .

School and home life were separate yet entwined, the edges blurring. As young teens we often played in the schoolgrounds on weekends, using the tennis court, basketball court. And although the extract from my poem "The waves turn" focuses on family life – the sea, Irish influences, Catholicism and the role of women are constant refrains, melodies often out of sync, off-key.

. . .

ii

As a small child,
I saw my great grandmother
Mary O'Brien (nee Powell),
who'd married Timmy O'Brien
from Tipperary
drifting towards Tamarama
looking for Feakle,
County Clare. Tall as each other
we passed on the street.
Her eyes were blue   startling

iii

Inside the house
of my Irish grandmother
her girls smiled
burgundy smiles from
blackening walls

Grandad and I sat outside in
the stillness of cracking stone.
Nanna didn't drink/smoke/smile
went to mass several times
on Sundays – stray sermons fell
from her splintered knees she
bore six beautiful daughters four
handsome sons
they had remarkable teeth
she said I looked more like my mother
. . .

iv

. . . (who) was
catholic   Irish in thoughts
laughter   destruction   sailed
down the Richmond River with her
father to Tamarama.
            Later
she worked for Jewish families

Polished their silver
badly washed/absorbed their stains.
                    Baby sitting
at nights
                    we listened to
black wood panels creaking along the
radio the dark ache of silver waiting
to be stolen black waves stirring
salt wandering   berserk
through the suburbs.

                    We slept in
their featherbeds waiting . . . My mother
hated housework. Yearly the
missionaries curdled
her blood with heavy words till
her sins seemed large as death
within that wooden box.
                    Later I went to the
winebar for sherry we walked out
together to pawnshops.
                    Absorbed by the sea
she swam at Bondi never beyond the 'heads'
                    turned back
with the waves   she is dead
                    the waves turn
they are   within me these women
          strong   the sea   sours
towards the shore
and waves   turn   within me
                                        breaking

          . . . .

I started work in the city at sixteen
discovered the harbour, the Domain.
Worlds opening up – inner cities.
different ways of living, seeing.
Hungry for the classics, novels, poetry,
belonged to three public libraries.

Read on buses, walking down the street, in parks.
Everywhere.

Talking the night away with friends in coffee shops at the Cross, a
novelty then.

After 6pm Sunday Mass at St. Mary's Cathedral, arriving late, leaving
early, we went to Russian films in William Street, *Ivan the Terrible*,
Crime and Punishment, the *Battle Ship Potemkin*.

In infamous pubs heard my first real Irish songs – rebel songs, *Kelly
the Boy from Killanne*, *The Foggy Dew*, *Roddy McCorley* – Gaelic songs *An
Bunnan Bui* (*The Yellow Bittern*), *Eamonn An Chnuic* (*Ned of the Hill*) –
overwhelmed by the passion, beauty, sibilant, harsh flow of the
language.

Over the years I've questioned, changed some of my beliefs, my life,
but being Irish is in my blood, imagination. When my brother
discovered I was no longer a Catholic, he said I must be Protestant, or
English.

I wrote my first poem on my typewriter at work when I was seventeen
and kept on writing despite frustrations, rejections –
somehow incomplete if I wasn't imagining, worrying at poetry.
Wrote in secret for many years and have never stopped writing
exploring poetry, what it means to be human;
women's lives
and only occasionally now

                    looking over my shoulder

Mother as Theatre

Mary Dempsey

A child. The mother. An implant. The child as implant. The child blocks the view of the mother. The mother's view. Her view. What can she see? The child. Who is the child? Who is the mother? Where is the child looking? Where is the mother looking? The child is small. She sees the floor more easily. She sees the legs of the table. What does the mother see? She sees the trees and the sky. What do they say to her? They say leave the child. With the child the world is small. With mother there are the trees and the sky. There is the other. The other is outside the orbit of the mother and child. The other is other people, a community that exists for the mother yet doesn't exist because of the child. The child is dominated by the mother's view. The child does not see this view. She is tied to the mother and the mother is tied to the other. The other is represented by the mother's yearning. The yearning is the knot and the not. She can't see the other. The other is not. There is only the yearning. The yearning for the outside. The not/knot of the mother is also the child's yearning. The yearning for the mother. The mother is not here. The mother is the there. The mother is a language the child does not speak. The mother is the other. The not here where the floor is where the legs of the table are. The mother is the trees and the sky. The yearning. Why is the mother? The mother is blocking the child's view of the trees and the sky. The other. The mother does not see the child. The child is the other. The yearning. Is it a question of size? The trees. The eyes do not meet. In the space both are looking for utopia. The utopia of the gaze. The looking into. They are looking out. The trees. The space is badly designed for seeing, for looking. Into the child. The child is looking into the child. The home is the child. The child is looking out for signs. Signs of praise. The mother is not praising. The mother needs praise. The child does not praise. The child cries. The mother is crying too. The more the mother cries the more the child cries. The more the child cries the more the mother cries. They are lost. Time. Where is time? Time does not heal. Time is absent. Time lingers like a long twilight. Mother and child, signalling out. Which signal works? They are both signalling the father. It is time. There is no telephone. Ring for an ambulance to heal time. To carry time away. To carry absence away. Call for someone to kill time. It stays too long. It won't go away. It belongs to another place. Time is here. The mother wants to be there. Where time is not. Where time goes away. Go away. The child stays. The mother stays. The child becomes the mother. The mother gets lost. The mother meanders among the trees. The trees are not real. They are her imagination. She does not believe in the trees. She pretends she likes them. She hides in the trees but they are her prison. They can no longer be her freedom. Her freedom dies. Time killed it. Someone else stayed. A body, an outline. A silhouette. The mother does not see the child the child does not see the mother. There is temper, resentment. No time for the other. Who cares about the other. Now it is the mother the child. They do not see into each other's eyes. It is not a question of size. Time stole the outside, the community. The theatre of play. Time stole the theatre. The improvisation, the play. Time stole the relationship. The other is warped, an enigma, a science. Who is who? What changed? The enigma of belonging to the other. I am the other. I rarely play. I have no theatre. Home was not a theatre it was a monologue of disparate, disrepair. The *Disparaître. Paraître, Pater*. A parody of the outside. A play without inside. Outside the play of looking in, not seeing, not looking in.. What strengthens the seeing? The play. The dialogue. Who speaks first, what is the order, what is the sequence? Who manages the arrest. *Arrêt*. I see. Seeing through play. The dialogue. Who sees? Speaking is seeing. The words see. I don't see. I use words to see. I play. I theatre. I create theatre. The mother. The theatre is my mother. The play. The play acts. I act. Who plays the mother. The conscious? The I? Overwhelmed by the I, the mother. The mother. The mother as I am.. The I of me. Me, the play. The theatre. I play me. The I. I don't see the other. The I. I have forgotten me, the mother. The I. I was the mother. Virgin mother. I not pater. The mother. The other. Time killed the mother, the other, the udder. The utter.

It seems. The play. The image. The yearning. The longing. The image of the I. I want communication. The I wants to communicate. The I of me. I long to communicate the blessing of the mother. The mother, the other I. I give. I take. I look I see the mother. The mother is hiding from the mother. I don't see. I don't see the mother. I play. I play in language. I move. I take I give. I play the other, the mother. I give I take I play the other the mother I play. I theatre. I am the theatre of the mother. I am the theatre where my mother plays. I play. The theatre of the mother. The props of the mother. The call. I call. She calls. In the theatre I see the legs of the table, the ground. She looks at the trees and the sky. I can't see the trees and the sky. I am tired of looking. I speak. The theatre. I imagine the mother. The mother the theatre. I play. The looking. The I ing. I achieve…. The mother lost in the trees. I achieve. I see. She doesn't see I. I love. I love. I love I I am I love. I love. I don't see, I love. II am the mother, achieving the mother. I achieve. I the mother I I love. I achieve the I. The theatre me.

CULTURE

Woman's Image Transformed: The Sufism of Ibn 'Arabi

A. Clare Brandabur

Recent studies show that Jalal al-Din Rumi, or Mevlana (1207-1273), was the most widely read poet in America in the 1990s. However, as Dalrymple points out in an article on Rumi's popularity, it is doubtful that many of those who hear his words sung by Madonna or read his poems in trendy English translations (like those of Coleman Barks) realise the nature of its origins as being composed originally in Persian, and that its appealing attitudes toward love, sexuality, and death, grow out of an orthodox Sunni tradition of Islamic mysticism (Arberry 1). Modern devotees might be even more surprised to learn that the poetry of Rumi contains within it a fusion of two distinct branches of Sufism, one Persian and the other Arabic, the latter from a tradition embodied in the work of Muhyiddin Ibn 'Arabi (1165-1240). At the same time as Rumi has been discovered in the English-speaking world, this Arab Islamic mystic poet, who was Rumi's contemporary, has also experienced what is perhaps a slightly more scholarly resurrection.

Muhyiddin Ibn 'Arabi was born in Murcia in Spain, but visited Rumi in Konya during his extensive travels and, like that of his younger colleague, his work has also recently become widely available in English translation. This paper will try to summarise what is now known of this confluence of the Persian and Arabic Sufi traditions, which came about through the interaction between Rumi and the Islamic mystic and poet Ibn 'Arabi.

Muhyiddin Ibn 'Arabi, or the Sheikh Al-Akbar ('the greatest teacher'), was a contemporary of Rumi, who left his home in Murcia, Spain, and travelled extensively through Andalusia, the Maghreb, and Saudi Arabia, before journeying on to Anatolia, Iran, Iraq, Palestine, and Syria. He visited Konya at the time of the great flowering of Sufism and the mystical tradition of which Rumi, also called Mevlana, and his community were at the centre. The inter-weaving of the two separate Sufi traditions was brought about primarily through the intermediary of an adopted son and spiritual heir of Ibn 'Arabi, Sadr al-Din Qunawi, who was nearer in age to Rumi than his father/mentor, and who became an intrinsic part of the community in which Rumi's thought achieved its mature development. As we shall also see, the two great mystics agree in finding love at the centre of all things: for example, Talat Halman, eminent Turkish scholar, poet, and translator, titled his essay on Rumi "Love is All: Mevlana's Poetry and Philosophy" (1992). In addition, central to the teachings of both Rumi and Ibn 'Arabi, is a profound respect for women.

Like Ibn 'Arabi, Jalal al-Din Rumi taught that the feminine is not opposed to the masculine, but encompasses and combines the two:

> Woman is a beam of the divine Light.
> She is not the being whom sensual desire takes as its object.
> She is Creator, it should be said.
> She is not a Creature. (Rumi cited in Corbin 160)

This elevation of woman to a high position in the divine plan correlates directly with the teachings of Ibn 'Arabi, and was expressed with great eloquence by Etel Adnan, a Lebanese-American feminist painter and poet who, having been asked by her friend Fawwaz to write an essay on women, told him that, though she did not have time for an essay, she would instead write him letters about the particular problems of women in the places to which she would be travelling over a period of months. Her letters are collected and published as *Of Cities and Women: Letters to Fawwaz*. Among them is a letter from Berlin in which she records seeing the white sheets flying from windows in protest at the American bombing of Baghdad during the first Gulf war, and another from a Greek island about a woman who had been taken away to a mental hospital, having been locked in her room for years as punishment for refusing to marry the man of her parents' choice. And she writes from Murcia in Spain recounting the ideas she learns in a conference commemorating the 750th anniversary of the death in Damascus of Ibn 'Arabi. What she discovers is an esoteric system of thought, which is in full flowering. From Murcia, Adnan writes:

> The first texts we hear throw us into the piercing clarity brought upon the invisible world that characterizes Ibn 'Arabi's thought. We hear his theorems on Divine essence, art, and attribute, and the relationships he establishes

amongst the modalities of the Divine. Also evoked are a kind of oneiric perception, the apparitions through dreams and sleep, the communications through the night which were linking the disciples of Ibn 'Arabi with each other and they, with the Master. It is as if they were surrounded by an abundance of Revelation. […]

This morning, among the speeches, there was one that was of particular interest to me: a remarkable discourse on the role of Woman in Ibn 'Arabi's thought. Ibn 'Arabi is the only great theologian of History that has given woman absolute equality within the Absolute. Thus for him, the world is held in balance because it is upheld by a human, living, pole–a qutb–who at his death is immediately replaced by another. If this pole were missing the world would falter into definitive chaos. And by affirming that this pole can be a woman, Ibn 'Arabi gives women a primordial function in the essential economy of the universe. The image of woman in Ibn 'Arabi represents – in the XIIIth century–a turning point in the genesis of the Notion of 'woman' in the Arabo-Islamic world and, by way of influence, in Western thought.

Divine wisdom, thought Ibn 'Arabi–before Dante, and those who followed him–is feminine; and human love is always a scandal because it is always a necessity; a model of divine love.

He starts from actual and concrete love: he writes: 'You have to be in love with a beautiful young girl. Through her you have experienced happiness and joy. Offering her beauty the wine of intensity, you have secretly conversed with the suns and discoursed with the full moons'. 'In front of she who radiates solar light when she smiles,' he says, 'adieu to the self, and to patience.' 'This woman's word restores life. She is indomitable'.

'Thanks to this human love the vision that unifies all love arises: Love as love is one, though the objects of this love are different.' The experience thus lived of Love's unity leads Ibn 'Arabi to the vision of the unity of the Whole, making him 'find in the most specific mountains and valleys a counterpoint to the divine stations.

Everything is exalted by the woman; she traverses the signs of the zodiac at their highest point. She is the   morning that rises into the sky, the rose that arises from tears. Her throne is a high mountain, for she transcends the world. And from there, the sky of light is under her feet, her diadem, beyond the spheres. She establishes – on the human, as well as mystic level – harmony and union.

Yes, my dear friend, a XIIIth century Arab sufi, in this old city of Murcia, has awakened in me the need to know where I stand with myself, and where we are in the face of things. The formidable questions he raised, with his clairvoyantly insane quest of the divine, the disquietude that must have underlined his apparent certainties, seem close to our sensibilities and torments. Are we going to exist? Will our civilization survive? (50-52) [1]

Adnan's reflections following this lecture are indicative of how much the discourse has influenced her, what vertigo it makes her feel, and she reflects:

I tell myself that we are terrorists, not terrorists in the political and ordinary sense of the word, but because we carry inside of our bodies–like explosives–all the deep troubles that befall our countries–and travelling doesn't change anything in any way. We are the scribes of a scattered self, living fragments, as if parts of the self were writing down the bits and ends of a perception never complete." (54).

Spain (or should I say the Inquisition?) has carefully erased the traces of its Arabs. And this cultural genocide was soon followed by the slaughter of the Indians . . . and Spain will tomorrow celebrate the quintcentennial of its conquest!

These last few days we have spoken of Ibn 'Arabi as if we were dealing with a ghost or a shadow. Where is his house? Where are the places he frequented, the libraries of his parents, the gardens in which he played?

Hearing the Arabic words behind the Spanish ones, I tell myself that Andalusia is the first loss, the death of the Mother, and of the orchards of which Lorca was the last tree.

[1] Permission to quote at length from Etel Adnan's *Of Cities and Women* was granted by the publisher, The Post-Apollo Press, in August 2005.

Ibn 'Arabi pursued the Whole when all the details were falling one after the other around him. He had foreseen the fall.

Spain has been a mirror for me. An enormous mirror in which my reflection is but a small fragment. There are a lot of people in this mirror: people of yesterday and people of today, women, men, children, animals, plants. In the memory of a woman there is always the memory of several others, as if to be woman and to be memory were one and the same thing. (55-56)

Speaking from multiple layers of identities – as a poet, as an Arab, as a woman, as an exile, as a lesbian – Adnan gives us the quality of Ibn 'Arabi's spirituality filtered through her own poetic sensibility, so responsive to the tragic history of Islamic Spain, its multi-cultural golden age shattered, not only by the Inquisition, but also by fratricidal conflicts among the disputed leadership of Andalusia in the Middle Ages, and set in the perspective of modern times – the rise of fascism, the Spanish civil war, the bombing of Guernica, and the murder of the poet Lorca.

Among many questions concerning the ecstatic celebration of woman to which Adnan has responded with such sympathy and recognition, is this: if this breakthrough in Islamic thought happened, where did it go? How much of it persists in the work of those who were influenced by Ibn 'Arabi? And further, how much of it, if any, accounts for the fascination of a contemporary generation with the poetry of Jalal al-Din Rumi? How much of it, in effect, was transmitted to the Konya or Eastern Sufi tradition, and is it possible to trace the circumstances of this influence?

Thanks to a resurgence of interest in this subject, there has been a proliferation of translations and commentaries concerning the work of both Rumi and Ibn 'Arabi. The late Annemarie Schimmel has written an insightful biography of Rumi, *As Through A Veil: Mystical Poetry in Islam* (2001). The major work of Rumi, *The Masnavi*, has been partially translated several times, but the first and most complete English edition is *The Mathnawí of Jalálu'ddín Rúmí*, edited from the oldest manuscripts available, with critical notes, translation and commentary by Reynold A. Nicholson; A.J. Arberry has translated Professor Badi' al-Saman Furuzanfar's 1952 edition of Rumi's prose writings, *Fihi Ma Fihi* as *Discourses of Rumi*; Reynold A. Nicholson's *Divan-i Shams-i Tabriz* is subtitled "Selected Poems from the Divani Shamsi Tabriz". Nicholson has also contributed to *A New Collection of Ecstatic Poems: The Soul of Rumi* by Coleman Barks, *et al*; in *The Essential Rumi*, Coleman Barks and John Moyne have published a fascinating selection in English translation from the *Mathnawi*, the six books of poetry dictated by Rumi to his scribe, Husam Chelebi, which the poet sometimes also called, Barks says, "The Book of Husam." An important study of Persian mystical poetry by Ahmed Ghazzali, *Sawanih: Inspirations from the World of Pure Spirits: The Oldest Persian Treatise on Love,* has been translated from the Persian with a commentary and notes by Nasrollah Pourjavady. These are only a few of the studies of Rumi and his work to appear in quick succession in the last few years. On at least one occasion, Rumi's work has been made to serve a political purpose: a dramatic reading from Rumi's *Mathnavi* was presented as 'Theatre for Peace' in 2005 by the Triangle Theatre in Phildelphia, and the Creative Alliance in Baltimore and the Centre for Global Peace.

Concerning Ibn 'Arabi also, there has been a steadily growing scholarship in several languages, including English. The impressive biography by Claude Addas has been translated from the French into English under the intriguing title *Quest for the Red Sulphur: The Life of Ibn'Arabi* (1993), with its mysterious overtones of alchemy. In the Introduction to his translation of Ibn 'Arabi's *Sufis of Andalusia (The Ruh al-Quds & al-Durrat at-Fakhirah)* (1971), R.W.J. Austin has provided a brief outline of his subject's life and prodigious output. Of Ibn 'Arabi's two major works, at the time of writing, Austin says, "his two most important works are the monumental *Futuhat* and the *Fusus al-hikam*: of these only the latter has been partially translated by Titus Burckhardt" (Austin 47). Importantly, especially for English readers, the Muhyiddin Ibn 'Arabi Society has been formed,[1] whose journal is an excellent source of further scholarly discussion and information.

According to Robert Briffault, Ibn 'Arabi's work provided a model for that of Dante Alighieri. In particular, Briffault demonstrates, Ibn 'Arabi's idealisation of the beautiful woman Nizam, whom Ibn 'Arabi met and heard preach in a mosque at Mecca, could conceivably

---

[1] PO Box 892, Oxford OX2 7XL, UK. E-mail: mias.uk@ibnarabisociety.org. Website: http://www.ibnarabisociety.org

have provided the pattern for Beatrice in the *Comedia*. Of the impact of Ibn 'Arabi on his own times, Briffault says:

> At the time when Brunetto Latini visited the Arabian academy at Toledo, the world of Islam had been thrown into a ferment by the doctrines of a mystic, Ibn Ali Ibn Arabi of Murcia, who had died twenty years earlier and had been raised to the rank of Saint and prophet. Ibn Arabi had begun his career as a Sufi poet [...] But Ibn Arabi had shortly after thrown all philosophical sobriety to the winds, and the expression of his mystical exaltation assumed the form of visions and allegories [...] His chief work, *Al-Futuhat*, 'Light' (or 'Emanation'), dealing with the 'Knowledge of God,' explains the effect produced on 'intelligences' by the radiations or emanations of the supreme sphere. Taking up an ancient traditional theme, developed by Muhammed Ibn 'Abd Allah Ibn Masarra of Cordova, Ibn Arabi describes the evolution of 'intelligence' under the similitude of the journey of a philosopher. Taking Jerusalem, the center of the earth, as his point of departure, he visited, under the direction of various guides, the circles of hell and Limbo and ascended to the height of the spheres of the Moon, Mercury, Venus, the Sun, Mars, Jupiter and Saturn, eventually reaching the throne of the *Primum mobile* (Briffault 175).

Following this, Briffault talks about the analogous pattern of Dante's *Convito,* and discusses the claim of Asin Palacios (in *Dante y el Islam*), that "Dante's *Comedia* is, in conception and in detail, completely derived from this legend of the voyage of Mahomet [sic] into the other world, as it was told by Ibn Arabi, in the *Futuhat*" (284). However, Briffault dismisses this claim, saying that, "the theme abounds in all of Celtic literature" (284), but then affirms a far more general and profound debt to Arab culture – on the part not only of Dante, but the whole of European culture – one rarely acknowledged in most discussions on the subject in a climate in which debts to the Arab world are easier to ignore than to acknowledge:

> However, it is also necessary in a different connection to keep in mind that *Dante's entire intellectual culture, and that of the Middle Ages as well, issued from Arabic works or was*

actually transmitted by the Arabs. Hence it is quite natural that, being imbued with a culture and thought of Arabic origin, Dante manifested this filiation of his spirit in his great poem as well as in the rest of his works. Although the notion of a voyage to the world beyond the grave is too widespread for it to be necessary to assume that Dante borrowed the Notion from the Arabic tradition, the same cannot be said for the manner in which he made use of it. The philosophical novel is a peculiarly Arabic type. Thus, for example, Ibn Tofail, when he presents his theory of the development of innate thought (a quite erroneous conception, by the way), did it in the form of a philosophical novel, a sort of Robinson Crusoe tale, dealing with a child who miraculously grew up on a desert isle.[...] Thus, if we have understood the sources of Dante's inspiration, we should not have been surprised to have noted that throughout the tour the whole arrangement and architecture of the world beyond the grave, the circles of the inferno, those of the hill of Purgatory and of the spheres of Paradise, as well as their location, and innumerable details of the punishment received by the damned and the pleasures enjoyed by the saints, correspond exactly to those which Al-Arabi gave in his elaboration of the Islamic legend. (284-5. My emphasis)

It is not clear whether Dante's Beatrice and Petrarch's Laura, like Ibn 'Arabi's Nizam, refer to real women or whether, by the time these Italian poets inherited the tradition, it had become merely a formula. 'L'aura' means light, and 'Beatrice' means the 'blessed,' that is, the one admitted into the presence of the Divine Light. Briffault takes up this question in detail concerning Petrarch's muse and concludes there is not a shred of evidence that any real woman was involved, noting that, "the name 'Laura' very likely is drawn from Arnaud Daniel, Petrarch's favorite troubadour, who enjoyed making puns on the word 'l'aura'" (288).

From the new information about the life of Ibn 'Arabi, we see a concensus, as we have already mentioned, that it was Ibn 'Arabi's stepson and spiritual disciple Sadr al Din Qunawi (1206-1274) who exerted the most direct influence on Jalal al-Din Rumi and his beloved Shams al-Din. Through his Commentaries on his Master's work, and through his personal example and conversation, Qunawi transmitted much of the theology and mystical teaching of his father to the Konya circle, which was an important centre of Eastern Sufi mysticism in the thirteenth century. This is the opinion of Claude Addas who, in a meticulously detailed chronology, establishes that Ibn 'Arabi lived from 1165 to 1240, while Jalal al-Din Rumi was forty-two years younger – born in 1207 and died in 1293. Rumi would have been born two years after Ibn 'Arabi's first visit to Konya in 1205 (Addas 296-310).

The sophisticated and geographically extensive achievement of the Islamic Sufi tradition is all the more astonishing when we realise that the period in which it developed and was maintained was one of upheaval and disaster. Because of military and political strife, Sufis became pilgrims and wanderers and, for many, Konya became a refuge under the relatively tolerant rule of the Seljuks. Because the Sufi orders were among the first to be targeted for persecution in times of strife, it was often they who were forced to leave during political conflict. The Crusaders were still arriving from the West, while the Mongols were moving in from the East, devastating whole cities and whole kingdoms. In the Fourth Crusade of 1204, the semi-literate Franks of the Fourth Crusade destroyed part of Constantinople by fire, and looted its libraries and churches of thousands of manuscripts and sacred works of art. The Mongols were laying waste to parts of the East – Ghenghis Khan reached the Yellow River in China in 1205 – close to the time of the Fourth Crusade and roughly the same year as Ibn 'Arabi's first visit to Konya. The years 1200-1202 saw famine in Egypt and severe earthquakes in Syria. The Crusaders attacked Hama and re-took Sidon in Syria. Meanwhile, in Spain, the so-called 'Reconquista' was underway, threatening and destabilising the Almohad dynasty. The city of Baghdad, and with it the Caliphate, finally fell to the Mongols in 1258 (Addas 141 cf, 208-9).

In addition to his important contribution to the mystical tradition of Rumi, the journey of Ibn 'Arabi to Konya is also responsible for documenting the history of representational painting in Konya in the thirteenth century, as Duggan has pointed out.[1]

---

[1] According to Duggan, the existence of a highly developed tradition of naturalistic art can be inferred from the detailed descriptions in the writings of Ibn 'Arabi like the example given above, though none of the paintings from that period is known to have survived.

Duggan bases his findings on the *Futuhat II*, of Ibn 'Arabi, Rumi's *Mesnevi*, and an account by Shemsed-Din Ahmet Dede Aflaki, whose book, *Menakkib al Arifin*, was begun in 1318 and completed in 1353 (Duggan 281-3). Duggan quotes from the *Futuhat* (a passage also cited by Austin) in which Ibn 'Arabi records an encounter with a painter in Konya whose life-sized, fully realistic painting of a partridge was attacked by a falcon, deceived by the perfection of the representation into thinking it a real bird (Duggan 283). No naturalistic paintings are known to survive from this period, but a graphic tradition developed later from a manuscript that was started forty-five years after Rumi's death, according to Talat Halman. Shams al-Din Ahmad al-Aflaki wrote of Rumi in Persian, recording miraculous achievements, which renowned Orientalist scholar Edward G. Browne admits are "quite incredible" (Halman 47). Aflaki's work, Halman says, was recast later by Abd al-Wahhab Ibn Jalal al-Din Muhammad al-Hamadani. This work, entitled *The Luminaries of the Legends* was, in turn, later translated into Turkish by Mahmud Dede, a follower of Mevlana, who presented his translation to Sultan Murad III (1588 or 1589). In its final version (1590), this work, *Translation of the Legends of the Luminaries*, contains twenty-two miniature paintings, many of which are beautifully reproduced in Halman and Metin And's book on Mevlana (59-74). Halman mentions copies of this manuscript in the Morgan library in New York and in the Topkapi Palace Museum in Istanbul (47).

If we compare the poetry of the *Tarjuman al-Ashwaq* or *Mystical Odes* of Ibn 'Arabi with the poetry of Rumi, in spite of the similarity of theme, there is an interesting difference in the selection of metaphors used to speak of the longing of the soul for the Divine Beloved. In the Persian tradition many images of the rose, the nightingale, of wine and the tavern occur as metaphors for longing for divine union. Whereas in the *Turjuman al-Ashwaq*, we find images taken from the pre-Islamic Arabic poetry centring on the lamentation over the campfires of the caravan of the departed beloved, and images of pilgrimages by camel caravans to Mecca, which provide metaphors for the sense of abandonment by the Divine. The second of the *Mystical Odes*, for example, begins: "On the day of parting they did not saddle the full-grown reddish-white camels until they had mounted the peacocks upon them" and, later, "the day when they departed on the road, I prepared for war the armies of my patience, host after host", and the stanza ends, "I exclaimed, when her she-camel set out to depart, 'O driver of the reddish-white camels, do not drive them away with her!'" (31). Ode VIII begins, "Their abodes have become decayed, but desire of them is ever new in my heart and decayeth not./These tears are shed over their ruined dwellings, but souls are ever melted at the memory of them" (63). According to Ibrahim Musa Al-Sinjilawi, in his book *The 'Atlal-Nasib in Early Arabic Poetry* (1999), many traditional Arabic odes express mourning for the dear ones who have left, the poet grieving over the abandoned abodes or camp sites of departed friends. For example, "Oh, abodes of the tribes in al- Barandan! Eight years have passed over them since I left./Nothing remains of them except a broken up trench and posts now buried in the sand like the wells" (89). Another example, given by Al-Sinjilawi, is the opening of an 'atlal by Mu'allaqah of Labid: "Effaced are the campsites, both the stopping points and the campgrounds, in Minan both Ghaul and Rijam have become the haunts of wild beasts" (93-4). These campsites would have been the resting places of the camel caravans, and it is this tradition that figures so largely in Ibn 'Arabi's *Turjuman al-Ashwaq*. For the much-travelled Ibn 'Arabi, the camel caravan generally, and the pilgrimage to Mecca in particular, hold a more important place in the poetic imagination than for Rumi who writes from within the Persian poetic tradition.

Another rich vein in the writings of Ibn 'Arabi, for the contemporary seeker of wisdom, concerns the work of spiritual direction. The guidance of novices in the Way was one of the most important aspects of the pastoral work of Ibn 'Arabi, as Addas records. In terms familiar to Christian aspirants to perfection, from the writings of John of the Cross and Teresa of Avila, Ibn 'Arabi recommended the practice of *muhasaba* or daily examination of one's conscience, a practice which he did not limit to reviewing of actions, but which extended even to thoughts (Addas 164).

According to Austin, Ibn 'Arabi stands at the crossroads of the Sufi tradition both in time and in space: he was the first of the Andalusian and Maghreb Sufis to record and systematise what had been largely oral history and practice, passed by *silsilah* from one Master to the other, in a tradition going back to the Prophet (57). And, at the same time, through his wide travels, which he undertook as his special vocation, he sought out, visited, spoke to, and prayed with an incredible number of the Folk, the initiates of the Sufi tradition, finally leaving the western European world and permanently relocating in the East – Saudi Arabia, Iran, Turkey, Palestine, and Syria, finally settling in Damascus where he lived for seventeen years and where he was to die (Austin 45). His motive for this constant travel seems to have been a sense that his vocation was to communicate the Sufi truth to the leaders of the whole world, rather than merely take refuge from political danger. However, in some places he was accused of heresy and threatened with imprisonment and even death, as, for example, in Egypt (Austin 39). Austin summarises Ibn 'Arabi's importance thus:

> The very great significance of Ibn'Arabi for the history of Sufism rests on two things: firstly, he was the bridge or link between two historical phases of Islam and Sufism; secondly, he was the link between Western and Eastern Sufism. (48)

Ibn 'Arabi, Austin argues:

> gave expression to the teachings and insights of the generations of Sufis who preceded him, recording for the first time, systematically and in detail, the vast fund of Sufi experience and oral tradition, by drawing on a treasury of technical terms and symbols greatly enriched by centuries of intercourse between the Muslim and Neo-Hellenistic worlds. (48)

Perhaps the synthesis he made of contemporary Sufism and its history would not have been made at all had it not been for the unique vocation of this itinerant mystic, who had been introduced to Averroes as a boy (Addas 107), and visited every holy person, some of them women, in Andalusia before travelling through Palestine, Arabia and on to Konya. In Austin's view:

> It was because he was also the link between eastern and western Sufism, and that, at a particularly important time, his influence was so profound and widespread. The link was forged, as mentioned above, during Ibn 'Arabi's visit to Konya in 607 / 1210 when he took as his disciple Sadr al-Din al-Qunawi. It was through the latter's links with some of the most eminent Persian Sufis that Ibn

'Arabi's teaching reached the East. Suffice it to say that he was master to Qutb al-Din al-Shirazi, the notable commentator on the Ishraqi philosophy of Suhrawardi, and Fakr al-Din al-Iraqi, the great mystical poet, and an intimate friend of Jalal al-Din Rumi, author of the monumental verse compendium of Sufi lore, the *Masnavi*. (49)

Austin summarises: "This influence of Ibn 'Arabi was not limited to the theoretical side of Sufism, but penetrated deeply into the fabric of Sufi life as a whole. Through Rumi in the East and Abu al-Hasan al-Shadhili in the West, two of the greatest Sufi orders were permeated by his teachings (Austin 48-49).

As Adnan suggests above, the source of Ibn 'Arabi's spiritual awakening, regarding the role of woman in the spiritual life, stems from a vision or epiphany in Mecca. Corbin provides a detailed account of this crucial experience, saying that a prayer for inspiration rose to the lips of the "interpreter of ardent desires" (Corbin 44) some years later when, on a night of pensive melancholy, he circumambulated the *Ka'aba*. For Corbin, it is unimportant whether this ritual was real or an interior or spiritual actuality: "That night in any case he heard the answer – from the lips of Her who, as long as he lived, would remain for him the theophanic figure of Sophia aeterna" (Corbin 44). According to Corbin:

> In 598/1201 when he reached Mecca, the first goal of his pilgrimage, Ibn 'Arabi was thrity-six years of age. This first stay in the holy city was to be so profound an experience that it formed the basis of what we shall read later on about the 'dialectic of love.' He received the hospitality of a noble Iranian family from Ispahan, the head of the house being a shaikh occupying a high post in Mecca. This shaikh had a daughter who combined extraordinary physical beauty with great spiritual wisdom. She was for Ibn 'Arabi what Beatrice was to be for Dante; she was and remained for him the earthly manifestation, the theophanic figure, of *Sophia aeterna* (Corbin 51).

This interpretation of Corbin is affirmed by Addas, who cites Corbin approvingly when he discusses the decisive role of Nizam for the spiritual life and the writing of Ibn 'Arabi, attributing to her inspiration the writing of the *Tarjuman* or *Mystic Odes*. Here, he quotes from the *Tarjuman* XI vv.13-6:

> My heart has become capable of all forms:
> For gazelles, a meadow, for monks, a monastery,
> A temple for idols, the pilgrim's Ka'aba,
> The Tablets of the Torah, the Book of the Qur'an.
> I profess the religion of Love, and whatever the direction
> Taken by its mount, Love is my religion and my faith.
> (Ibn 'Arabi cited in Addas 211)

This exaltation of woman, in Ibn 'Arabi's mystical poetry, seems to have carried over into the practice and everyday life of this great mystic. According to Addas, all three of the people he mentioned as wanting to take with him to Paradise were women (87). His biographers agree that he was married several times, the first at a very young age to a woman to whom he attributed great sanctity. Her name was Maryam bint Muhammad b.'Abdun. In Austin's biography we find a long quotation from Ibn 'Arabi himself, in which he describes the spiritual experience of his saintly wife, attributing to her, without the least sign of jealousy or doubt, the attainment of mystical insight, which he himself had not achieved (22-23). Later, he attributes to his tiny daughter, Zeinab, a precocious mystical understanding when she was barely able to walk (Austin 46).

After his experience with Nizam at Mecca, his colleagues warned him about what had happened three centuries earlier to Mohammed al-Hallaj, the quintessential Sufi mystic, who had been too open in his ecstatic utterance that 'I am He and He is I' and had been killed for his blasphemy. Thus, Ibn 'Arabi had to disguise his intuition about the role of women to avoid being condemned as a heretic. He even warns his reader that he will disguise his insight: "Every time I mention a name it is her I am naming. Every time I refer to an abode (dar) it is her abode I am describing" (Addas 209). However, he immediately cautions the reader, "in composing these verses my allusions throughout were to divine inspirations and spiritual revelations" (Addas 209).

The nature of Ibn 'Arabi's relationship with the Persian Sufis at Konya is detailed in Addas's *Quest for the Red Sulphur*. First of all, his biographers agree that Ibn 'Arabi was married to the mother of Sadr al-Din Qunawi, the widow of the Sheikh Qunawi, who was Ibn 'Arabi's close friend. Thus, depending on what year the child was born, it is likely that Sadr al-Din was either Ibn 'Arabi's child, or that he adopted him, having married the boy's widowed mother. The latter would seem most likely, since Ibn 'Arabi is quoted as saying he was dearer to him than an actual son by the flesh (Addas 228).

That the boy felt himself the spiritual son of Awhad al-Din Kirmani, the man to whom his step-father entrusted his education, is indicated by the fact that, as an adult, Sad al-Din Qunawi told his friends to "lay out Kirmani's prayer rug in my tomb" (Addas 230). In addition, Qunawi said, in a letter to a friend, that Kirmani had been his master, "in certain respects and for two years at Shiraj I was his companion and in his service" (*ibid.*).

The spiritual inspiration of the poetry of Jalal al-Din Rumi, then, in addition to his scholarly father and his own family heritage from Balkh, was further enriched by the input of Qunawi who was destined to play a crucial role in transmitting to the Konya circle the teachings of Ibn 'Arabi. As the adopted son of Ibn 'Arabi, and the ward of Kirmani, he was the recipient of a double spiritual inheritance – Arab from Ibn 'Arabi, and Iranian from Awhad al-Din (Kirmani), which pre-disposed him to become the pivot or link between these two aspects of Islamic esotericism. Qunawi himself used to say, "I have tasted milk from the breasts of two mothers!"(Addas 230).

There is one final respect in which these mystics may seem topical and contemporary to today's reader of poetry. As Edward G. Browne notes, in the passage already quoted from Halman (47), many of the achievements of these mystics were frankly incredible. Perhaps such marvels would be recognised today under the rubric of magic realism. In *Alone with the Alone,* Corbin recounts a typical example in the life of Ibn 'Arabi, which took place in Tunis when, one evening, withdrawn in a prayer niche of the Great Mosque, he composed a poem which he communicated to no one. In fact, he did not even write it down, but noted the day and the hour of his inspiration in his memory (47). A few months later, in Seville, a young man unknown to him, approached him and recited the verses. Overwhelmed, Ibn 'Arabi asked him "who is their author?" and the other replied: "Muhammad

Ibn 'Arabi" (Corbin 47). The young man had never seen Ibn 'Arabi and did not know who was standing before him, so how did he know the verses? A few months before (the very day and hour when the inspiration had come to Ibn 'Arabi in Tunis) a stranger, an unknown pilgrim, had mingled, in Seville, with a group of young men, and had recited a poem which they, delighted, had begged him to repeat in order that they might learn it by heart. Having done so, the stranger had disappeared without making himself known or leaving any trace. Similar events were well known to the masters of Sufism (Corbin 47). In this Sufi life, it was apparently commonplace to meet people who came from "the World of Mystery [...] the home of spirits," says Addas, citing an occasion on which "Ibn 'Arabi encountered the son of Caliph Harun al-Raschid, who had been dead for four centuries"(Addas 215; Corbin 53). It is particularly touching that, on his way to Mecca, Ibn 'Arabi travelled by way of Palestine, visiting al-Arish, Gaza, Hebron and al-Quds, since this mystic regarded Jesus as the One through whose teachings he first entered on the Way (Addas 197-9).

Both Ibn 'Arabi and Mevlana hold a profound appeal for many who are caught up in the violence and the materialism of this time. The rediscovery of their work and its availability in translation makes accessible to us their recognition of the spiritual value of women: for Ibn 'Arabi, the vital role of the Pole or *Qutb* could be held by a woman as well as by a man, and this provides a resource of inestimable value at a time when women are denigrated, brutalised, and exploited. Today's reader finds refreshing the Sufi insistence that the Way was open to everyone, regardless of religious sect, a principle for which they were often persecuted by their more dogmatic contemporaries. These Sufi mystics were also regarded as dangerous heretics by religious authorities who took a strictly literal approach to spiritual matters. As Halman says, "when all is said and done, it is conceivable, beyond the tragic eras and the happy ages of history, that the most profound truth, perhaps the only irreducible value inherent in human existence is the one expressed so eloquently in a line from a poem by Mevlana: 'Live in love's ecstasy, for love is all that exists'" (46).

References

Addas, Claude. *Quest for the Red Sulphur: The life of Ibn 'Arabi.* Trans. Peter Kingsley. Cambridge UK: Islamic Texts Society, 1993.

Adnan, Etel. *Of Cities and Women: Letters to Fawwaz.* Sausolito, California: Post Apollo Press, 1993.

Al-Sinjilawi, Ibrahim Musa. *The 'Atlal-Nasib in Early Arabic Poetry: A Study of the Development of the Elegiac Genre in Classical Arabic Poetry.* Nasser Al-Hasan 'Athamneh, ed. Irbid, Jordan: Yarmouk University Publications, 1999.

Arberry, Arthur J. "Introduction." *Discourses of Rumi.* Richmond, Surrey: Curzon Press, 1993.

Austin, R.W.J. Introduction and Notes to *Sufis of Andalusia by Muhyiddin Ibn-'Arabi.* Roxburgh: Beshara Publications (Harper Collins), 1971.

Badi' al-Saman Furuzanfar. *Fihi Ma Fihi* as *Discourses of Rumi.* Trans. A.J. Arberry. Richmond, Surrey: Curzon Press, 1993.

Barks, Coleman and John Moyne. *The Essential Rumi.* London: Penguin, 1999.

Barstow, Anne Llewellyn. *Witchcraze: A New History of the European Witch Hunts.* London: Pandora Harper-Collins, 1994.

Benaissa, Omar. "The Diffusion of Akbarian Teaching in Iran during the 13th and 14th Centuries" Trans. Zahra Benaissa and Cecilia Twinch. *Journal of the Muhyiddin Ibn 'Arabi Society*, Vol. XXVI, 1999: 89-109.

Briffault, Robert. *The Troubadours.* Lawrence F. Koons, ed. Bloomington: Indiana UP, 1965.

Burckhardt, Titus. *Fusus al-hikam.* Paris: Sagesse des Prophetes, 1955.

Corbin, Henry. *Alone with the Alone.* Princeton, NJ: Princeton UP, 1997.

Dalrymple, William. "The Popularity of Rumi." *The Guardian.* 5 Nov. 2005: 1-5. www.books.guardian.co.uk/departments/classics/story/o

Duggan, T.M.P. "Representational Painting and Drawing From Life in 13th Century Rum Selçuk Anatolia." *Adaliya* (Ayri basım) (Research Institute on Mediterranean Civilizations) No. IV/1999-2000. 281-286.

Ghazzali, Ahmed. *Sawanih: Inspirations from the World of Pure Spirits: The Oldest Persian Treatise on Love.* Trans. Nasrollah Purjavady. London: Kegan Paul, 1986.

Halman, Talat and Metin And. *Mevlana Celaleddin Rumi and The Whirling Dervishes.* Istanbul: Dost Yayinlari, 1992.

Ibn al 'Arabi, Muhyiddin. *Tarjuman Al-Ashwaq. A Collection of Mystical Odes by Muhyiddin Ibn Al-Arabi.* Trans. Reynold A. Nicholson.

Preface by Dr Martin Lings. London: Theosophical Publishing House, 1978.

Ibn al-'Arabi, Muhyiddin. *Sufis of Andalusia: The Ruh al-Quds & al-Durrat at-Fahirah by Muhyiddin Ibn'Arabi.* Trans. and Introduction by R. W. J. Austin. Roxburgh, UK, 2002.

Nicholson, Reynold, ed. Trans. *The Mathnawi of Jalálu'ddín Rúmí.* 8 Vols. London: Messrs Luzac, 1925-1940.

Palacios, Asin. *Dante y el Islam.* Madrid: Voluntad, 1927.

Queller, Donald E. and Thomas F. Madden. *The Fourth Crusade: The Conquest of Constantinople.* 2nd Ed. Philadelphia: U of Pennsylvania Press, 2000.

Rumi, Jalal al-Din. *The Essential Rumi.* Trans. Coleman Barks and John Moyne. London: Penguin Books, 1999.

Rumi, Jalal al-Din. *Discourses of Rumi.* Trans. A. J. Arberry. Richmond, Surrey: Curzon Press, 1993.

Safi, Omid. "Did the Two Oceans Meet?" *Journal of the Muhyiddin Ibn 'Arabi Society.* Vol. XXVI 1999: 58-88.

Schimmel, Annemarie. *As Through a Veil: Mystical Poetry in Islam.* Oxford: One World, 2001.

Schimmel, Annemarie. *Rumi's World: The Life and Work of the Great Sufi Poet.* Boston and London: Shambala, 2001.

Sonography and Family Photography Online

Julie Palmer

Julie Palmer is supported by the Arts and Humanities Research Council (UK).

Obstetric ultrasound has become routine and so has the practice of giving pregnant women a picture from their scan. What people chose to do with this image varies; perhaps some people discard it, but anecdotal evidence suggests that many others keep it in wallets and photo albums, display it at home or at the office or, increasingly, on the World Wide Web. The social practices developing around displaying and viewing ultrasound pictures puzzled me at first. Having studied ultrasound as prenatal tests, I wondered how these images functioned outside the clinic. After all, sonographers undergo extensive training in order to make sense of ultrasound data and to the lay observer there is little, if any, informational value to the image. This would seem to render it meaningless outside the clinical context, but this is clearly not the case.

Here, I consider the ways in which ultrasound has been incorporated into family iconography. My focus is on a specific context in which the take-home ultrasound image is found – online family albums. The Web is one of the means by which people share their take-home ultrasound pictures and Web pages can be seen as popular cultural texts that both reflect the dominant meanings of ultrasound and create new and varied meanings from the image.

For me, the social practices around take-home sonograms make more sense when they are thought about in relation to photographic theory. I think that our understandings of photography, and specifically family photography, have a huge role to play in the ways we understand sonography. Although the foetal image draws on both photographic codes and medical-scientific codes, it is primarily by being treated as a photograph that the image has moved outside medicine to become a cultural object.

Drawing on Hayles' (2002) work on media-specific analysis – in which she argues that media imitate one another, incorporating aspects of competing media while promoting the specific advantages of their own form of mediation – I explore the technological ecosystem in which ultrasound and photography co-exist. I am interested in the ways in which family photography and ultrasound both imitate one another and incorporate aspects of one another, and I ask what this means for our understanding of both imaging technologies.

While ultrasound, as the original "inscription technology" (Hayles 24), remains pertinent to the analysis of sonograms in an online context, this context also provides an excellent opportunity to explore ultrasound in (one small section of) its medial ecology (Hayles 5). I am using the term medial ecology as Hayles does, to mean the relationship between media interacting with one another in a given social, cultural and temporal context. I explore the ways in which family photography and ultrasound both imitate one another and incorporate aspects of one another. This requires technological precision and yet also attention to interplays and imitations. I am drawing on Hayles' 'Media-Specific Analysis', which promotes an attention to technology that illuminates the kinds of tensions and disjunctures that I have hinted at. An understanding of ultrasound as a technology that involves high frequency sound waves that are differentially reflected by tissue and bone in a way that can be composed into an image, marks the inclusion of that image in family photography as remarkable. It defamiliarises these pictures and these practices so that we can pay critical attention to them.

Figure 1

My first example is perhaps fairly typical of the sites that I have read. While much of the website is devoted to the mother's hobbies – crafts, cooking, gardening – there are several pages devoted to her children, with picture galleries that begin with scan pictures and continue to document the child as she grows. The example here is from the earlier of two scans. The heading tells the reader that this is an 'ultrasound scan photo' of the couple's first child. It gives the baby's full name and date of birth. It tells us the baby was six days late. A simple caption provides an informative label for the image. A colourful background depicting teddy bears, baby's bottles and alphabet blocks frames the black and white image. The colours are baby-ish – pales pinks, blues and yellows.

At first glance it would seem that there is an almost total lack of medical context to this image. A closer look reveals that the 'baby' is eleven weeks and four days old (and presumably this is according to the measurements taken at the ultrasound examination); she was born 'late' (a clinical judgement). In this re-presentation of the sonogram, the medical and the sentimental are combined. The techno-foetus is constructed as 'baby', at least in part, by the surrounding 'wallpaper' and captions. Sentimental and affectionate language, 'baby' colours and pictures work to recode the sonogram in non-medical terms. This is an 'ultrasound scan photo'. The picture was 'taken' on May 20th. The language is that of photography rather than prenatal testing, or at least any distinction between the two technologies is blurred. So perhaps 'ultrasound scan photo' is not a bad description. This is a hybrid artefact. So, if we can agree that the sonogram's primary meaning is not medical in this context, what does it communicate?

Firstly, an ultrasound image provides evidence of pregnancy. I think this has to be considered in the light of its routine clinical use. It is often only after the first scan that people tell family and friends that a child is expected, and the ultrasound picture becomes a 'tangible and portable sign' that the foetus exists and is normal (Mitchell 2001, 148). A later scan picture might be used to announce the sex of the baby. A number of websites feature scan pictures with the caption 'It's a girl!' or 'It's a boy!' This is a different kind of announcement. Ultrasound is highly significant in terms of assigning gender. A gendered identity can begin to be constructed for the child; a name can be chosen and clothes bought.

What is interesting about this is that ultrasound images have the status of evidence irrespective of whether they are visually comprehensible. The sonogram provides (visual) evidence of gender, even though an untrained viewer is unlikely to be able to tell the sex of the foetus from the scan picture.

Figure 2
Source: Clive Banks' Science Fiction Databank
http://clivebanks.co.uk accessed 24/05/05
The author of this site asks us to see the baby in the picture. We are given the clinical measurements – the 'baby' is 63.2mm long – but the rest is up to us. It is the bracketed text that interests me most here: 'Okay, I know it's a bit fuzzy, but if you squint you can make out the head on the right, its little waving arms, and its legs over there on the left.' The author's instruction to 'squint' is not unusual. Another

author advises: 'If you tilt your head over to the left, you can see it better' (anon). It is quite usual for sonograms to be displayed with captions to help the viewer make sense of the image. Body parts may be labelled for the unskilled viewer and the position of the foetus may be annotated in terms of movement and 'intention' – the foetus is waving or kicking or sucking its thumb.

These kinds of captions acknowledge the limitations of the technology, but it is an acknowledgement of limitation in terms of photographic aesthetics. Presumably the scan was successful in obtaining the desired clinical data, but the resultant image is 'a little fuzzy'. So, I did not find an assumption of the part of these Web authors that the image is immediately comprehensible to their audience, and yet it is meaningful nonetheless. Some authors even show a sense of humour about the clarity, or otherwise, of the image.

Figure 3
Source: http://www.flickr.com/photos/rockdude/sets/43759
accessed 24/05/05

The Web author names this picture 'Bigfoot'. The fascinating caption is humorous yet it seems to play with the idea that a sonogram is self-evident. The viewer is asked to guess, but the presumption is that we will guess correctly. The image is comprehensible because it is black and white and it is produced by Philips; it has clinical markings in the margins that suggest to any reader familiar with this technology that this is an ultrasound, and probably an obstetric ultrasound. We guess correctly and yet it could almost be a bizarre footprint.

I understand this by thinking of homepages as the art of 'making do' (Fiske 1994). Unlike the domestic photo, the sonogram can only be produced by a professional, a sonographer. It is more akin to the professional photograph than the amateur snapshot. Pictures must be 'taken' in the clinic or hospital; they are limited by appointment times and restricted in number. So, there is less opportunity for editing. Despite the aesthetic standards in operation, expectant parents have little chance to choose the 'best' shots. While there is some evidence that sonographers will try to get a 'good' picture for parents-to-be, the number of 'shots' is fairly limited and unless parents-to-be chose to go to a private 'studio' to have more extensive pictures of the baby 'taken' (and there are places were this can be done) the scan picture has to stand for something, however unclear it may be.

But the value of the sonographic image is symbolic and ritualistic. Perhaps like other photographs, they are not so much informative as "invitations to deduction, speculation, and fantasy" (Sontag 23). Annette Kuhn observes that a photograph is material for interpretation, "evidence in that sense: to be solved, like a riddle; read and decoded, like clues left behind at the scene of a crime" (Kuhn 12). To show you what it is evidence of, a photograph must always point away from itself and generate meaning in an intertextual network (Kuhn 12). But more than this, our contemporary visual culture seems to need images: everything must be illustrated. Although at one time vision was not trusted to make perceptual judgements by itself (Mirzoeff 5), it has become hypervalued (Slater 221).

Many scan pictures appear online as illustration to the documentation of pregnancy. Significant landmarks and experiences are shared with an audience and saved for posterity. An account might begin, 'I went for my first scan today…' In these cases the image serves as illustration to a narrative.

Figure 4
Source: Blog from a Baby
http://www.wittydomainname.com/BlogJr.html accessed 17/05/05

Lisa adds this narrative to her sonogram:

> I promise you, that is actually a baby…Pip was very quiet for the entire scan…The baby was snuggled into a little space in my womb, and taking after its mother, really couldn't bother to be entertaining at 8.20 in the morning. The lovely ultrasound lady first told us that there was only one baby in there, and then pointed out the heartbeat. That's when I burst into tears that didn't stop flowing for the duration of the scan. Pip has two arms and two legs, is measuring 13 weeks and 1 day…and was kind enough to give us a bit of a wave…We're so relieved and it's really nice to finally be able to go "public". Now I think I can just enjoy being pregnant. Well done, little Pip.

Lisa records her first scan on her weblog. She has decided that now she can 'go public'; with the scan 'passed' the baby can be introduced to family and friends. The idea of family resemblance is even raised, but in terms of behaviour rather than anything that can be seen from the static image. Nonetheless, the visual image is central to the account. The baby is introduced as 'Our little star of the screen', and 'Presenting Pip'. The language is that of Hollywood film. In this way, Lisa introduces the baby to family and friends.

Janelle Taylor has noted that sharing the sonogram image is important as a means of establishing or strengthening kinship links with the foetus (32-33) and my online data supports this. The existing literature argues that 'bonding' is one of the perceived key benefits of ultrasound examination. The notion of bonding emerged in the early 1970s and, by 1983, it was applied to ultrasound. There was a shift from an understanding of bonding as being concerned with spending time with an infant to an understanding based in spectatorship (Taylor 21-22). It is thought that anyone might bond with a baby by seeing the ultrasound scan pictures. But in this model, the mother-to-be no longer has a privileged relationship to the foetus. We can all be spectators.

While this suggests a turning away from the pregnant body – a devaluing of embodied knowledge and experience – online, I have observed a fascination with the changes of pregnancy. For example, Lisa includes six 'belly pics' – at 13, 14, 24, 29, 33 and 39 weeks.

Figure 5
'Belly pic' at 24 weeks.
Source: Blog from a Baby
http://www.wittydomainname.com/BlogJr.html accessed 17/05/05

The author's comment "I keep forgetting to take pictures of my bump" suggests that this is something that she ought to be doing. The primary reason for the pictures is the pregnancy. Close-up portraits detail the progression of the 'bump'. Such images demonstrate a fascination with the physical changes associated with pregnancy. They are often playful, perhaps bemoaning the loss of a waistline or delighted with new maternity clothes.

In most of the websites that I looked at, the sonogram is presented amongst other photographs without any sense of difference or disjuncture. In detailed accounts of pregnancy, the scan pictures often seem supplementary because they are outnumbered by photographs. Changes in a woman's body can be documented very frequently, particularly with a digital camera. The juxtapositions go largely unremarked upon because of the mobilisation of discourses of photography. I think that the conventions of family photography and family photograph albums inform how we see and understand images in this context, so I want to consider these conventions in a little more detail.

Family photographs are socially constructed artefacts with visual rules about composition. They traditionally represent individuals with ties of kinship or household and tell stories of growth and changes in family configuration' (Matthews and Wexler 81). Family photographs are usually ordered in a linear series, chronological, except for the cyclical repetition of 'climactic moments' (Kuhn 17) such as births, christenings, weddings and holidays (but not deaths). Images and text are carefully arranged in relation to one another.

If collating the family album is kinship work, so, presumably, is presenting it online. Here the audience is much less bounded but, as we have seen, many other features remain the same. The conventions of the album are circumscribed, but, as Kuhn notes, there is always room for manoeuvre in a genre; people make use of the rules of the album in their own ways (Kuhn 17). With the advent of foetal imaging, people are adding sonograms to the very beginning of a series of family pictures; they introduce a new family member even before they are born.

The conventions of displaying family photographs, when applied to sonograms, help them to mimic photographs and so to 'pass'. But there are also other conventions at work here. Bricolage is typical of Web pages. They combine the personal and the professional – a CV shares online space with holiday pictures and wedding pictures, perhaps recipes and knitting patterns. Tim Berners-Lee envisioned the Web as a computer network that could function in a way that suited the human brain, a network that could make connections, even if those connections seem arbitrary. The dream behind the Web, then, is of a common information space in which we communicate by sharing information. Its universality is essential: the fact that a hypertext link can point to anything, be it personal, local or global, be it draft or highly polished (Berners-Lee).

Connections are achieved through hypertext – non-sequential blocks of text are connected with electronic links resulting in texts that are not linear, but multi-linear (see Landow 1997 on the nature and potential of hypertext). Ultrasound pictures are integrated through both (the act of) bricolage and (the technology of) hypertext links. The click of a mouse might lead us, as readers, from scan pictures to a family wedding to a beach holiday and back again. We chose where to look next.

I want to suggest that hypertext links potentially reconnect the techno-foetus with many other aspects of life and autobiography. Perhaps it is just that Berners-Lee's utopianism is contagious and I do not wish to suggest that hypertext is the solution to all our (feminist) problems with foetal imaging, but perhaps the specificities of the online text allow another way of thinking about the issue. What I observe is that many Web authors re-present ultrasound images in a complex web of their lives and their bodies. It is often not disconnected from the pregnant body, from kinship and parenting, and it is not even disconnected from the author's interest in craftwork or science fiction. In hypertext, anything can be connected to anything else and perhaps this isn't good enough, perhaps we only want the techno-foetus connected to very specific things, but it does raise intriguing possibilities.

References

Berners-Lee, Tim. *The World Wide Web: A Very Short Personal History.* http://www.w3.org/People/Berners-Lee/ShortHistory.html (accessed 12/02/05)

Fiske, John. *Understanding Popular Culture.* London: Routledge, 1994.

Haraway, Donna J. "The Virtual Speculum in the New World Order" in *The Gendered Cyborg: A Reader*, G. Kirkup, L. Jones, K. Woodward and F. Hovenden, eds. London: Routledge, 2000.

Hayles, N. Katherine. *Writing Machines.* Cambridge, Mass.; London: MIT Press, 2002.

Kuhn, Annette. *Family Secrets: Acts of Memory and Imagination.* London: Verso, 1995.

Landow, George P. *Hypertext 2.0: The Convergence of Contemporary Critical Theory and Technology*. Baltimore: The John Hopkins UP, 1997.

Matthews, Sandra & Laura Wexler. *Pregnant Pictures*. London: Routledge, 2000.

Mirzoeff, Nicholas. *An Introduction to Visual Culture*. London: Routledge, 1999.

Mitchell, Lisa M. *Baby's First Picture: Ultrasound and the Politics of Fetal Subjects*. Toronto: U of Toronto Press, 2001.

Slater, Don. "Photography and Modern Vision: The Spectacle of 'Natural Magic'" in *Visual Culture*. C. Jenks, ed. London: Routledge, 1995.

Sontag, Susan. *On Photography*. London: Penguin Books, 1979.

Taylor, Janelle S. "Image of Contradiction: Obstetrical Ultrasound in American Culture" in *Reproducing Reproduction: Kinship, Power and Technological Innovation*. S. Franklin and H. Ragoné, eds. Philadelphia: U of Pennsylvania Press, 1998.

The Fun Fearless Female: Real or Fantasy?

Janneke Fernhout

As part of a project on language and globalisation, forty-four national versions of the magazine *Cosmopolitan* were investigated. In order to place the magazine and its discourses into a social context, textual analysis, interviews and ethnographic research were undertaken. The interviews gave insights into the way that young women (18-30) felt affected by discourses of sex, independence and self-confidence found in *Cosmopolitan*, which claims to be about empowering the woman. This discourse can also be found in television series like *Sex and the City*.

In order to establish to what extent the women were able to recognise the magazine's discourse, they were shown some images and articles that were representative and characteristic of those generally found in the magazine and asked to comment on them. The images are from a common database, shared by all of the international versions of *Cosmopolitan*. Initially, the interviewees were keen to point out that they were above the kinds of representations of the world that appeared in the pages of the magazine, seeing it as trivial. However, it became clear in the data that many of the values promoted in the magazine were important to them in how they wished to represent themselves.

What follows is an analysis of a sample of the selected images followed by a summary of some comments given by the interviewees. After this, their reactions are looked at in-depth and embedded in a broader social context. Here we show how the women feel empowered by certain discourses, which draw on certain feminist concepts. *Cosmopolitan* uses these concepts in a way that does not raise more serious questions about society, women and political freedom.

Reactions on Cosmo-*images*

In previous *Cosmo*-research, Machin and Thornborrow (2003) argue that *Cosmo*-images create a fantasy world through idealised and abstract representations that are of a sensual nature (459). The interviewees were asked to comment on the selected images (taken from the Dutch *Cosmopolitan*, July 2003). Below is a description of the images used, and the reactions of the interviewees follow:

Image 1: Woman on a Beach Surrounded by Men

In this image, a woman dressed in a bikini has her arm draped around the shoulder of a man. While half-sitting/half-leaning on his belly, arm, and raised knee, she has moved her head slightly backwards, her eyes are closed and she is laughing. The man's head is turned towards her and he looks at her face. Three other men are looking at her as well: one man (only his head is shown) from the left middle of the image, one man behind the first man and woman, and finally a sitting man on the right who is bending towards the woman. The first two men are laughing and the third man seems to be looking straight at the woman. The setting is on a beach: indicated by sand (the woman has also some sand on her hand and leg) and in the background is visible the sea, beach chairs and other people. The beach is located near to a city with high buildings, hotels perhaps. The setting of this image can be characterised as generic: it displays a non-descript city (Machin 2004). The image has a sensual nature, as the woman is the central object of the picture, enjoying the attention of four men. The sensual elements here are the fact that she is dressed in a bikini and the movement of her head being thrown backwards. A fantasy world is created being created due to the exact location of the picture being unrecognisable, as well as the fact that four men are interested in one woman. As no other women are present, the other men seem to have no other option but to turn their attentions to this woman, who, in this way, becomes the centre of attention and appears to be empowered by her capacity to attract all male attention.

Responses: The interviewees did not associate with this image and could not identify with the woman nor with the way she was behaving. She was described as an 'attention seeker', 'arrogant' and 'dominating the men'. The interviewees distanced themselves by labeling her as an 'attention seeker', a label which they would not give to themselves.

Image 2: Working Woman

This image, appearing on the 'working girl page', displays a woman sitting on an office chair, her feet on the desk. Her head, like the woman on the beach, is leaning backwards slightly, and she is laughing. It is not clear whether she is laughing at someone (who would be at the right side of the scene), or is just enjoying herself. The woman is dressed in grey and her hands are in her pockets. She is more or less lying in her chair. The setting of the image can be classified as an office, though there are no other employees present. The background shows other office chairs and desks, with papers and an object that could be a telephone. There is a window, through which part of a flat or a skyscraper can be seen. It is dark outside, since there are lights burning in the flat/skyscraper. These elements form a good basis to establish the setting as an office (probably also located in a skyscraper). In this image, the typical *Cosmo* fantasy world is created, in which women ('Fun Fearless Females') always act alone. In this respect, they are never distracted from their goals by religion, family and friends, as may be the case in the real world. Furthermore, the fact that she is not working enhances the fantasy.

Responses: This image evoked positive remarks. The interviewees stated that they could identify more with this woman as she looked 'ordinary' to them, like a person one could see walking in the street. She was described as wearing 'dull clothes', which was considered to be refreshing for images in a glamourous magazine. In addition, they mentioned that 'she is having fun', 'enjoying herself' and 'is self-confident', in coherence with the core themes of *Cosmopolitan* in general. They also mentioned that 'she dares to be relaxed', despite the fact that the depicted woman is located in an 'office' and ought to be working.

Even though the smiles of the women on the two images are very similar they are not recognised by the participants as such. Whereas in the first image the smile was considered as 'exaggerated', the smile in the second image is labeled as 'happy'. Another interesting remark concerning the second image is that one of the interviewees stated that this image is 'more realistic' in contrast with the first image. This last comment seems to be questionable. In an office (as the formal background indicates), one is supposed to work and this woman does not show any signs of working at all. The interviewed young women admired her for 'daring to be that laid back' at work, indicating that they would not dare to behave in this way themselves. Her daring attitude and self-confidence at work was considered to be empowering and something they strived for themselves, as will become clear later on.

While the first image evoked negative reactions and was rejected, the second picture was regarded far more positively. These forms of distancing and relating to the *Cosmo*-discourse was constantly recurring theme throughout the interviews.

Distancing/Relating to the Cosmo-*discourse*

The reactions to the first image correspond with the initial reaction of the interviewees to the magazine itself; they all agreed that *Cosmopolitan* was not really a magazine they liked, as it has 'little to read' and 'a lot of advertisements' plus, they said, they 'cannot take this magazine seriously' (in comparison to other magazines). They did not consider themselves to be the target group, which they described as (too) 'hip', 'modern' and 'trendy'.

They were keen to point out they were not like other young women in society. This became clear in their answers to a question asked previously that concerned the dominating values for young women in society today. Their answers, among others, included 'independence', 'looks/ beauty', 'money/ career', 'happiness', 'enjoyment of life' and 'freedom'. They considered these values to be shallow and stated they cared more about things 'that really matter in life' like 'looking after each other', 'respect', 'equality', 'family' and 'health'. Therefore, the first image stood for everything they despised and considered shallow. They perhaps did not want to admit that they would actually enjoy the depicted amount of attention if it were given to them for fear of being considered selfish. The women reacted with some hostility to the image, perhaps a reaction to the threat the depicted woman poses ('this woman is getting all the attention').

In this respect, literature about feminism of the nineties appeared to be applicable to contemporary society. For example, Cels (1999) states that the female collective went down with the previous generation and that young women do not feel like a group anymore (as women in the seventies did). She states that they stand, think and speak for themselves and are proud of this (39). Cels questions if there ever really was such a thing as sisterhood. To investigate this, several young women were interviewed wherein one of them stated that instead of forming a group, women are more likely to be one another's rivals. Another woman stated that women do not like each other, as they always seem to criticise and envy each other. A feeling of competition is mentioned as the most important reason for the absence of solidarity. When it comes down to having a partner or a job, there are women who swear by competition. This is endorsed by the hostile reaction to Image 1.

The woman in Image 2 was easier for the interviewees to identify with and did not pose a threat to them. Later in the interview, one of the interviewees stated that she would like to have a certain degree of all of the characteristics attributed to the *Cosmo*-woman: intelligence, beauty, trendiness, self-confidence, an ability to relax, and independence. The other interviewees agreed with this statement. They stated that despite the fact that they did not possess the perfection that [the woman in the] *Cosmopolitan* radiates, it was something they strived for in their lives. The same applied for the values of being independent, gaining power and being self-confident, also classified as feminist values. Nevertheless, they were eager not to label themselves as feminists.

Feminism in Practice

When specifically asked about their view on feminism, the women made statements such as 'Feminism is something of the past'; 'I live my life as I want to live it, thanks to previous movements' and 'Feminism has nothing to do with me'. Nevertheless, feminist discourse was all around in statements made later: 'Women should have as much right to pleasure as men', and 'I want to be able to live my life as I want to'. When asked in-depth about these commonly heard statements, it appeared that these statements caused conflicting and problematic concerns, as they admitted that these ideals can, in practice, be hard to integrate into their own lives. They realised that they could only live their lives independently to a certain extent, as interests of family, colleagues and religion were involved in their lives and decisions too. As well as this, it appeared that their claimed sexual freedom was in fact a tool to overcome grief or hurt. This finding will be placed in a broader social context below.

The central idea of contemporary feminism, according to the young women interviewed, is that women want to make their own choices: in relationships, at work, and regarding looks, study and sexuality. Only salary is regarded as an agenda item in contemporary emancipation.

This is confirmed in a Dutch documentary ('Waar is mijn paarse tuinbroek'/ 'Where is my purple dungaree?') about current feminism. The maker of this documentary was reassured by how women are active today and how emancipated they are and her only concern was the emancipation of immigrant women. There was no real critical stance taken on how new kinds of freedom are integrated; sexual freedom, for example. From my data, it appears that sex was a way to be considered attractive and a tool to (try and) forget one's loneliness. Independence seemed to become linked to looking good and to sex. The interviewees had one-night-stands and felt empowered thereby. They stated it functioned as some sort of confirmation that they mattered, still looked good, and were appreciated by men. In this sense, these women still depended on the approval of men. A quotation from the *Daily Mirror*, about a woman who enjoys having sex with younger men also illustrates this:

> There was something about my basic insecurity and the confidence that comes with the young that made it work. It was the combination of youthful lust and the experience of a woman of a certain age. Certainly, once I'd been made to feel like the most gorgeous creature in the world, there was nothing to hold me back.' And since then? ' When I don't think about not having a partner, I'm fine.' Says Lynda. 'And then someone will say: 'Do you mind being on your own?' (18 June 2004)

Here, both loneliness and the need for confirmation become very clear. The concept of being independent seemed to rise on the personal agenda, after a broken relationship. With the pain of a break-up, the dependence and/or emotional attachment that formed part of the relationship suddenly felt like a bad thing. It looked like these women decided to prevent future pain by acting independently and transforming sex into empowerment rather than linking it to emotional attachment. Consequently, they felt they took control of their lives (and emotions) again, as they had felt rather powerless before. By using their sexuality in this way, they found a tactic that enabled them to forget their pain. In *Cosmopolitan*, the Fun Fearless

Female uses her sexuality in the same way. The young women felt 'in control (again)' when they decided who their 'sexual victim' would be.

Despite the discourse about being happily single and independent, it appears that, deep down, the interviewees longed for true love and fulfilling relationships. However, it was considered a weakness to say this. Being single, as opposed to life in the sixties, was something one should enjoy. A woman can/should be happy without a man/woman in her life.

When asked, many interviewees said that 'an independent confident woman' is someone who 'has everything under control' and 'decides everything in her life.' It is questionable to what extent one can control life in the first place but, more importantly, is wanting to have control over everything not simply a means to suppress the insecurity of what will happen when one does not have the situation under control? Being insecure appeared to be a taboo. Insecurity for many of the women is something that should be dealt with by performing the act of self-confidence or trying to 'control the situation.' These solutions are not really dealing with the insecurity *per se*, but apparently provides a good way to handle insecurity. The interviewees stated they used the strategy of self-confidence mostly in work situations. Insecurity was not considered as something that could actively be worked on, in order to take away the insecurity. These models of dealing with insecurity are also to be found in *Cosmopolitan* (Machin & van Leeuwen 2003). *Cosmopolitan* cleverly portrays the models people (want to) relate to in society nowadays. During discussion of the *Cosmo*-images, the depicted women were considered 'self-confident' and when asked how this was apparent, the interviewees simply answered: 'because of her pose'. This pose was always of a sensual nature and again draws on the concept of using looks/sexuality for empowerment. This confirms that according to the interviewees, self-confidence is not something that derives from the inner self (professional competence, for example), but is a pose, as opposed to something one has.

Conclusion

Although *Cosmopolitan* addresses the naïve reader, its brand reader is the 'Fun Fearless Female'. This image is created in *Cosmopolitan* by women who take control of emotions rather than situations, are independent, self-confident and use their power through looks rather than by professional competence. At the same time, the naïve woman is addressed with manuals, 'hot tips' and expert advice. In a perfect world, a truly confident woman would naturally not need magazines like *Cosmopolitan*, as the confidence would come from within herself. The interviewees were conscious of the fact that the Fun Fearless Female is a Fantasy (as they could never reach her 'perfection'), yet they tried to integrate this fairy tale into reality in the hope that they would overcome powerless emotions.

References

Breakwell, G.M., Hammond, S., Fife-Schaw, C. *Research Methods in Psychology*. California: Sage Publications, 1995.

Cels, S. *Grrls! Jonge vrouwen in de jaren negentig*. Amsterdam: Prometheus, 1999.

Ceulemans, M.J. *Women and Mass Media: A Feminist Perspective. A Review of the Research to Date on the Image and Status of Women in American Mass Media*. Leuven: Katholieke Universiteit, 1979.

Costera Meijer, I. *Het persoonlijke Wordt Politiek. Feministische Bewustwording in Nederland 1965-1980*. Amsterdam: Het Spinhuis 1996.

Ferguson, M. *Forever feminine. Women's Magazines and the Cult of Femininity*. London: Heineman, 1983.

Hermes, J. *Reading Women's Magazines. An Analysis of Everyday Media Use*. Cambridge: Polity Press, 1995.

Hopman-Rock, M., Staats, P.G.M., Weidema, I.M. *Focusgroep-Interviews Met Artrosepatiënten. Groepsinterviews Met 11 Artrosepatiënten*. Leiden: TNO Gezondheidsonderzoek, 1992.

Krueger, R.A. FocusGroups. *A Practical Guide for Applied Research*. California: Sage Publications, 1994.

Machin, D. "Building the World's Visual Language: The Increasing Global Importance of Image Banks in Corporate Media' *Journal of Visual Communication* (2004).

Machin, D. and Thornborrow, J. "Branding and Discourse" in *Discourse and Society* 14 (2003): 453-471.

Machin, D. and Van Leeuwen, T. "Global Schemas and Local Discourses in *Cosmopolitan*.' *Journal of Sociolinguistics* 7/4 (2003): 493-512

McRobbie, A. *In the Culture Society, Art, Fashion and Popular Music*. London: Routledge, 1999.

Morgan, D.L. *Focus Groups as Qualitative Research*. Newbury Park: Sage Publications, 1988.

Nussbaum, M.C. *Love's Knowledge. Essays on Philosophy and Literature*. Oxford: Oxford UP, 1990.

Röling, H. "Zedelijkheid" in *Nederland in de Twintigste Eeuw. Een Boeiend Beeld van Een Bewogen Tijdperk*. Utrecht: Stichting Educatieve Omroep Teleac, 1995.

Santhakumaran, D. "Talking to Strangers: Taking Advice from Women's Magazines." Conference paper. SS15, Newcastle, 1-3 April 2004.

Schagen, K. (director). *Waar is de Paarse Tuinbroek?* VPRO, 2004 http://www.vpro.nl/programma/geluk/afleveringen/16641827/ (16.06.04)

Vegt, R. "Vriendinnen van Papier. Vrouwentijdschriften Tussen 1934 en 2003. Van Zeep tot Soap". *Continuïteit en Verandering in Geïllustreerde Tijdschriften*. 1 (2004): 38-53.

Vonk, H. Avenue en Elegance in de slag om de AB-doelgroepen. De Journalist. 39 (1988): 22-23.

Wassenaar, I. *Vrouwenbladen. Spiegels van een mannenmaatschappij*. Amsterdam: Wetenschappelijke Uitgeverij b.v., 1976.

Willems-Bierlaagh. C. *Nederlandse vrouwentijdschriften 1800-1945*. Bibliografische lijst Amsterdam: Internationaal Informatiecentrum & Archief voor de Vrouwenbeweging IIAV, 1992.

Sport and Lesbianism; 'Say Nothing and Don't Forget to Grow Your Hair and Fingernails'

Linda Greene

This paper evolved during the course of my PhD research in Ireland. I initiated the study because of the dissonance I felt between the theoretical and empirical work on gender and sexuality and the sports experiences of nine self-identified Irish lesbian athletes. As I interviewed these particular women on their sports experiences, something began to emerge. There was a reinforced clarity from the interview data that, although there is some support and acceptance of women's sport, it still holds a tenuous and secondary position in society. Ireland is no exception, as internationally concerted efforts are still made to portray a socially acceptable image of 'appropriately' female athletes. This image is predictably feminine and heterosexual and exerts enormous pressure on female athletes to conform or be ostracised (Krane and Barber 2003; Sykes 1996, 1998).

The recent debate (Summer 2005), sparked over comments made by the GAA president, Sean Kelly, regarding female fashion parades in Croke Park, suggests that women's involvement in sport continues to be limited on fundamental levels that are poorly disguised with a tokenistic ill-informed speech regarding gender and sporting equality. Historically, sport has been presented as a male-dominated arena where men are rewarded for displays of conventional masculinity, and research suggests that women's successful participation in sport threatens male hegemony. Michael Messner, for example, contends that successful female participation in sport is controlled as it threatens the maintenance and reproduction of traditional masculinities via sport.

However, sexism and homophobia are not the sole territory of officials and GAA representatives. These are often so ingrained that athletes readily and enthusiastically police the sexuality of team-mates. As my interviews with the women athletes progressed, many of the interviewees expressed the notion that not only was their gender being contested as women participating in a male dominated arena, but also that their athletic credibility was fundamentally linked to a heterosexual litmus test of sorts. In order to access their chosen sport and maintain respect, the athletes felt that they were expected to present an 'air' of heterosexuality. Evidently another difficult battle for many of these women is a non-athletic contest influenced greatly by hetero-normative politics.

Take this data from a recent interview I carried out in Ireland[1]:

Q. In your opinion do you feel that you are or have been categorised/pigeon-holed in any way as a lesbian athlete? If so, by whom?

A. I'm quite careful about who knows I'm a dyke, I just have to be. I'm a teacher and I work lots with kids and there are an awful lot of bigots out there so I have to try to strategise to protect my income, and my family. I come from quite a tough area and my parents still live there and I wouldn't want them to experience any kind of intimidation because their daughter's a lesbian so I have to be careful on some level. On other levels I'm very out and proud... it's a constant negotiation of safe territory.... As a young girl I was bullied a lot with name calling – tomboy, lezzer and other such things. So in that sense I was pigeon-holed and categorised from a very young age by others... (Kate)

Drawing on interviews carried out in 2004 and 2005, I would like to use this paper to explore the evolving hypothesis that the social and athletic credibility of the female athlete is intrinsically linked to her sexuality, and to ask why it is that some muscular women are welcomed in sport while others are shunned and ridiculed? What type of muscle (strength) is permissible, and how is gender performativity and sexuality linked to an acceptable athletic performance and, finally, to an athletic and social credibility? One interviewee, who is also one of Ireland's most prominent GAA athletes, strongly felt that she was moved from a position of authority to a relegated position within the team, and she firmly believes that this 'demotion' was linked to her 'rumoured' homosexuality. Team-mates evidently began reacting differently to her, and one 'all star' player, with whom she felt great mutual respect had existed, actually stopped talking to her. In team sports in particular, what your team-mates think of you can negate or enhance your athletic performance (consider the recent demise of the

---

[1] Names have been changed to protect the identity of the interviewees.

'great' Roy Keane in November of 2005 when he supposedly lost the respect of the Manchester United dressing room). According to Pat Griffin:

> The closets in sport are deep because so many women in sport are hiding there. These deep closets are full of not only lesbians, but also heterosexual women who fear that women's sport is always one lesbian scandal away from ruin. These strong women coach and compete in the shadow of a demonized stereotype so reviled that all women in sport are held hostage by the threat of being called a lesbian. (x)

Many female athletes are understandably concerned by how they are perceived by the general public. Evidence supports this. For instance, marathon runner and 1984 Olympic Champion, Jean Benoit, has been documented as saying that: 'When I first started running, I was so embarrassed that I'd walk when cars passed me. I'd pretend I was looking at the flowers,' (Avery 2). Some of the interviewees articulated their distaste for the recent camogie campaign, 'Chicks with Sticks'. One interviewee remarked that while on the way to the biggest game of their lives, they were 'mortified' travelling on a mini-bus covered with the slogan 'support our chicks with sticks!'

I suggest that coaches and potential sponsors routinely monitor an elite female athlete's credibility, which is often disguised as 'suitability' or 'compatibility', but is always and without doubt linked to a monitoring of sexuality. Research by Smith (1986) and Coakley (1986) suggests that homophobia and heterosexism influence the self-esteem, confidence, stress levels and performance of female athletes. This interviewee discusses the potential anxiety involved in building a rapport with younger more 'vulnerable' team mates:

> [y]ou know, I thought that maybe it's because of my sexuality, because of what she's thinking, that her opinion has changed of me... and unfortunately it's guilty by association that a lot of players think that just because I happen to be talking to them or whatever... (she pauses then continues) I get on with some younger players ... it's a mentoring kind of affect that I'd have (from) when I was captain and I was probably the most popular one within the county... and you know again I kind of feel guilty

that people are going to associate them because there now seen talking to me and I feel terrible about it and I'm very apprehensive about actually becoming very close friends with them because maybe they're at the influential age of maybe 18, 19, 20 and you're just afraid of people thinking something different you know?' (Claire)

Research suggests that intimidation takes place in an effort to control women's sexual and sporting liberation (Cahn). According to interviewee 'Ciara':

There was what you would call the religious lesbians who thought you know that gay was bad. It was evil, even though they were doing it themselves you know. But they thought well they're not going to let the kids ['kids' implies 17-20 year-old women] get involved again. But again they just weren't letting the kids make up their own minds. They were leading them down the path they wanted them to go down. I mean there was a really bad case of it a few years back where a lot of kids were really messed up by it. This group of women thought that they were doing the kids a favour but they weren't. They were messing with their heads messing with minds and should have just let them alone… I mean these women were telling these kids not to do this and yet they were doing it themselves behind closed doors but telling the kids that it was bad, it was evil it was wrong. Those places were evil places don't go in there and threatening them, you know if you go in there you're not playing for this team, which was just horrible. (Ciara)

This data suggests that much work remains to be done as Irish female athletes continue to be controlled by an invasive hetero-normative and sexist dominant cultural policy. Griffin suggests that a strong resistance to women's participation in sport and the need to marginalise and control the growth of women's athletics is socially encouraged and maintained, and that, historically, one of the most effective means of controlling women's participation in sport is to challenge the femininity and heterosexuality of that athlete:

The lingering association of women's sports with lesbianism makes many women in sport defensive about their athleticism and insistent on being perceived as heterosexual. This sensitivity to the negative connotation of the 'lesbian label' and the association of women's sports with lesbians create a hostile athletic climate in which many lesbian athletes and coaches hide their identities to protect their access to sports. (ix)

According to Judith Halberstam, when a woman is perceived to be 'masculine' or 'unfeminine', she becomes explicitly aware that she has crossed a gender boundary and, thus, threatened a particular male privilege (2, 6). Griffin argues that, "because most women are afraid to be called lesbian or have their femininity called into question, their sport experience can be controlled by using the lesbian label to intimidate them" (20). Clearly, a woman's successful participation in sport is problematic to conventional gender ideology as it threatens stereotypical masculinity and conventional gender roles. However, I suggest that muscle is only permissible and welcomed when wrapped in the safe pony-tailed induced looks or mannerisms of athletes like Mia Hamm, Maria Sharapova or Anna Kournakova. Evidence suggests that hetero-normative politics are greatly involved in creating socially acceptable athletic heroines (Halberstam 1998; Messner 1990).

Consider the anxiety behind this televised statement made by WNBA basketball star Sheryl Swoopes: "My biggest concern is that people are going to look at my homosexuality and say to little girls – whether they're white, black, Hispanic – that I can't be their role model anymore.... I don't want that to happen" (Swoopes). Much debate regarding gender-appropriate behaviour has been contested via sport and athleticism. Critical to this debate is the idea that, traditionally, sport serves many important social functions for men, including the defining and reinforcing of conventional masculinities; like war, it acts as a place where men can become heroes. It also provides an acceptable and safe space for male homo-social behaviour. Similar to race, class, and physical ability, sexuality can be another defining and crucial factor in the experience of athletes, as one is reminded of complex strands, interactions and 'Bird Cage' metaphors (Marilyn Frye/ Feminist theorist). According to Griffin:

> Understanding how sport helps to teach boys to embrace masculinity and to avoid what is labelled feminine provides a social context for describing the experiences of lesbian in athletics.

There are reasons why athletic women are called lesbians and why there is so much fear and silence among lesbians in athletics. There are reasons why there is such resistance to the acceptance of lesbians in athletics. All of these reasons relate to the maintenance of male power and privilege and the fear that is instilled among women about challenging that power. (2)

My earlier suggestion that women's sport is a non-athletic contest loaded in sexist, hetero-normative assumptions is supported by much theoretical data to date. Research by Messner (1990), for instance, suggests that categories, such as masculinity and femininity, are used to control the participation of women and girls in sport, while Butler (1997) explores the rhetoric involved in a gender normative performance. In 1987, Adrienne Rich suggested that, "lesbian experience is perceived on a scale ranging from deviant to abhorrent or simply rendered invisible" (26), and Judith Halberstam's research suggests that a lesbian's successful participation in sport continues to subvert gender roles and threatens male hegemony (1998). Indeed, according to Halberstam, female masculinity is viewed as most threatening when coupled with lesbian desire. There is no doubt at the beginning of the twenty-first century that women continue to use sport to develop broadened definitions of womanhood and contest rigid concepts of femininity (Cahn 1994, 343): it is a battleground where you can almost get away with it, but not quite. Consider this 2005 data from an Irish athlete and prolific soccer player:

Q. So you've been involved in women's soccer here in Dublin for about twenty odd years is that safe enough to say?
A. Yeh I'd say about twenty-five years. The women's soccer now. Ye see I started off with schoolboys when I was younger.
Q. Ok could you tell us a bit more about that?
A. Well that was tough I had to pretend I was a boy coz girls weren't allowed play with boys when I was a kid. It's different now, they're encouraging the girls to play with the boys, but I had to pretend I was a boy when I played with them.
Q. And when you say pretend you were a boy does that mean like you had to act like a boy?
A. Act like a boy, talk like a boy walk like a boy.
Q. And under whose direction was that? Who had told you?

A. That would be the coach 'cause I was better than most of the boys and he couldn't risk losing me off the team! So I had to pretend to be a boy. (Joan)

According to prominent sport Sociologist Michael Messner:

> Influenced by feminist scholarship, women began to develop a critical analysis of male sport including its effects on women, and of the contributions of male sport to   the reproduction of male hegemony in society... sport is a male institution as it actively promotes values and behaviours and ultimately naturalises stereotypical masculinity. The social attention and acclaim that are given to athletic males help to confirm patterns of male privilege and female subordination that seep into mainstream culture and continue to be applauded in this broader arena. Since the 1970's sport has been interrogated for its contributions to historical patterns of male empowerment and female disadvantage. (20)

The vested interests of masculinity are clearly visible from the contested space that continues to be women in sport. Some researchers believe that queer theory opens up a boundless solution for exploring identities. Yet, according to Joshua Gamson:

> as queer theory becomes increasingly contested within the academy, identities are being interpreted as multiple, contradictory, fragmented, incoherent, disciplinary, unstable, fluid – hardly the stuff that allows a researcher to confidently run out and study sexual subjects as if they are coherent and available social types. (347-348)

I suggest, however, that this makes an analysis of the connections between female masculinities and athletic credibility increasingly important. Discourse surrounding gender, sexuality, and identity politics is infused with critiques of masculinities, and such analyses could be instrumental to a more coherent study of women's experiences of organised sport. On analysis, it is clear that women's participation in organised sport stands for a changing social dynamic and a visible challenge to male hegemony. Halberstam notes:

Masculinity in this society inevitably confines up notions of power and legitimacy and privilege; it often symbolically refers to the power of the state and to uneven distributions of wealth. Masculinity seems to extend outward into patriarchy and inward into the family; masculinity represents the power of inheritance, the consequences of the traffic in women and the promise of social privilege. (2)

Drawing on the theories of Merleau-Ponty and R.W Connell, David Whitson contends that masculinising and feminising practices associated with anatomy are fundamental to a conventional gender order:

> In contending that our sense of who we are is firmly rooted in our experiences of embodiment, it is integral to the reproduction of gender relations that boys are encouraged to experience their bodies, and therefore themselves, in force-full, space occupying even dominant ways. It may be suggested that maculating and feminising practices associated with the body are at the heart of the social construction of masculinity and femininity and that this precisely why sport matters in the total structure of gender relations. (23-24)

Conventional understandings of masculinity naturalise masculinity (not masculinities) within the sporting male to the extent that masculine females are, at the very least, considered subversive. Historically, within the Olympic Games, violently invasive sex tests are carried out in the name of 'fair play'. Supported by so-called 'medical expertise,' every effort has been made to limit female athletic participation. The underlining argument is that the 'true nature' of a girl is not to be a boy and the true nature of a boy is never to be a girl, and if you must play sport, at the very least you're obliged to grow your hair and fingernails.

In a recent interview published in *Diva* magazine, ex semi-professional soccer player Carla Di Maria, who played in Italy in the 1980s estimates that "at least half the league were lesbians and everyone knew it – players, fans, officials and owners – but we were never allowed to talk about it. It was where I met my girlfriend; it wasn't a problem as long as we never made it obvious" (17). In the same article, boxer Michele Aboro contends that she is unable to have a professional career in England, where her 'butchness' is considered a problem, and she is forced to fight in the Netherlands where her looks and sexuality aren't such a problematic issue. In this same article, 'elite' international athletes openly stated that they kept their lesbianism quiet for fear of missing out on the Commonwealth Games. Silence or lying is often considered by many as the best or safest 'policy', but what happens when 'passing' is not an option. What happens when the 'say nothing and make sure you grow your hair and fingernails' option is not an option:

> Q. We've looked a little bit at what's going on for women dating women in your sport... (can't name the sport for confidentiality reasons). Have you ever experienced any direct harassment as a gay individual from your family or from your community?
> A. No but I've experienced it from a manager's point of view.
> Q. Can you elaborate?
> A. I'll elaborate but I'm not naming names.
> Q. No that's fine.
> A. He was the Manager of (International competitive level) sometime during the nineties. He knew that I was gay but he just didn't like it. Yeh and he just... this was my first bad experience of being getting prejudiced against because I was gay. And he basically just dropped me because I was gay not because I wasn't good enough to play on the team. I was left off the team for three years because of it and I wanted to do something but people wouldn't back me up. And that's annoying in the sense that, I'm back with the international team now whereas I could have had more and more experience but because people wouldn't stand up for me because of who I am he just continued to do what he was doing and it really annoyed me. And to this day I still think about it and I am going to do something about but I don't know what way to go about it...So it really did impact like...It had a very bad impact on me, he is the first man that ever made me cry... He's the only man that ever made me cry and it was over I wasn't heterosexual and I didn't want to sleep with him. I thought it was very unfair of people who didn't   back me up I asked people to meet me to   discuss what he's doing to discuss who he's with. They wouldn't have it. (Jane)

Griffin writes:

> Sport is a passion for many lesbian athletes. For these women, being denied the opportunity to coach or play is unthinkable. Many lesbian coaches and athletes accept as   fact that being publicly out and being in athletics are entirely incompatible this certainly was my experience as a high school and college coach. (134)

Women must learn to toe the line of heterosexual femininity or risk falling into a despised and liminal category of mannish (not-women) women. Contemporary sponsorship deals epitomise the type of 'feminine' women that are welcome in sport. Consider Maria Sharapova's recent sponsorship deal with a leading manufacturer of deodorant. Gamson writes:

> The history of social research on sexualities has elements familiar from the histories of women's studies, Ethnic studies and the like: It is a history intertwined with the politics of social movements, wary of the ways 'science' has been used against the marginalised, and particularly comfortable with the strategies of qualitative research – which at least appear to be less objectifying of their subjects, to be more concerned with cultural and political meaning creation, and to make more room for voices and experiences that have been suppressed. Thus on the one hand, the coming-of-age of the field is a coming-to-voice of new sexual subjects on the terrains of both politics and academia. It is about invisible people becoming visible. (347-348)

By juxtaposing powerful women with a bypassed male authority, skilled women athletes continue to threaten 'man's' engendered physical superiority and, thus, his ability to dominate. One outcome of a heterosexist society is the prevalence of homophobia and, so, a social violence particularly targeted at 'non-feminine' or 'butch' women is actively encouraged. In "Female Masculinities", Halberstam explores the notion of 'toeing the line', linking its intensity to age and the perceived extremity of 'gender trouble':

> Tomboyism is punished, however, when it appears to the sign of extreme male identification (taking a boy's name or refusing a

girls clothing of any type) and when it threatens to extend beyond childhood and into adolescence. Teenage tomboyism presents a problem and tends to be subject to the most severe efforts to reorient. We could say that tomboyism is tolerated as long as the child remains prepubescent. As soon as puberty begins, however, the full force of gender conformity descends on the girl. (6)

Research that is not afraid to address sexism and heterosexism in relation to the drop-out point for many girls needs to be urgently conducted in Irish sports. I asked all of the interviewees in my study:

Q. So in your experience, do women athletes sometimes get a response in terms of how they look as opposed to their talents?
A. Yeah, mostly how they look. I mean you could be Maradonna and ugly and they're like is it a man or is it a girl? And then you see this lovely feminine girl and she could be gay and they're like she's massive she's lovely, what's she doing playing football? And this girl is gay and when they find out they're in shock whereas the girl the butch she comes off and she's not gay so what do they do then, there in shock do you know what I mean. Ye see you can't tell people like that.
Interviewer. Yeah it throws a lot of things up in the air.
Interviewee. Yeah it throws them in the air they're like Jesus what happened there? I took her as being gay and she's not. (Jane)

Golfers Muffin Spencer-Devlin and Rosie Jones chose to come out toward the end of their careers. For many it is an obvious choice in that, at the end of their careers, the financial implications are less pronounced. There is some hope, however, in athletes such as tennis player, Amelie Mauresemo, who is an 'out' lesbian during her playing career. Caution is required simply because the current reality that heterosexuality is the norm and that homosexuality must be articulated/confirmed or, indeed, denied is quite problematic and requires careful analysis. Much work remains, for in 2002-2003, the men in charge of the Women's Tennis Association launched, 'Get in touch with Your Feminine Side', a marketing campaign designed to sell women's tennis. The campaign slogan suggests that looking glamorous rather than muscular or athletic was all that is needed to bust ratings and female 'athletic' (i.e. financial) success. According to Krane and Barber, "Commercials utilizing high profile women athletes tout the 'softer side of Sears' and the joys of using 'Clean Shower'. Promoters focus on the message, 'you can be an athlete and be feminine too" (328-29). In 2002/2003, in fact, this was the primary theme of the initial promotional campaign for the Women's National Basketball Association (WNBA) and the Women's United Soccer Association' in North America (WUSA) (*ibid.*). Data resulting from interviews I am conducting for my PhD research suggests that this understanding is rampant in sport and affects the potential successes of female athletes, leaving no doubt that athletic credibility is linked to sex and sexuality. Consider this data arising from the question:

> Q. Is it your experience that women athletes sometimes get a response in terms of what they look like as opposed to their talents? (Or In your experience do you know of any athlete that has been applauded or discredited for their athletic abilities where you feel their ability was not taken into account but rather there sporting image)?

Answers varied from:

> 'Oh yes definitely,' to, 'are you kidding me of course' to, 'Yes I believe remarks would be made of how athletes look as opposed to their talent. In my opinion this is an experience more likely to effect butch athletes.' And finally to, 'of course, that's just the way it is'.

Research conducted by Coakley suggests that traditional gender stereotypes and the stigmas attached are powerful mediators of anxiety and stress to female athletes, and this is invariably linked to identity suicide. Coakley (1986) argues that burnout occurs in elite adolescent athletes as the result of controlling social-structural demands on these athletes. Smith (1986) defines burnout as a psychological and emotional withdrawal from an activity in response to excessive stress or dissatisfaction. Griffin explores silence and shame as a mediator for anxiety and stress:

> In that silence, shameful things happen. Young women who are confused and scared about their sexual identity suffer in isolation and sometimes kill themselves (identity suicide); women who are

harassed and discriminated against have no support or legal recourse. Heterosexual women are afraid or contemptuous of their lesbian and bisexual team-mates and women coaches; some women choose to avoid sport altogether out of fear of lesbians; and many women in sport are afraid of being called a lesbian or being associated with lesbian. (11)

In strategising to 'blend in' or be considered 'normal,' women often quit sport or turn on their more butch or masculine team-mates in an effort to become accepted or notably seen as straight:

> I was on a road trip with two 'straight friends' from my soccer team. When we reached the house I walked in on my 'team-mates' arguing over who would 'share' the bed with me. I slept on the floor and cried myself to sleep. The next morning I made my way to the (names the place) bus station and continued my journey alone. After all I was in a serious relationship and on my way to see my girlfriend to whom I was deeply committed. We never spoke about it… they changed in the other room… (Kate)

Further analysis is required as sport continues to be a key site where cultural conceptions of 'masculinity' and 'femininity' are constructed, re-constructed and contested. According to Messner:

> Economic structures, urbanization, race relations, sexuality, and nationalism are also fundamentally important aspects of the structure and ideology of organized sport,' (17, 1990). Cahn writes, 'Women received praise for their physical strength and ability only when it made them better mothers or more attractive mates. The athletic beauty-queen model depended on cultural images and practices outside sport - beauty contests, pageantry, and sexual appeals - for legitimacy. In the end women athletes found acceptance not simply for their skill, but for their usefulness and attractiveness to men. (82)

As a key site in the production and maintenance of conventional masculinities and, thus, a breeding ground of the modern day heroic male, sport endures tremendous surveillance and state control. Whitson draws on R.W. Connell's idea of sport as a 'masculising' practice, tracing how sport as a social institution helps to construct men's power over women as well as heterosexual men's privileges over gay men. Despite women's progress in sport, Whitson argues that, "sport continues to bolster hegemonic masculinity by ritualising and embedding aggression, strength, and skill in the male body and linking it with competitive achievement" (18). However, despite the challenges, women in sport have encountered another potential site to rigorously contest and reconstruct the potential of femininities, masculinities, and the concepts of 'natural' and scientific 'neutrality'. Twentieth century women's unapologetic athleticism proposes a physical dimension to questions about the proper spheres, qualities and relative power of men and women (Cahn). Research supports this as self-identified lesbian Irish women continue to contest and reconstruct gender and sexual boundaries as they love and perform in and out of Irish sport:

> Q. Ok so when you played in the boy's leagues what was the general reaction of the parents or other coaches or other teams to you?
> A. Well they just assumed I was a boy. I got my hair cut short the whole lot. My mother cried. But I had to do it for the love of my soccer. So the hair was cut. Wore boys clothes, acted like a boy. Forgot I was a girl for a while.
> Q. And when you say acted like a boy?
> A. Well I mean there wasn't much acting involved at that age because we were all so young we all pretty much acted the same just messing and stuff a bit of rough and tumble with boys I just fitted in quite well.

Sex, according to Kate Millett, is always a status category with political implications – political implications referring to a politics of, "power structured relationships, arrangements whereby one group of persons is controlled by another" (23). Such political agendas are particularly visible in Irish women's sporting participation. As I conduct my research, it is becoming increasingly evident that the female athlete represents a powerful political challenge to a shrinking male hegemony, and the masculine female is considered particularly threatening as perameters surrounding sex and sexualities become increasingly fluid. With regard to finance and sponsorship, the credibility of the woman athlete is particularly vulnerable and dependant upon a public embrace: an acceptance that is often dependent upon the woman playing a particular role. According to Martina, an International level athlete:

> Q. How do you think lesbians impact women's sport in Ireland?
> A. Those who do play at a high level are usually in denial of their sexuality in order to gain grants/scholarships etc. Being a known lesbian in sport in Ireland I think would limit all types of support...both financial and social.

When financial and social barriers fail, other gate-keeping devices, such as gender passports, femininity cards or the direct abolishment of women in sport, are used to prevent women from accessing athletics and gaining some level of control over their own bodies and social embodiment. In 2000, the International Olympic Committee stopped mandatory sex testing at the Olympic Games. However, now that there is no accurate measure of gender *per se*, a different physic management of gender has come into play. For example, athletes are drug tested and a visual test is carried out under the guise of drug testing, leading me to conclude that, although muscle itself does not have an agenda, conventional understandings of appropriate gender behaviours definitely carry some muscle. Despite the fact that athletic bodies, by definition, are in transition (as they shape and bulge and reform), the aggressive 'non-confining' athlete continues to be 'read' as deviant. Bryson suggests that, "as long as sport continues to be linked with conventional masculinity women in sport will continue to be viewed as trespassers on male territory" (413). Research in a paper delivered by Heather Sykes on Transgender sporting bodies states, 'the fetishistic engagement with the normative Olympic body is upset when it is interrupted by bodies that defy a categorical gender binary. The underside of the fetish reveals itself as a transphobic response to athletes who do not mirror a normative gender template' (1, 2005).

It is not surprising that homophobic discourse penetrates Olympic athletes and committees alike, it seems all 'non mainstream' athletes from the Gay Games, the Gay Olympics, The Special Olympics, The Paralympics are being directed away from 'major' or 'mainstream' competition toward sub-categories or subdivisions almost ghettoised in their efforts to become visible. Many of the interviewees, early in the interview declared that they themselves had not been affected by heterosexism only to reveal later in the interview that they had been banned from teams or had trouble in the workplace simply because of their perceived or blatant homosexuality (note prominent US coach Rene Portland and her 'no lesbian' policy). On reflection, ethics regarding gender performance and female sexuality seem so ingrained that conscious, strong women sometimes failed to note the conflictive discourse in their lives and unconsciously refused to make the correlation. One interviewee, a lesbian P.E teacher and excellent athlete, responded that butch was 'great', butch is fine as long as everyone understands and sees that I'm 'really' femme. When asked if she felt restricted in her job because of her sexuality she responded 'no not at all' only to divulge later that she was terrified of some of the 'kids' finding out because she has a lot of one-on-one interaction with them while encouraging sporting participation. When I asked her what she was terrified of, she said, "the parents finding out and thinking that I was up to no good?"

Even as women athlete's bodies morph and change they are expected to maintain rigid gender templates (or at the very least a safe feminine persona and manner are required). Increased muscle mass is to be disguised, its impact softened to the general public by exaggerated displays of hyperbolic femininity. Take 'Flo-Jo' (Florence Griffith Joyner), 100m and 200m sprinter, for example, with polished nails and jewels, or think female body-builders bikini clad, foundation intact, big hair! Despite real athletic success, traditional gender templates must be adhered to by modern day sporting icons and the women are often under tremendous pressure from families, lovers and sponsorship deals to maintain the *status quo*. I'm thinking specifically of the cocktail style dress appearance of the 1999 US Women's Soccer team on Jay Leno, the polished and 'femmed up' English footballer Karen Walker as a presenter on ITV for the 2005 European women's soccer championship, and the soft non-offensive interview style of Venus and Serena. I would argue that all are performers of an expected gender performance that is required by sponsors and society alike: it is a pre-requisite for athletic and financial legitimisation. Evidently a woman's, and in particular a lesbian woman's, athletic credibility is entrenched not only in her athletic performance but also in her gender performance:

Q. Is it your experience that women athletes sometimes get a response in terms of what they look like as opposed to their talents? In your experience do you know of any athlete that has been discredited or applauded for their athletic abilities where you feel their ability was not taken into account but rather there sporting image).

A. (laughs...Oh Yeh)... I've been on teams where the real leader a butch lesbian will captain the team but a second captain a pretty straight girl who commands no respect amongst her peers will be the coaches choice to soften the impact. (Claire Interview).

In-fact the 2005 'man of the match' in the final of the Irish Women's National basketball tournament went to the one woman on the court holding a child on her hip. A coincidence? Perhaps!

Part of my current research effort is to document how Irish lesbian athletes manage/experience homophobia and how they strategise for athletic credibility and survival. It aims to document and explore the experiences of some Irish lesbian athletes while involved in high level organised sport. According to Adrienne Rich:

It] is not enough for feminist thought that specifically lesbian texts exist. Any theory or cultural/political creation that treats lesbian existence as a marginal or less 'natural' phenomenon, as mere 'sexual preference', or as the mirror image of either heterosexual or male homosexual relations, is profoundly weakened thereby, whatever its other contributions. Feminist theory can no longer afford merely to voice a toleration of 'lesbianism' as an 'alternative lifestyle' or make token illusions to lesbians. A feminist critique of 'compulsory heterosexuality' is long overdue. (2)

As Irish society becomes increasingly 'diverse,' it is worrying indeed to consider the not-so-unique experience of this lesbian athlete:

Q. Ok. So would it be safe to say that a lesbian identity as an athlete has been positive mostly for you with some negative experiences dotted throughout that?

A. Yeah it has always been positive for me I've always been comfortable in that environment, bar when I was getting into it first they thought I was a boy.

Q. Have you ever experienced any kind of violence in your life because of your sexuality?

A. Not through soccer. Em… that would be more through just walking down the road having things shouted at you. I have been attacked a couple of time yes but I tend not to dwell on things like that I just get up and get on wit it. That's part of life when you're a lesbian I suppose. Or you're different. (Lucy)

The evidence suggests that in an effort to seek grants, scholarships and, indeed, athletic legitimacy, women in sports are often forced to conform to heterosexuality or are at least expected to 'maintain the dignity of passing'. It is clear from research conducted to date that the social-cultural structure of sport, the social-cultural structure of Irish society, and the social organisation of sexual orientation all require careful analysis when exploring the sports experiences of Irish lesbian athletes.

References

Avery, Janet. "Transforming the Silence on Lesbians in Sport: Suggested Directions for Theory and Research in Sport Psychology" in Robin S. Vealy, ed. *1997 Women in Sport and Activity Journal.* New York: Simon & Schuster, 1997: 21-24.

Butler, Judith. *Excitable Speech; A Politics of the Performative.* New York. Routledge, 1997.

Bryson, L. "Challenges to Male Hegemony in Sport" in D. Sabo and M. Messner, eds. *Sport, Men and the Gender Order: Critical Feminist Perspectives.* Illinois. Human Kinetics, 1990.

Cahn, S. "Crushes, Competition, and Closets: The Emergence of Homophobia in Women's Physical Education" in S. Birrell and C. Cole, eds. *Women, Sport and Culture.* Leeds: Human Kinetics, 1994: 327-340.

Cahn, S. *Coming on Strong. Gender and Sexuality in Twentieth-century Women's Sport.* Harvard : Harvard UP, 1994.

Coakley, J. "Sport in Society: Issues and Controversies." *Journal of Sport Psychology.* 8 (1986): 36-50.

Connell, R. "A Very Straight Gay: Masculinity, Homosexual Experience and the Dynamics of Gender." *American Sociological Review* 57 (6) (1992): 735-751.

Diva Magazine. 17 (2005).

Gamson, Joshua. "Sexualities, Queer Theory, and Qualitative Research" in *Handbook of Qualitative Research.* 2nd Ed. Norman K. Denzin and Yvonna S. Lincoln, eds. California: Sage Publications, 2000.

Griffin, Pat. *Strong Women, Deep Closets: Homophobia and Lesbians in Women'sSsport.* California: Human Kinetics, 1998.

Halberstam, Judith. *Feminine Masculinity.* Durham: Duke UP, 1998.

Kosovsky Sedgewick, E. *The Epistemology of the Closet.* Berkeley: U of California P, 1990.

Krane, Vikki. & Barber, Heather. "Lesbian Experiences in Sport: A Social Identity Perspective." *Quest* 55 (2003): 328-346.

Messner, Michael. A. & Sabo, Donald. F., eds. *Sport, Men and the Gender Order: Critical Feminist Perspectives.* Illinois, Human Kinetics Books, 1990.

Millett, Kate. *Sexual Politics.* New York. Simon & Schuster, 1990.

Peper, K. "Female Athlete = Lesbian: A Myth Constructed from Gender Role Expectations and Lesbiphobia" in *Queer Words, Queer Images.* J. Ringer, ed. New York: New York UP, 1994.

Rich, Adrienne. *Blood, Bread and Poetry: Selected Prose 1979-1985.* London: Virago Press, 1987.

Rich, Adrienne. "Compulsory Heterosexuality and Lesbian Existence." *Signs: Women in Culture and Society* 631 (1980): 647-648.

Smith, R.E. "Toward a Cognitive-Affective Model of Athletic Burnout." *Journal of Sport Psychology*, 8. 1986: 36-50).

Swoopes, Sheryl. NBC. 5 Nov. 2005.

Sykes, H. "Discources on the Bioethical Limits Surrounding Transgender Sporting Bodies." Unpublished paper presented at the Queer Theories Seminar, Women's Educational Research and Resource Centre, University College, Dublin, 5 Nov. 2005.

Sykes, H. "Turning the Closets Inside/out: Towards a Queer-Feminist Theory in Women's Physical Education." *Sociology of Sport Journal.* 15 (1998): 154-173.

Sykes, H. "Constr(i)(u)cting Lesbian Identities in Physical Education: Feminist and Post-structural Approaches to Researching Sexuality." *Quest.* 48 (1996): 459-469.

Whitson, David. "In Sport the Social Construction of Masculinity" in Messner & Sabo, *Sport, Men and the Gender Order: Critical Feminist Perspectives:* 17-24.

Searching for Feminine Esteem

Gayle Owens[1]

> My very soul yearns with intensest passionate emotion
> [for]...the true ennoblement of women, the full
> harmonious development of her unknown nature, and the
> consequent redemption of the whole human race.
> Dr. Elizabeth Blackwell, 1871 (cited in Beilenson 46)

A hundred and twenty years after Dr. Blackwell's words, I set out to find a way to stop apologising to myself for being a woman. And, what was the problem? It was that pesky identity with the feminine archetype. I loved being a mother. I liked living in a female body. I liked being fast and smart and independent. I could be analytical, make good decisions, buy my own house and car. But, in the back of my mind, I was on guard lest my feminine side would show I was, after all, weak, a dingbat, or unreasonable.

I had to admit I had this pejorative opinion of the feminine, and I could see it skulking in the minds of other women who were successful but still didn't have good self esteem. The culprit, of course, is western culture. Shouldn't we suspect and scrutinise everything we have learned in a patriarchy, and, most especially, how the feminine is viewed? My criticism of the feminist movement is that there's been a tendency to strive for a bigger and more equitable piece of the cultural pie without seriously examining if we even like the way the pie is baked. For example, hiring a woman to be the minister within a patriarchal religion does nothing to change the belief system of that religion. Or studying women within the academic tradition means that the feminine archetype is dismissed as irrelevant. So, I invite you to

---

[1] Author's Note: For the conference I scrapped the talk that is laid out in this paper. Instead I led a discussion of the feminine archetype. I wanted the medium to be an example of the message. I was not the 'expert' imparting the truth, but a member of the group searching for my truth. While the discussion included analysis and facts (the way of the masculine,) it also allowed feeling and intuition (the way of the feminine.) It seems to me that there's a huge disconnect between academic programmes about women and women who are living in the world. Academia is mainly based on masculine principles. Women are finding that they must live out the feminine principles as well in order to have a full and authentic life.

quest with me for a bit. Is it possible to find appreciation and respect for the feminine if we take off the cultural filters? Could we actually be proud to embody the feminine?

One way to think about the merits of the feminine (and the masculine) characteristics is the way the Taoists think of them. Yin and Yang are interdependent and complementary. Vulnerability exists only in contrast to protection, receptivity only in contrast to assertiveness, bliss to moral force. No characteristic could exist without its opposite. Active makes no sense without passive to act upon. Passive means nothing unless it is contrasted with activity. One aspect of a quality cannot exist – indeed has no significance – without its opposite. The opposites are dependent on each other with each contributing equally to the whole and to balance.

> The Tao Te Ching says:
> When people see some things as beautiful
> other things become ugly...
> Being and non-being create each other.
> Difficult and easy support each other.
> Long and short define each other. (Mitchell 2)

A second argument raises the possibility that what we have learned has been wrong in several ways. Our scientific paradigm judges masculine characteristics as superior to feminine characteristics. In other words, intellect is better than instinct, active is better than passive, logic is superior to passion. But eastern philosophy tells us just the opposite, that the essence of life lies in the intuitive, the emotions, the mysterious.

Who is right – East or West? Many thoughtful people have concluded that both polarities are important to how we live our lives. Either approach, when one-sided, leads to dehumanising conditions. In many third world countries, for instance, there is a deplorable standard of living because rationality and knowledge have not been developed along with logic, science, technology or self-determination. In the United States, there is depression, alienation, and violence because the 'not rational' – intuition, instinct, wisdom – has not been advanced; thus, we also ignore compassion, interdependence and mystery.

A third argument is a sub-set of the second. We view the feminine pejoratively because we have been conditioned to view feminine characteristics that way. If we were to step out of our old learning, we might see the positive value of these characteristics. With masculine characteristics, our tendency has been the opposite – to focus on their positive aspects. But we forget that masculine principles, taken to extreme, can be absurd, or, if used in the wrong circumstances, even harmful. For me, yoga has been a grand metaphor for this. I have learned the hard way in yoga class that not only do I not make progress, but I have even hurt myself when I've pushed the masculine (strength, force, muscling my way through) at the expense of the feminine (yielding, knowing when to back off, working within my capacity for that day).

'Passive' was one of the terms on the list of feminine qualities that initially gave me a queasy feeling. As a woman, I did not want to be identified with such a characteristic. Why? Because we equate passive with weakness and ineffectiveness; besides, we live in a society that values action and power. We believe there's nothing we can't do if we just work hard enough.

But those of us who are students of human behaviour, as leaders, therapists, or teachers, have learned the importance of being passive. We have learned to wait to intervene, or not to intervene at all. We wait until the student is ready to do her work. We trust the process, trying not to interfere with it. We have learned that approaching certain situations with force or control can cause polarisation and harmful outcomes. In fact, yielding to resistance can be our most effective tactic. Gandhi and Martin Luther King, Jr., for example, showed us how awesome passive non-resistance could be.

'Surrender' is closely related to passive, but is possibly even more frightening to women who have felt powerless. Paradoxically, the reason Twelve Step programmes (for example, self-help groups, spiritually-based: the most popular in the U.S.A. is Alcoholics Anonymous.) which, to date, have impacted on many more men than women, have been extremely effective and popular is because they hinge on the process of surrendering. Surrendering is badly needed by egos that have become too grandiose in their own separateness and assumed power – for example, egos that used alcohol, drugs, or food to escape feelings and the unconscious.

Step One of such programmes says: "We admitted we were powerless over alcohol – that our lives had become unmanageable" The alcoholic or the addict is in trouble because she has convinced herself that she is invincible. The laws that apply to ordinary humans do not apply to her. She has a touch of megalomania. Surrender and humility are necessary if she does not want to be sick and miserable. She must lay down the masculine attitude of 'I can conquer anything' and accept the feminine attitude which tells her she cannot, does not and should not have power over certain substances, situations, and people.

Another cornerstone of Twelve Step programmes is relationships, probably the most widely recognised attribute of the feminine. Relationships with a higher power, relationships with the group, relationships with other recovering alcoholics or addicts, and relationships with those who need help, are continually fostered and nurtured by the steps, the traditions, and the literature of the programme. The ability to relate – to children, to women and men, to Mother Earth, to Spirit— is there any other human capacity which is as vital for the survival of our families, our society, our planet?

I used to live in fear that I would be seen as irrational. Now I see that reasoning has actually been highly overrated. Irrationality is beneficial, compelling and absolutely essential. Consider a human who is only and totally rational, one for whom all decisions and behaviour are based strictly on reason and logic (I have met him, and he is boring and 'nonhuman'!)

Yes, the zest of life, the joy and spirit of life spring from imagination, feelings, intuitions – the unconscious – all irrational. Spontaneity, playfulness, love, and creativity are irrational functions without which no community could survive or would want to survive. Many great scientific discoveries have broken through from the irrational – from dreams, hunches, accidents, or an idea that suddenly leaps into a scientist's mind. Without the irrational for inspiration, the rational would simply dry up.

Our conscious lives are small islands anchored in enormous oceans of unconsciousness. Whether or not we are aware of the connection, we are mostly the living ocean rather than the visible island. Indeed, it is when we try to be so rational with no psychic backgrounds that our troubles intensify; extreme rationality leads to neurosis or, even, evil. One way or another, irrationality will be lived out.

One last thought. Spirituality, by definition, is derived from the irrational and can be killed with too much reason. Perhaps this is why we have so much rule-based religion in our society. And the patriarchy is afraid of spirituality because spirituality, by definition, rises above the bounds of any culture.

The words we use to describe the feminine are humble attempts to capture the essence of an archetype. They can only be pieces of the truth, but at least they entice us to listen and ponder. Our culture has strained these words through its negative filter, attempting to strip them of all vitality and validity. But we have the capacity to remove the cultural filter, to discern the feminine wisdom contained in these words.

My quest has led me to equanimity. The feminine is the hidden treasure, kept from us to perpetuate a way of life that is no longer viable once she is brought forth.

Black is beautiful. Water is as powerful as fire. The feminine lives.

> Such a sage awakes to light in the night of all creatures.
> That which the world calls day is the night of ignorance to the
> wise. *Bhagavad Gita* (Iknath 134)

References

Beilenson, Evelyn and Ann Tenenbaum, eds. *Wit and Wisdom of Famous American Women*. White Plains, New York.: Peter Pauper Press, 1995.

Eknath, Easwaran. *The Bhagavad Gita for Daily Living. Vol. 1: The End of Sorrow*. Petaluma, CA: Nilgiri Press, 1975.

Mitchell, Stephen. *Tao Te Ching*. New York: Harper Perennial, 1988.

Contributors

Elisabetta Bertolino is a PhD student in the School of Law, Birkbeck College, University of London.

Aida Diaz Bild is from the University of La Laguna, Canary Islands.

A. Clare Brandabur is a Lecturer in English at Doğup University, Istanbul, Turkey.

Fiona Buckley, Neil Collins, and Theresa Reidy are Lecturers in the Department of Government, University College Cork, Cork, Ireland.

Colleen Z. Burke is an award-winning poet and author from Sydney, Australia.

Eduardo de Gregorio-Godeo is Assistant Professor of Modern Languages at the University de Castilla-La Mancha.

Mary Dempsey is a writer, film-maker and photographer from Galway.

Jenneke Fernhout is in the Department of Language & Communication, Cardiff University, Wales.

Linda Greene is a PhD student in the Women's Research and Resource Centre (WERRC), University College Dublin.

Devin Kuhn is from Claremont Graduate University, California.

Mary O' Donoghue is in the School of Arts & Humanities at Babson College, Boston.

Ornaith O' Dowd is in the Department of Philosophy, Brooklyn College, New York.

Gayle Owens is a Psychologist with over twenty years experience as a Psychotherapist. .

Julie Palmer is a PhD student in the Centre for Women's Studies, University of York, England.

Eva Perez is in the Department of Spanish, Modern and Latin Philology at the University of the Balearic Islands, Mallorca.

Mary Power is in the English Department, University of New Mexico, Albuquerque.

Tara Prescott is a PhD student in Twentieth Century American Literature at Claremont Graduate University, California.

Georgia Rhoades teaches Women's Studies at the English Dept, Sanford Hall, Appalachian State University, Boone.

Lorraine Ryan is in the Department of Language and Cultural Studies, University of Limerick.

Katherine Side is in the Department of Women's Studies, Mount Saint Vincent University Halifax, Nova Scotia, Canada

Ailbhe Smyth is Director of the Women's Research and Resource Centre (WERRC) at University College Dublin.